"I enjoy reading Phil Moore's books. [...]
Christian life with percepti [...]*"*
- Nicky Gumbel - Vi[...]

"In taking us straight to the heart of the text, Phil Moore has served us magnificently. We so need to get into the Scriptures and let the Scriptures get into us. The fact that Phil writes so relevantly and with such submission to biblical revelation means that we are genuinely helped to be shaped by the Bible's teaching."

- Terry Virgo

"Fresh. Solid. Simple. Really good stuff."

- R. T. Kendall

"Phil makes the deep truths of Scripture alive and accessible. If you want to grow in your understanding of each book of the Bible, then buy these books and let them change your life!"

- P. J. Smyth - *leader of Covenant Life Church, Maryland, USA and the Advance Movement of Churches*

"Most commentaries are dull. These are alive. Most commentaries are for scholars. These are for **you***!"*

- Canon Michael Green

"These notes are amazingly good. Phil's insights are striking, original, and fresh, going straight to the heart of the text and the reader! Substantial yet succinct, they bristle with amazing insights and life applications, compelling us to read more. Bible reading will become enriched and informed with such a scintillating guide. Teachers and preachers will find nuggets of pure gold here!"

- Greg Haslam, *Westminster Chapel, London, UK*

"A strong combination of faithful scholarship, clear explanation and deep insight make these an invaluable tool. I can't recommend them highly enough."

- Gavin Calver - *Director of Mission, Evangelical Alliance*

"The Bible is living and dangerous. The ones who teach it best are those who bear that in mind - and let the author do the talking. Phil has written these studies with a sharp mind and a combination of creative application and reverence."

- Joel Virgo - *Leader of Newday Youth Festival*

For more information about the Straight to the Heart series, please go to **www.philmoorebooks.com**.
You can also receive daily messages from Phil Moore on Twitter by following **@PhilMooreLondon**.

Luke

60 BITE-SIZED INSIGHTS

Phil Moore

MONARCH
BOOKS

Oxford, UK & Grand Rapids, USA

Published by Monarch Books
an imprint of
Lion Hudson plc
Wilkinson House, Jordan Hill Road,
Oxford OX2 8DR, England
Email: monarch@lionhudson.com
www.lionhudson.com/monarch

ISBN 978 0 85721 799 8
e-ISBN 978 0 85721 800 1

First edition 2017

Acknowledgments

Scripture quotations taken from the *Holy Bible, New International Version* Anglicised. Copyright © 1979, 1984, 2011 Biblica, formerly International Bible Society. Used by permission of Hodder & Stoughton Ltd, an Hachette UK company. All rights reserved. "NIV" is a registered trademark of Biblica. UK trademark number 1448790. Both 1984 and 2011 versions are quoted in this commentary.

p. 64, extract from *Christianity Rediscovered* © 1978, Vincent Donovan. Used by permission of SCM Press and Orbis Books.
p. 90, extract from *What Shall this Man Do?* © 1961, Watchman Nee. Used by permission of CLC Publications. May not be further reproduced. All rights reserved.
p. 95, extract from *Signs of the Apostles* © 1973, Walter Chantry. Used by permission of Banner of Truth (banneroftruth.org).
p. 139, extract from *Evangelism in the Early Church* © 1970, Michael Green. Used by permission of Eerdmans.
p. 144, extract from *The Unnecessary Pastor: Rediscovering the Call* © 2000, Eugene Peterson. Used by permission of Eerdmans.
p. 151, extract from *Center Church* © 2012, Tim Keller. Used by permission of Redeemer City to City.
p. 161, extract from *Mere Christianity* © 1952, C. S. Lewis. Used by permission of The C. S. Lewis Company.

A catalogue record for this book is available from the British Library.

This book is for my children: Isaac, Noah, Esther and Ethan. The Father, Son and Spirit are calling you to join the family.

CONTENTS

About the *"Straight to the Heart"* Series

On his eightieth birthday, Sir Winston Churchill dismissed the compliment that he was the "lion" who had defeated Nazi Germany in World War Two. He told the Houses of Parliament that *"It was a nation and race dwelling all around the globe that had the lion's heart. I had the luck to be called upon to give the roar."*

I hope that God speaks to you very powerfully through the "roar" of the books in the *Straight to the Heart* series. I hope they help you to understand the books of the Bible and the message which the Holy Spirit inspired their authors to write. I hope that they help you to hear God's voice challenging you, and that they provide you with a springboard for further journeys into each book of Scripture for yourself.

But when you hear my "roar", I want you to know that it comes from the heart of a much bigger "lion" than me. I have been shaped by a whole host of great Christian thinkers and preachers from around the world, and I want to give due credit to at least some of them here:

Terry Virgo, Dave Holden, Guy Miller, John Hosier, Adrian Holloway, Greg Haslam, Lex Loizides and all those who lead the Newfrontiers family of churches; friends and encouragers, such as Stef Liston, Joel Virgo, Stuart Gibbs, Scott Taylor, Nick Sharp, Nick Derbridge, Phil Whittall, and Kevin and Sarah Aires; Tony Collins, Margaret Milton, Jenny Muscat, Jessica Scott and Simon Cox at Monarch Books; Malcolm Kayes and all the elders of The

Coign Church, Woking; my fellow elders and church members here at Everyday Church in London; my great friend Andrew Wilson – without your friendship, encouragement and example, this series would never have happened.

I would like to thank my parents, my brother Jonathan, and my in-laws, Clive and Sue Jackson. Dad – your example birthed in my heart the passion which brought this series into being. I didn't listen to all you said when I was a child, but I couldn't ignore the way you got up at five o' clock every morning to pray, read the Bible and worship, because of your radical love for God and for his Word. I'd like to thank my children – Isaac, Noah, Esther and Ethan – for keeping me sane when publishing deadlines were looming. But most of all, I'm grateful to my incredible wife, Ruth – my friend, encourager, corrector and helper.

You all have the lion's heart, and you have all developed the lion's heart in me. I count it an enormous privilege to be the one who was chosen to sound the lion's roar.

So welcome to the *Straight to the Heart* series. My prayer is that you will let this roar grip your own heart too – for the glory of the great Lion of the Tribe of Judah, the Lord Jesus Christ!

Introduction: All of This Happened for You

I too decided to write an orderly account for you, most excellent Theophilus, so that you may know the certainty of the things you have been taught.

(Luke 1:3–4)

Luke is the odd man out of the New Testament. We need to grasp that if we want to understand the message of his gospel. He was so unlike the other New Testament writers that many people doubted he was qualified to write Scripture at all, and the apostle Paul had to defend him by stating explicitly that his gospel was as much Holy Scripture as the Old Testament.[1] Luke was an outsider to the Jewish faith, yet God inspired him to compile an account of the life of Jesus in order to prove to people all around the world that what Jesus said and did he said and did for everyone. The astonishing message of Luke's gospel is that what happened to Jesus happened for us all.

Luke was the only New Testament writer who was not a Jew. Paul was a Jewish rabbi. Peter and John were Jewish fishermen. Matthew, Mark, James and Jude were Jewish too. We do not know who wrote the book of Hebrews, but one thing at least we know for certain: its writer was a Jew. As an uncircumcised Greek from the pagan city of Antioch in Syria, Luke was therefore a glaring anomaly. When Paul lists his

---

[1] Paul quotes from Luke 10:7 in 1 Timothy 5:18 and describes it as *graphē*, the same Greek word that is used throughout the New Testament to describe the Old Testament as God-inspired *Scripture*.

teammates, he lists Luke among those who had once been worshippers of the pagan gods of Rome.[2]

It wasn't just Luke's ethnicity that set him apart from the other New Testament writers. Matthew, Peter, Mark and John had been eyewitnesses to the ministry of Jesus. James and Jude had grown up in the same house as him in Nazareth. Even the latecomer Paul had seen such glorious visions of the risen Jesus that he could claim in 1 Corinthians 15:8 that *"last of all he appeared to me also, as to one abnormally born"*. Luke, on the other hand, had still been worshipping Luck, the patron goddess of Antioch, when Jesus gave his Sermon on the Mount and fed the five thousand on the shores of Lake Galilee.

Luke also differed from the other New Testament writers when it came to education. Peter and John were unschooled fishermen. James and Jude were the sons of a common carpenter. They were the kind of people the Greek philosopher Celsus had in mind when he dismissed the early Christians as *"foolish, dishonourable and stupid – nothing but slaves, women and little children"*.[3] Luke defied this stereotype. As a qualified doctor, few could rival his level of education.[4] He was living proof that Jesus didn't merely come to save the weak and the poor. With Luke in his team, Paul had been able to convince many rich and powerful Romans that the coming of Jesus was good news for everyone.

This is important because it made Luke the ideal author of his gospel and of its sequel, the Acts of the Apostles.[5] The fact

---

[2] When Paul lists his Jewish and Gentile co-workers separately in Colossians 4:10–11 and 4:12–14, Luke appears in the second list. The fourth-century historian Eusebius also tells us that he was a Gentile in *Church History* (3.4.7).

[3] Celsus wrote this in his book *The True Word* in c. 175 AD. It is quoted by Origen in *Against Celsus* (3.49).

[4] Paul tells us Luke was a doctor (Colossians 4:14). Eusebius confirms this in his *Church History* (3.4.7).

[5] Since Luke does not name himself at the start of either book, Luke and Acts are technically anonymous. However, the early historical accounts are unanimous in attributing authorship of both books to him. For example, a

that he was a misfit among the New Testament writers made him perfectly fitted to defend Christianity when the apostle Paul was arrested in Jerusalem and taken in chains to Rome.

Luke dedicates both of his two books to Theophilus. Since the name is Greek for *Friend of God* or *Friend of the Gods*, some readers see it as nothing more than a poetic name for Christians, but Luke drops several hints that it means far more than this. We are meant to hear the echo of *"most excellent Theophilus"* (Luke 1:3) when the lawyer Tertullus addresses a judge as *"most excellent Felix"* (Acts 24:3) and when Paul addresses another judge as *"most excellent Festus"* (Acts 26:25), because Theophilus was the judge who had been picked to preside over Paul's trial before Caesar's court in Rome. Why else would the so-called Acts of the Apostles ignore the actions of nine of the twelve apostles? Why else would it ignore the actions of the other three after the halfway mark in order to concentrate instead on the actions of Paul? Why else would Acts end so abruptly, with Paul waiting for the verdict of a judge in Rome? Why else would Luke work so hard to prove that neither Jesus nor Paul has broken any Roman laws? All of this only makes sense if Luke is writing to provide background for Judge Theophilus in Rome.[6]

When we understand this, we begin to see God's wisdom in choosing Luke to write this gospel. He made no secret of the fact he was a core member of Paul's team but, as a Greek, his words could not be dismissed out of anti-Semitism.[7] The fact that he was not an eyewitness to the life of Jesus made him all the more

---

manuscript of Luke's gospel which dates back to 170 AD contains a prologue that tells us, *"Luke was an Antiochan of Syria, a physician by profession. He was a disciple of the apostles and later accompanied Paul until his martyrdom. He served the Lord without distraction, having neither wife nor children, and at the age of 84 he fell asleep in Boeotia, full of the Holy Spirit... The same Luke wrote Acts of the Apostles."*

[6] This becomes clearer and clearer in Luke's second volume, so I explore the implications in much more detail in my book *Straight to the Heart of Acts* (2010).

[7] Note the way that Luke uses the words *"we"* and *"us"* while describing the activities of Paul's team in Acts 16:10–17, 20:5–21:18 and 27:1–28:16.

intriguing to Theophilus. Luke was a man just like himself, who through careful investigation of the facts had been persuaded to throw away the idols of Rome and to worship the Jewish Messiah. The fact that Luke was an educated doctor also made his testimony all the weightier. If a qualified physician believed that a virgin had conceived a child, that crowds of invalids had been healed and that a corpse had been raised from the dead, then Theophilus could not dismiss the reports of those miracles as fairy tales, believed too readily by the ignorant rabble. Luke's medical training and his two years of careful research gave him enough credibility with Theophilus to make him wonder if what he had heard was true.[8]

In Act 1 of his gospel, Luke records the early life of Jesus and assures Theophilus that this isn't someone else's story: **he came for you (1:1–8:56)**. In Act 2, he urges Theophilus to say yes to Jesus, assuring him that **he can use you (9:1–19:27)**. In Act 3, Luke explains to Theophilus that this invitation has been made possible because **he made a way for you (19:28–24:53)**.[9] The first volume of Luke's two-part history of the Christian faith therefore introduces Theophilus to the founder of Christianity and repeatedly challenges him to respond to the fact that *all of this happened for you*.

So let's read Luke's gospel together. Knowing that his book would gain a wider audience than Theophilus, Luke filled it with many things that will fuel your own faith too. Whether you are a seasoned Christian or a hardened sceptic, Luke wrote his book to help you to discover that what Jesus said and did he said and did for you.

---

[8] Luke undertook the research he describes in 1:1–4 during the time that Paul was imprisoned in Israel from 57 to 59 AD. Having met Theophilus on his arrival in Rome, he then wrote Luke and Acts from 60 to 62 AD.

[9] Some commentators prefer to view Luke's structure in terms of geography: *Galilee* (1:1–9:50), *Judea* (9:51–13:21), *Perea* (13:22–19:27) and *Jerusalem* (19:28–24:53). However, I will show you that Luke's structure is far more about his challenge to us than it is about the geographical backdrop to that challenge.

Act One:

He Came for You

From Where I'm Standing (1:1–25)

The angel said to him, "I am Gabriel. I stand in the presence of God, and I have been sent to speak to you and to tell you this good news."

(Luke 1:19)

Matthew, Mark and Luke are often referred to as the "synoptic" gospels because they "share a common perspective", whereas John wrote three decades later to fill in the gaps in their story.[1] Although this is a helpful distinction, it can also blind us to the major differences between Luke and the other three gospels, because in many ways it is Luke that stands apart from Matthew, Mark and John. We see this clearly in the opening verses of his gospel.

In 1:1–4, Luke tells us that he is standing in the spectators' gallery. He is not like Matthew, Mark and John – an eyewitness to the events that he describes. He presents himself instead as a classical Greek historian, introducing his work in the same style as Herodotus, Thucydides and Xenophon. Using the best Greek of any New Testament writer, he explains that his account is the result of a careful investigation of all the evidence.[2] Jewish witnesses could give oral histories of what they saw and heard,

---

[1] Clement of Alexandria says that this was John's purpose in writing (Eusebius, *Church History*, 6.14.7).

[2] Luke writes perfect classical Greek when he wants to (1:1–4), but he is also skilful enough to write Greek with a Hebrew flavour at other times. He deliberately echoes Hebrew turns of phrase in his Greek when he writes that *"he added to send"* (20:11, 12) and *"I have eagerly desired with eager desire"* (22:15).

but only Luke could distil a thousand personal testimonies into a single Greek history book.[3] His two years of painstaking research while his friend Paul was in prison in Caesarea from 57 to 59 AD had uniquely qualified him as a historical biographer of Jesus.[4]

In 1:5–10, Luke introduces us to a man who stood at the very heart of Jewish history. Zechariah was one of the priests who stood before the Lord in the sacred inner room of the Temple in Jerusalem. None of the other gospel writers mentions him, but Luke uses him as a historical benchmark to pinpoint the date for us as June or July 6 BC.[5] Whereas Matthew, Mark and John start their gospels by proclaiming that Jesus is the Jewish Messiah, the Son of God and the eternal Creator, Luke starts by showing how these events fit in with where we ourselves are standing. All of this happened for us.[6]

Zechariah is standing in front of the altar of incense in the inner sanctuary of the Temple, but what fills his gaze is disaster. He and his wife Elizabeth are devout believers in the God of Israel and have been blameless in keeping his laws, yet their prayers have gone unanswered. They are old and childless in an age that saw infertility as a disgrace, an outward sign of God's displeasure. He is as confused about his own life as the

---

[3] Luke says he aims to write (*graphō*, 1:3) an orderly account of what has been *taught orally* (*katēxeō*, 1:4).

[4] Whereas Matthew, Mark and John tend to group their material by theme, Luke is a stickler for exact chronology. His *ordered* account (*kathexēs*, 1:3) is easily as reliable as any other ancient work of history.

[5] Herod the Great ruled from 37 to 4 BC and was still alive when Jesus was born. Since John the Baptist was 6 months older than Jesus (1:26) and Jesus was aged 30 in 27 AD (3:1 and 23), John must have been conceived in 6 BC. 1 Chronicles 24:7–19 tells us that Zechariah's division of priests was only ever on duty in June or July.

[6] It also happened for those all around us, so we cannot keep this good news to ourselves. Luke tells us in 1:2 that believers become *"servants of the word"*. Sharing is not optional.

Jewish nation that he represents is confused by its defeat and occupation by the Romans.[7]

In 1:11–17, God does not leave Zechariah standing all alone in his confusion. The priest is suddenly terrified to see an angel standing next to the altar of incense. It is Gabriel, the same angel who appeared to the prophet Daniel and whose name is Hebrew for *God's Warrior*.[8] He calms Zechariah with an assurance that he brings good news. God has heard his anguished prayers and will grant him the son he longs for. More than that, he will make his son a herald of God's salvation to the nation of Israel. The last two verses of the Old Testament promise that the Messiah's arrival will be preceded by a prophet like Elijah, who *"will turn the hearts of the parents to their children, and the hearts of the children to their parents"*.[9] The angel quotes from those verses to inform Zechariah that his son will be that prophet. In answering Zechariah and Elizabeth's prayers, the Lord will also answer the prayers of Israel. As a proof that their baby will preach salvation to the Jews, he will be filled with the Holy Spirit even as a foetus in his mother's womb.[10]

Note what Luke does here at the start of his historical biography of Jesus, writing as a Greek outsider from the spectators' gallery. He grounds the story of Jesus in the Jewish Scriptures and in the Jewish Temple in the Jewish city of Jerusalem. He explains that the coming of Jesus is good news for

---

[7] Zechariah means *The Lord Has Remembered* and Elizabeth means *God's Oath*. The Lord had made them infertile, not to curse them, but to make them a channel of his blessing and to fulfil his promises to Israel.

[8] Daniel 8:16; 9:21. The time between the completion of the Old Testament in 432 BC and the appearance of Gabriel to Zechariah in 6 BC is known as the "400 years of silence". Suddenly the silence is over.

[9] Malachi 4:5–6. John would not echo Elijah's miracles (John 10:41) so much as the revival that Elijah brought to Israel in 1 Kings 18. See Matthew 11:7–14; 17:10–13.

[10] Luke 1:15 deliberately echoes the words of an angel to another infertile couple in Judges 13:4–5. Luke wants us to view his words as Scripture. The God of the Old Testament is now giving the world a New Testament.

the Jewish nation, but even as he does so he announces that the coming of the Jewish Messiah is also good news for everyone. The angel tells Zechariah that his son's task will be *"to make ready a people prepared for the Lord"*. John the Baptist would preach that no amount of Jewish ancestry could make anybody part of God's true people. Similarly, no amount of Gentile blood could ever shut them out.

In 1:18–25, Zechariah struggles to see things from where the angel is standing. He points out that he and Elizabeth are far too old to have children.[11] He demands proof from Gabriel. Instead of giving him proof, the angel makes him deaf and mute so that he will learn to listen.[12] He needs to stop talking and to start seeing things from heaven's perspective, like the angel: *"I am Gabriel. I stand in the presence of God, and I have been sent to speak to you and to tell you this good news."* From where the angel is standing, this announcement makes perfect sense. The essence of the Gospel is that God helps those who cannot help themselves.[13] Zechariah would only hear and speak again when he named his son John, which is Hebrew for *The Lord Is Gracious.* Elizabeth understands the Gospel faster than her husband. She declares that *"The Lord has done this for me. In these days he has shown his favour and taken away my disgrace among the people."*

If you are Jewish, the start of Luke's gospel is fantastic news. It proclaims that God has fulfilled his promises to your nation through the birth of John the Baptist and of Jesus. If you

---

[11] Luke uses the same Greek words in 1:7 and 1:18 that are used in the Greek Septuagint translation of the Old Testament to say that Abraham and Sarah were *well on in years* (Genesis 18:11; 24:1). He wants us to see his gospel as Scripture and as the promise of a new and better seed of Abraham (Genesis 18:10–15).

[12] The Greek word *kōphos* in 1:22 can mean either deaf or mute. We can tell that it means both from the fact that people have to communicate with Zechariah using sign language and a tablet in 1:62–63.

[13] Gabriel uses the verb *euangelizō* to tell Zechariah literally in 1:19 that he has come to *evangelize* him.

are not Jewish, like Luke and Theophilus, the start of this gospel is fantastic news for you too. It calls you to come down from the spectators' gallery and to take your place in the people that God is preparing for himself. Luke starts his gospel by calling all of us to change our perspective and to see things from where the angel is standing: all these events in the summer of 6 BC happened for you and for me.

The Impossible (1:26–38)

*"How will this be," Mary asked the angel, "since
I am a virgin?" The angel answered… "Nothing is
impossible with God."*

(Luke 1:34–37)

A judge like Theophilus must have heard some tall stories in his
time. The courtrooms of the ancient world were full of them.
But in all his years as a judge he cannot have heard a more
impossible claim than this one. Luke said a virgin had given
birth to a baby.

Even today, many people struggle to believe that this really
happened. Rob Bell asks if it might just be *"a bit of mythologizing
the Gospel writers threw in to appeal to the followers of the Mithra
and Dionysian religious cults that were hugely popular at the time
of Jesus, whose gods had virgin births?"* He queries whether *"in
the Hebrew language at that time, the word 'virgin' could mean
several things"* or whether *"in the first century being 'born of a
virgin' also referred to a child whose mother became pregnant
the first time she had intercourse?"*[1] Rather than skim over these
verses, we therefore need to slow down to consider carefully
what Luke is saying. What made him risk his credibility at the
very outset of his gospel by asking Theophilus to believe the
impossible? These verses suggest at least four reasons.

First, Luke says this as a historian. He knows we will find
it difficult to believe what he says happened, so he provides us
with a time, a place and a name. He pinpoints the date by telling
us that the virgin conceived six months after Zechariah's wife

---

[1] Rob Bell asks these questions in *Velvet Elvis* (2005).

– in other words, in January 5 BC.[2] He pinpoints the location as the town of Nazareth in Galilee – not a city where such things might be missed in the crowd, but a close-knit community of a few hundred people.[3] He also tells us the name of the woman involved – the same Mary who was engaged to Joseph, the descendant of David. Luke expects us to believe him because his two years of research forced him to conclude that the impossible had really happened to a particular woman at a particular place and time.

Second, Luke says this as a doctor. When the former tax collector Matthew describes the birth of Jesus in his gospel, he instinctively focuses on how events unfurled for Joseph. Jewish society was segregated by gender, so he naturally told the story from the perspective of the man. Luke's profession transcended gender barriers. As a doctor, he instinctively approaches childbirth from the woman's point of view. His reference to *conception* and *delivery* in verse 31 serves to remind us that these are not the words of a primitive fool, but those of someone who has been trained in first-century gynaecology. Luke is fully aware that what he is saying here is medically impossible – that one of Mary's eggs was fertilized by divine miracle without there being any need for human sperm.

Third, Luke says this as a student of the Old Testament. He does not quote explicitly from the Jewish Scriptures, since that would mean very little to Theophilus, but he clearly has the early prophecies of Isaiah in mind. The angel's words echo the promise that God would cause a virgin's son to rule forever on David's throne over God's people. Yes, that would be humanly impossible. It would have to be a miracle from God. But the

---

[2] Jesus was therefore born in September or October. It's just tradition to celebrate his birth on 25th December.

[3] Matthew 2:23 emphasizes the spiritual significance of Nazareth for Jewish readers. Luke emphasizes its geographical location to help Roman readers to find it on a map and believe what he is saying is real.

prophet declared in triumph that *"The zeal of the Lord Almighty will accomplish this."*[4]

Fourth, Luke says this as a scientist who has come to believe in something bigger than science. We might have expected a physician to play down all talk of the supernatural in his gospel, but in fact we find the opposite is true. Luke uses the words for "demons" and "healing" and "the Holy Spirit" more often than any of the other gospel writers. He uses the word "angel" almost as often as the other three combined. He adds several new miracles to those already recorded by Matthew and Mark. Nobody is more diligent than Luke in questioning facts, but nor is anyone more convinced than Luke that heavenly facts trump earthly facts every time God issues a simple command.

Luke explains that Mary conceived through God's power, because salvation always starts with him and not with us. God announced his plan to her through Gabriel, the same angel that appeared to Zechariah and whose name means *God's Warrior* or *God's Strongman.*[5] Gabriel responds to her horrified expression by assuring her that *"The Lord is with you"* and that *"Mary, you have found favour with God."* She is to call her baby Jesus, which is Hebrew for *The Lord Saves*, because her virgin birth is the fulfilment of God's ancient prophecy to Eve that he would save the world through the offspring of a woman, without needing the help of any man.[6]

Mary asks the obvious question: *"How will this be, since I am a virgin?"* She isn't voicing unbelief, like Zechariah in the Temple, but bewilderment in the face of the impossible. The angel explains that *"The Holy Spirit will come on you, and the*

---

[4] Isaiah 7:14; 9:6-7. While Luke just states the facts, Matthew quotes from Isaiah for his Jewish readers.

[5] Gabriel's appearance proclaims God's irresistible power, which is why Daniel, Zechariah and Mary all react with fear to seeing him (Daniel 8:17; Luke 1:12).

[6] God prophesies over Eve in Genesis 3:15 and declares in Hebrew that *"her seed"* will be the Saviour. He does not prophesy about Adam's seed because the Saviour would be born without the sperm of any man.

power of the Most High will overshadow you. So the holy one to be born will be called the Son of God."[7] He doesn't use the language of modern medicine, but Gabriel essentially informs her that the same Holy Spirit through whom the Lord created the physical universe in Genesis 1 will perform a creative miracle inside her womb. He will create a male gamete out of nothing to fertilize the egg within her. Her child will be the Son of God physically as well as spiritually. Luke is not denying medical facts. He is simply insisting that God can overrule them. He is inviting us to believe that God is truly this passionate to save us.

Mary believes that if God can provide a baby for Zechariah in the barren womb of Elizabeth, he can also provide a baby for her in her virginity. She believes that if God's Word was powerful enough to create the universe out of nothing at the dawn of time, it is also powerful enough to create whatever physical matter is needed in her womb to create a baby, without the need of help from any man. She believes the angel's promise when he assures her in verse 37 that *"Nothing is impossible with God."* Although she knows it may mean being rejected by Joseph and by her neighbours in Nazareth, she submits to God's plan: *"I am the Lord's servant. May your word to me be fulfilled."*[8]

Luke assures us as a historian and as a doctor that the impossible took place in the town of Nazareth in 5 BC. He invites us to respond with the same humble faith as Mary. He wants us to believe that God is this committed to saving us. All of this happened for you.

---

[7] The angel's words in 1:35 are meant to echo the Old Testament accounts of the glory of the Lord descending on the Tabernacle and Temple. The virgin birth singled Jesus out as the holy Son of God.

[8] Mary was even at risk of being killed by her neighbours. See Deuteronomy 22:21 and John 8:1–11.

The Lowest of the Low (1:39–45)

*As soon as the sound of your greeting reached my
ears, the baby in my womb leaped for joy.*

(Luke 1:44)

When Nelson Mandela emerged from twenty-seven years in
prison, he declared that *"A nation should not be judged by how
it treats its highest citizens but its lowest ones."*[1] In that case the
Roman Empire was terribly guilty. Its male citizens ill-treated
their wives as much as they ill-treated one another. They denied
citizenship to the foreign tribesmen they conquered in their lust
for empire and they denied legal personhood to their slaves.
Rome was a place where the strong grew stronger and where
the weak were often simply left to die.

This was the world in which Luke had been raised, a world
in which the poet Lucan complained that *"Poverty is shunned
and treated as a crime."*[2] When he came to faith in Jesus, Luke
repented of his Roman ways and became a champion of the
lowest of the low. One of the distinctive features of his gospel
is how much he sides with outcasts and with rejects, insisting
that what Jesus said and did he said and did for them as much
as for anyone.

Roman society viewed women as second-rate to men. It is
therefore striking that Luke begins the story of Jesus by focusing
on a woman. He mentions Mary by name more than the other

---

[1] He says this in his autobiography *Long Walk to Freedom* (1994).

[2] Writing at the same time that Luke wrote his gospel, the poet Lucan says
this in *Pharsalia* (1.166).

three gospel writers put together, describing her inner thoughts and her interactions with her relative Elizabeth.[3] Throughout the rest of his gospel Luke sees himself as a voice for the many voiceless women of the world. He includes at least ten women in the story of Jesus who do not feature in Matthew, Mark and John. He records two new parables about women and he notes that many women followed Jesus alongside his twelve disciples.[4] Don't miss this, because it was revolutionary.

Roman society also looked down on the poor. It is therefore very striking that Luke begins his story with a Nazarene so poor that she brought the very cheapest offering to the Temple when her son was born.[5] Luke speaks up for the despised paupers of the world by recording more of Jesus' teaching about money than any of the other gospel writers: *"Blessed are you who are poor, for yours is the kingdom of God... But woe to you who are rich, for you have already received your comfort."*[6] Mary has very few material possessions yet Elizabeth assures her in verses 42 and 45 that she is more blessed than the rich in their palaces. Luke turns Roman attitudes towards poverty on their head.

Roman society also despised outcasts. It viewed most of the empire's population as "barbarians", so Luke challenges this racism by telling us that a Samaritan leper was the only one who remembered to thank Jesus for healing him and that Samaritan travellers could teach the Jewish priests a thing or two about God's compassion. He describes the love of Jesus towards lepers and slaves and beggars and prostitutes and tax collectors.[7] The fact that they were deprived of a voice in Roman society did not

---

[3] Mary and Elizabeth were relatives despite the fact that one came from the tribe of Judah and the other was a Levite (1:5, 36). By 5 BC the twelve tribes of Israel had intermarried.

[4] See 2:36–38; 7:11–17; 8:1–3; 13:10–13; 15:8–10; 18:1–8; 23:27–31; 24:1–11.

[5] Leviticus 12:8 says that the offering brought by Mary in Luke 2:24 was reserved for the poorest of the poor.

[6] Luke 6:20, 24. See also 11:37–41; 12:13–21, 33–34; 14:12–14; 16:14–15, 19–31.

[7] Luke 5:12–14, 27–32; 7:1–10, 36–50; 9:51–56; 10:30–37; 17:12–19; 18:9–14, 35–43; 19:1–10.

make them any less worthy of salvation. Jesus came into the world for the likes of them.

It is easy to imagine what effect Luke's love for the lowest of the low might have had on a Roman reader like Theophilus. As a judge in one of the capital's crowded courtrooms, he must have had more experience of the rotten underbelly of society than a producer on *The Jeremy Kyle Show*. However much he might have wished to resist Luke's claim that he was a sinner in need of God's salvation, he must have felt convicted by the gulf between the gospel writer's attitudes and his own. Luke expects us to feel the same way when we read his gospel, convicted that we are also sinners in need of God's forgiveness. To help us he challenges one of the biggest blind spots in our own day.

We don't keep slaves. We pride ourselves on our liberal attitudes towards gender and racial equality. We champion the rights of the disabled and of sexual minorities. But our attitude towards one of the voiceless groups that Luke defends in the first chapter of his gospel is no more enlightened than the attitudes of first-century Rome.

Luke made a revolutionary statement in verse 15. Did you spot it when he told us that Zechariah's son would *"be filled with the Holy Spirit even before he is born"*? Roman society denied that foetuses were fully human. Many women took the silphium herb to procure an abortion, and many men kicked their women in the abdomen if they refused. Once born, there was still a one-in-three chance that a Roman baby would be abandoned by its mother and left to die.[8] Luke is therefore defending another type of outcast when he tells us in verse 15 that God's Spirit can fill a foetus in the womb. He goes one step further in verses 39–45, since Mary has only just fallen pregnant when she visits Elizabeth. Jesus is still a tiny embryo inside her, yet the foetus of John the Baptist leaps for joy in his mother's womb in response

---

[8] See "Child Abandonment in European History", published in the *Journal of Family History* (January 1992).

to his arrival.[9] His reaction provokes Elizabeth to welcome Mary as *"the mother of my Lord"* – not as the mother of a cluster of cells that has the potential to become her Lord. Jesus does not yet have ears or fingers or toes, yet Elizabeth hails him as Yahweh.[10] In our world of easy access to abortions and the morning-after pill, that ought to challenge us every bit as much as it challenged Theophilus and his first-century friends.[11]

At the end of the *Hunger Games* trilogy of novels, Katniss Everdeen reflects that

> *I no longer feel any allegiance to these monsters called human beings, despite being one myself. I think that Peeta was onto something about us destroying one another and letting some decent species take over. Because something is significantly wrong with a creature that sacrifices its children's lives... You can spin it any way you like... But in the end, who does it benefit? No one. The truth is, it benefits no one to live in a world where these things happen.[12]*

Luke therefore tells us good news. We have all sinned but, unlike Katniss Everdeen, God has not given up on us. Instead of rejecting humans for exploiting one another, despising one another and aborting one another, God has decided to save us by becoming a better kind of human being. He became a zygote, then an embryo, then a foetus in a poor Jewish girl's womb. The Creator became the weakest of creatures to save humanity from its sinful self-destruction. So don't be offended when Luke insists that we are all sinners who need saving. Admit that you are as guilty as everyone else. The first step towards experiencing the good news of Jesus is to confess that he came for you.

---

[9] The Bible also tells us that foetuses are able to interact spiritually in Psalm 22:10, 58:3 and 139:13–16.

[10] The Greek word *kurios* in 1:43 is the word used throughout the Greek Septuagint for *the Lord*.

[11] Luke is not trying to single you out if you have had an abortion. He is encouraging you that the entire human race has blood on its hands. All of us have sinned and all of us need saving.

[12] Katniss says this in the Suzanne Collins novel *Mockingjay* (2010).

Every Single One (1:46–80)

Mary said: "My soul glorifies the Lord and my spirit rejoices in God my Saviour."

(Luke 1:46–47)

Desiderius Erasmus provoked outrage at the start of the sixteenth century when he retranslated the first chapter of Luke's gospel into Latin. For centuries the angel's words to Mary in verse 28 had been used as a prayer: *"Ave Maria, gratia plena"*, or *"Hail Mary, full of grace"*. Erasmus had gone back to the Greek text and had discovered that this translation was in fact very misleading. The angel did not say that Mary was *gratia plena* – full of grace in the sense that she was sinless and empowered to dispense grace to us. Gabriel declared that she was *gratiosa* – that she herself had received grace from God.[1] Erasmus declared that even the Virgin Mary was a sinner. It didn't make him very popular in medieval Europe.

Luke honours Mary more than any other gospel writer, but he also makes it clear that Erasmus was right: she was a sinner who needed saving. When the foetus in Elizabeth's womb leaps in recognition of the embryo in hers, Luke records Mary's excitement. Her prayer explains why the angel's greeting had troubled her so much and why she had needed his reassurance: *"Do not be afraid, Mary, you have found favour with God."* Mary's prayer celebrates that we are all sinners, every single one.

In 1:46–55, Mary confesses freely that she needs a Saviour. She was not conceived immaculately as some kind of sinless

---

[1] The Greek word *kecharitōmenē* in 1:28 is a "perfect passive participle". It is God who dispenses grace in this verse, not Mary.

demigoddess. She confesses that she was born in the same *"humble state"* as us and that she needs God to fulfil his salvation promises to Abraham as much as any other sinful human.[2] As it dawns on Mary that the baby in her womb is the Messiah that was promised, she praises God that her Saviour has finally come. She exclaims in gratitude, *"My soul glorifies the Lord and my spirit rejoices in God my Saviour."*[3]

It is vital that we take this to heart because Mary's confession lies at the heart of Luke's message. One of the key words in his gospel is *salvation*, a catch-all word for all God's promises throughout the Old Testament that he would one day come in person to right what Adam had wronged and to rid the world of the toxic consequences of human sin.[4] Mary's prayer warns us that only those who admit that they are sinners who need saving can ever have a share in God's salvation. Those who are proud and rich and full of themselves will be sent away empty, but those who empty themselves of all other hopes but God will be filled with the same grace as her. Mary does not present herself as our mediator with God, but as a sinner who points our way to his salvation.[5]

Now the spotlight shifts. In 1:57–80, Mary goes back home and Zechariah resumes centre stage. His wife Elizabeth gives birth to their baby and he demonstrates how much he has learned through being deaf and mute throughout her

---

[2] Mary says in 1:38 and 48 that she is nothing more than God's *doulē*, or *slave-girl*. Instead of looking to her, she urges us in 1:49 to look to the Lord as *ho dunatos – The Mighty One* or *The One Who Is Able* to save us.

[3] The Latin word for *glorifies* is *magnificat*. Since it is the first word of Mary's prayer in Latin, these verses are often referred to as the "Magnificat". Although it is sung in many churches, Luke technically records that Mary said them rather than sang them.

[4] See 19:10. Luke is the only gospel writer to use the Greek words for salvation – *sōtēria* and *sōtērion*.

[5] The Greek for *servant* in 1:54 can be translated *child* and the word for *descendant* in 1:55 is literally *seed* (*pais* and *sperma*). God's salvation would come to Israel through the true Son of God and true seed of Abraham.

nine months of pregnancy.[6] Despite the fact that nobody in his immediate family has ever borne the name that the angel told him to call his son, he writes instructions for the boy to be named John, which means *The Lord Is Gracious*.[7] Suddenly he can hear and speak again. While his neighbours look on in amazement, he uses his new-found voice to follow up the words of Mary. Filled with the Holy Spirit, he prophesies a salvation celebration of his own.

Howard Marshall observes that these prayers at the start of Luke's gospel *"function like an overture, setting out the main themes of the following drama, but doing so with their own distinctive music. One of the most characteristic tones here is that of salvation."*[8] Zechariah uses the word salvation three times as he explains to his startled neighbours the meaning of his sudden supernatural healing.[9] Some of his Old Testament allusions may have been lost on Theophilus, but don't miss the way they root what is happening in the salvation story of Israel. They proclaim that the Lord is still *"the God of Israel"* and that the Saviour in Mary's womb is the one God talked about to Abraham and to David and to the other prophets in the Jewish Scriptures.[10] Zechariah proclaims that his own baby John is the prophet whose coming is promised in the final two chapters of the Old Testament. He is the one that God refers to as *"the messenger, who will prepare the way before me"*. He is not the main event, but the warm-up act for the Messiah. He is the one who will prepare Israel for its Saviour.

---

[6] Note Luke's provision of historical pointers in 1:5, 8, 26 and 56. They date the birth to about April 5 BC.

[7] There had been several priests named John, or *Johanan* in Hebrew (1 Chronicles 6:10; Nehemiah 12:22–23), but there had never been a man of that name in Zechariah's immediate family.

[8] He says this under "Salvation" in Joel B. Green's *Dictionary of Jesus and the Gospels* (1992).

[9] *"The Lord's hand"* in 1:66 is an Old Testament name for the Holy Spirit (2 Kings 3:15). Note the repeated activity of the Holy Spirit in this chapter. See 1:15, 17, 35, 41, 66, 67, 80.

[10] See Malachi 3:1, 4:2, 5–6; 2 Samuel 7:8–16; 22:3; Isaiah 9:1–2; 40:3–5.

Zechariah and Elizabeth are about to exit the stage. Verse 80 speeds the life of John the Baptist forward thirty years.[11] They have completed their part in Luke's story. They have shown us that the life of Jesus is rooted in the national history of Israel and in the pages of the Jewish Scriptures. Since Luke told us in verse 6 that *"Both of them were righteous in the sight of God, observing all the Lord's commands and decrees blamelessly,"* and yet they have confessed freely that *"He has raised up a horn of salvation for us,"* they echo Mary's statement that each of us needs saving, every single one. If those who are born Jews need to be taught the way of salvation so that they can receive forgiveness for their sins, how much more do we? As Zechariah and Elizabeth finish their part in the story, they invite us to confess that we too are sinners and that God's Saviour didn't just come for other people. He came for us.

When Erasmus pointed this out to sixteenth-century Europeans, many of them were furious. One of his friends wrote to warn him that he had heard an angry denunciation of his work: *"You could hardly imagine the abhorrence he expressed for your translation of that word as 'Ave gratiosa.'"*[12] Some people will do almost anything to convince themselves that they do not need saving. They want to point to Mary or Zechariah or Elizabeth or some other saint in order to insist that human sinfulness is not universal, but Luke will have none of this. He begins his gospel by calling us to accept that Jesus came for us, because every single one of us needs a Saviour.

He tells us in 11:27–28 that *"As Jesus was saying these things, a woman in the crowd called out, 'Blessed is the mother who gave you birth and nursed you.' He replied, 'Blessed rather are those who hear the word of God and obey it.'"* That's the Gospel: Jesus came for sinners just like you and me.

---

[11] Luke 1:80 is meant to echo Judges 13:24–25. The God of the Old Testament is back on the move.

[12] Johann von Botzheim wrote this from the Austrian city of Linz in April 1530.

Good News (2:1–20)

The angel said to them, "Do not be afraid. I bring you good news that will cause great joy for all the people."
(Luke 2:10)

In March 44 BC, the eighteen-year-old Octavius received some astonishing news. Julius Caesar had made a new will shortly before his assassination and, much to the surprise of both friend and foe, it had named him as his great-uncle's heir. He was instantly catapulted from obscurity into such wealth and power that, after years of civil war and deft political manoeuvring, he became the first emperor of Rome. A single piece of good news had transformed a nobody into the ruler of the world.

Renaming himself Caesar Augustus, he began a propaganda campaign to convince the world that what had happened to him was good news for them too. Much of it revolved around two Greek words: the word *sōtēr*, which meant *saviour*, and the word *euangelion*, which meant *gospel* or *good news*. You can see both words in one of his inscriptions:

> *Providence, which orders all things and is deeply interested in our life, has set things in perfect order by giving us Augustus... and by sending him as a **Saviour** for us and for our descendants that he might end war and make all things beautiful. Since by his appearing Caesar has exceeded the hopes of all who awaited this **Good News**... the birthday of the god Augustus marks the start of the **Good News** about him for the world.*[1]

---

[1] This inscription from the city of Priene in Asia Minor in 9 BC proposes that people ought to revise their calendars around the birth of Augustus, just as they later did around the birth of Christ.

It helps to understand this if we want to read the second chapter of Luke's gospel in the same way that Theophilus must have read it in propaganda-saturated Rome. Luke pinpoints the birth of Jesus at a particular place in history – midway through the reign of Augustus Caesar, during the first of the two terms that Quirinius served as governor of Syria.[2] That concurs with chapter 1 to date events to September or October 5 BC.[3] Caesar has decided that he wants to count the subjects in his empire, so Mary and her fiancé Joseph are forced to make the 100-mile journey from Nazareth in Galilee to Bethlehem in Judea.[4] By the time they arrive Mary is in labour, but every guest room in the town has already been filled by people eager to register as the emperor has ordered.[5] Mary is forced to give birth to her baby in the stable of one of the inns and to use a cattle feeding trough as a makeshift crib.[6] It's hardly an impressive start to the story of Jesus.

But Luke has news for Theophilus and for the rest of the Roman Empire. What happened in that stable was far better news than the birth of Augustus Caesar. Look out for the two words *sōtēr* and *euangelion* in the angel's announcement to the shepherds:

---

[2] Quirinius was governor of Syria from 6 to 4 BC and from 6 to 12 AD. Luke mentions the census that was taken in his second term as governor in Acts 5:37.

[3] Some readers are surprised that Jesus was not born in 0 AD, but there never was a year 0 AD! 1 BC was followed by 1 AD, so the sixth-century scholar who first calculated "Anno Domini" was only out by four years.

[4] Since Bethlehem is Hebrew for *House of Bread*, some readers attribute great significance to the fact that the Bread of Life was served to the town in one of its feeding troughs (John 6:35, 48–58).

[5] Luke seems to want to use this detail to challenge us to make room for Jesus in our own hearts. See John 8:37; 2 Corinthians 7:2.

[6] Luke does not actually say that the manger was in a stable. As a doctor, he is more concerned about the type of diaper used on the baby and the cot it slept in than he is about the lesser non-medical details.

*Do not be afraid. I bring you **Good News** that will cause great joy for all the people. Today in the town of David a **Saviour** has been born to you; he is the Messiah, the Lord.*[7]

Shepherds were despised in the ancient world as light-fingered vagabonds. A judge like Theophilus knew that their testimony was regarded as unreliable in a court of law.[8] He therefore knows that Luke would never have invented such a story but is simply recording history as it unfurled. The Messiah's first palace was a stable and his first courtiers were shepherds, but nonetheless he was a better Saviour for the world than anyone who ever sat on Caesar's throne.

The angel uses the Greek word *laos* in verse 10 to announce that Jesus has come to be the Saviour of *"the people"*. The word is nearly always used in the Greek Septuagint translation of the Old Testament to describe the Jewish people, as opposed to the *ethnē*, the foreign nations of the world. The angel therefore echoes Zechariah's prayer by declaring that Jesus is the Saviour of the Jews, but his angelic colleagues appear to help him complete his song: *"Glory to God in the highest heaven, and on earth peace to those on whom his favour rests."* The angels declare to a world that is rushing about to earn the fickle favour of Caesar that King Jesus is conducting his own roll call among the nations. He is inviting everyone, both Jew and Gentile, to seek his favour and to discover that he offers something far better than the *Pax Romana*. He has come to broker peace between heaven and earth.[9]

---

[7] The angel uses the verb *euangelizō* rather than the noun *euangelion*. This is the first time that Luke has used the title *Christos*, which is the Greek equivalent of the Hebrew word *Messiah*, or *Anointed One*. Since the name *kurios*, or *Lord*, was also one of Caesar's titles (Acts 25:26), Luke's words were radical to Roman ears.

[8] For an example of this, see Genesis 46:33–34. Micah 4:6–8 had prophesied that outcasts from Migdal Eder, or *The Tower of the Flock*, just outside Bethlehem, would be first to respond to the Messiah (Genesis 35:19–21).

[9] The angels do not say in Greek that God's favour is on all people, but that all people can receive his favour.

The outcast shepherds have no proof that any of this is true. The angels tell them that they will only know for certain *after* they have proved their faith with their feet.[10] The angel army that announced this Good News is more than capable of protecting their flock if they trust God enough to leave it unprotected in the fields.[11] The shepherds conclude that the angel's story is so bizarre that, if they find a baby in a manger, they will know for sure that everything else they were told must also be true.[12] When they find what they are looking for, they lead the neighbourhood in worship as they head back to the fields. They proclaim the Good News to all they meet: a better Saviour than Caesar has come.

These verses have inspired countless Christmas songs of praise. As we read them now, Luke wants us to let the shepherds lead us in songs of faith-filled worship too:

Our God, heaven cannot hold Him nor can earth sustain;
Heaven and earth shall flee away when He comes to reign.
Yet in the bleak midwinter a stable place sufficed
For the Lord God Almighty, Jesus Christ.

What can I give Him, poor as I am?
If I were a shepherd I would bring a lamb;
If I were a wise man I would do my part;
Yet what I can I give Him – give my heart.[13]

---

[10] The rest of the Bible tells us that this is quite normal. We only get absolute proof that the Gospel is true when we start putting it into practice. Luke 2:12 is echoed by Exodus 3:12, 2 Kings 19:29 and John 7:17.

[11] Luke describes them as *"a great company of the heavenly host"* or *"a great multitude from heaven's army"*. Since a single angel overcame 185,000 Assyrian soldiers in 2 Kings 19:35, their sheep were quite safe from wolves.

[12] Luke seems to be hinting in 2:19 that the circumstances of Jesus' birth caused Mary to question in her heart whether he was truly the Messiah. The arrival of the shepherds must have encouraged her as much as them.

[13] Taken from "In the Bleak Midwinter", a carol by the nineteenth-century English poet Christina Rossetti.

Right Under Our Noses
(2:21–40)

Simeon took him in his arms and praised God,
saying... "My eyes have seen your salvation."

(Luke 2:28–30)

Sometimes it's hard to see what we have right under our noses. Take the man who sold a picture at a flea market in Pennsylvania in 1989. He was so unimpressed with its depiction of a country scene that he sold it for a mere $4. The man who bought it later confessed that he only did so to reuse the frame. But when he got home and removed the picture, he discovered a folded document between the canvas and the backboard of the frame. It was a first-edition copy of the Declaration of Independence, which he went on to sell at Sotheby's in June 1991. When the auctioneer's gavel fell, the man's $4 purchase had just netted him a tidy $2.42 million.[1]

That's an astonishing story, but before you rush off to the flea market yourself, consider what is under your nose as you read Luke's gospel. One of its recurring themes is how easy it is for us to miss what God is doing.[2] Who would have imagined that real action in the Roman Empire would take place, not in Caesar's palace, but in the Temple of one of the many nations Caesar had subdued? Who would have dreamed that God would use the wombs of an infertile old woman and of a virgin to herald

---

[1] This astonishing windfall was reported in *The New York Times* on 14th June 1991.

[2] For example, John the Baptist's life appeared tragic, yet 1:15 says he was *"great in the sight of the Lord"*.

a New Testament for Israel? Who would have imagined that at one point in history the person the most full of the Holy Spirit would be a foetus? Who among the busy people of Bethlehem was aware that Caesar's census was merely a historical footnote to something far bigger that was happening in the stable outside? Luke wants to use the topsy-turvy events of these early chapters to warn us not to miss what is under our noses as we read his gospel. He wants us to behave like Mary, who *"treasured up all these things and pondered them in her heart"*.

As Luke continues his story, he encourages us not to miss what is right under our noses. He tells us in 2:21 that when Mary and Joseph obeyed the Law of Moses by bringing their eight-day-old baby to be circumcised at the local synagogue (presumably the one in Bethlehem), the townspeople who had missed him a week earlier missed him again. Even when they stated to the rabbi that his name would be the one the angel gave him – Jesus, which is Hebrew for *The Lord Saves* – the rabbi failed to recognize the subject of his sermons. David's heir came to the synagogue in David's city, but David's people failed to notice the arrival of the true and better King of Israel.

In 2:22–38, the backdrop shifts towards the Temple in Jerusalem, where the priests offered their sacrifices and where the teachers of the law explained the meaning of the Old Testament prophets. None of them spot that there is something different about the baby that is being dedicated or the mother that is being purified by offering the sacrifices demanded by the Jewish Law.[3] The priest fails to notice that right under his nose is the one who will put an end to the Temple sacrifices. The teachers fail to look up from their books long enough to notice that the one they are reading about has finally arrived.

But Simeon is different. He is *"righteous and devout"* and *"waiting for the consolation of Israel"* – that is, longing for the

---

[3] Luke's two quotations in 2:23–24 come from either Exodus 13:2 or 13:12, and from Leviticus 12:8. If he had added a third quotation in 2:21, it would have come from Leviticus 12:3.

coming of the Messiah.[4] He is not alone in this but here's the crucial difference: *"the Holy Spirit was on him."* A big theme in Luke's gospel is that faith in God isn't at its core about books or rituals or religious activity, but about obeying the command, *"Since we live by the Spirit, let us keep in step with the Spirit."*[5] Simeon has learned to keep his eyes open to what God's Spirit is doing all around him. As a result, even during the so-called "four hundred years of silence" he has heard the Spirit reassure him that he will glimpse the Messiah before he dies.[6] While the city of Jerusalem misses the arrival of Jesus, Simeon senses the Spirit stirring him to leave his house and go into the Temple courtyards. When he sees the baby Jesus, he senses the Holy Spirit telling him that this is the long-awaited Messiah. He takes Jesus in his arms and he begins to worship God for what is under his nose.

Simeon's song moves the story up a gear.[7] Perhaps inspired by being told that the baby is to be named *The Lord Saves*, he exclaims that he has God's salvation resting in his arms. He echoes Zechariah that this is good news for the Jews (the baby is *"the glory of your people Israel"*), but that it is also *"destined to cause the falling and rising of many in Israel"*. While many native-born Jews will reject God's offer of salvation, Simeon predicts that many pagan outcasts will accept it and be saved.[8] If the Jews fail to see what God is doing right under their noses then

---

[4] Luke uses the language of the Jewish rabbis in this chapter (*"the consolation of Israel"* in 2:25 and *"the redemption of Jerusalem"* in 2:38) in order to convey to Theophilus the Jewish historical context.

[5] Galatians 5:25. We can tell that Paul and Luke were teammates from the way this gospel echoes his letters.

[6] Simeon means *The One Who Hears* and Anna means *Grace*. Both of them lived up to their names.

[7] These words have traditionally been regarded as a song, but Luke technically tells us that Simeon said them. They are known by the first two words of the song in Latin – *Nunc dimittis*, or *"You may now dismiss"*.

[8] The "sword" in 2:35 is a warning that Mary will also feel the pain of the Jewish rejection of her son.

the Gentiles will see it instead. Jesus has been *"prepared in the sight of all nations: a light for revelation to the Gentiles"*.[9]

An old lady named Anna also spots what God is doing in the Temple courtyards. Luke emphasizes that, like Simeon, this is only because she too is full of the Holy Spirit. Ever since the death of her husband after only seven years of marriage, she has devoted herself for decades to prayer and fasting in the Temple courtyards. She has become a prophet, and now she reaps her reward.[10] Whether through a direct revelation from the Spirit or through having learned to keep her eyes wide open to what God is doing, she hears what Simeon is saying and comes over to add some prophecies of her own.[11] She cries out to those who are praying for the restoration of Jerusalem's fortunes not to miss what is under their noses. She tells them to open their eyes to the fact that God's salvation has finally come.

So before you read on in Luke's gospel take a moment to pray that God will open your eyes to all that he wants to say to you. Ask his Spirit to guide you, just as he guided Simeon and Anna. Ask him to reveal what it means to believe that all of this happened for you.

---

[9] Luke 2:10 told us that Jesus came for *ho laos* – that is, *the people* of Israel, as opposed to the *ethnē*, or *Gentiles*. Luke 2:31–32 tells us literally that he came for *hoi laoi* – that is, for *the peoples* – as well as for the *ethnē*.

[10] Luke's Greek can be translated two ways. Anna was either a widow *until she was 84* or a widow *for 84 years*.

[11] The Greek word *anthomologeomai* in 2:38 means *to respond with praise*. Anna spoke her words in response to those of Simeon.

Lessons from a Twelve-Year-Old (2:41–50)

They found him in the temple courts, sitting among the teachers, listening to them and asking them questions.

(Luke 2:46)

Jesus was incredibly excited. The past few millennia had felt like trying to play the piano wearing ski gloves, but now his moment had finally come. No longer did he need to speak through prophets to capture the attention of the people he had created. Gone was the need to rely on men like Jonah, who ran away instead of prophesying, or like Jeremiah, who spoke the truth but was largely ignored. Jesus was now a twelve-year-old. He was on the brink of his bar mitzvah and the moment when he would be taken seriously in Jewish society as a man. This was the moment he had been waiting for. He could finally speak with his own human mouth to the world that he had come to save.

I know how I would have done it. I wouldn't have come in through the main gate. I would have performed a mighty miracle to command an audience from the very start. I would have performed a miracle to blast open one of the locked entrances and I would have burst into the courtyard, hovering like Yoda in *Star Wars*, while Handel's "Hallelujah Chorus" blared out all around me. When you are the Son of God, that's the kind of thing that you can do. I wouldn't have had any trouble drawing a crowd fast.

That's why I find these verses so surprising. That's not what the twelve-year-old Jesus does at all. Instead, we find him sitting and listening and asking questions. Remember that the next time you have a chance to share the Gospel. If you aren't a believer in Jesus, you already know how inept Christians can often be at trying to share their faith with you. It's because they don't yet know Jesus and his methods as well as they should. If you are a believer, Luke includes this event in his story in order to train you in how to share your faith with others. He wants to teach you a few lessons from a twelve-year-old.

When Jesus wants to share the Gospel with people, he starts by *loving them*. He is still a child – old enough for his parents to trust him and not start looking for him during the first day of their journey back to Nazareth, but still too young to be taken seriously by the teachers of the law if he simply blurts out what he knows.[1] He is in the same boat as us whenever we try to share our faith with others, so he sits down and shows the teachers that he likes them, that he respects them and that he honours them. It's a simple principle: Nobody cares how much you know until they know how much you care.[2]

When Jesus wants to share the Gospel with people, he also starts by *listening to them*. Luke's gospel has been full of surprising statements so far, but don't miss this one. What on earth did Jesus have to learn from the teachers of the law? These are the blind guides who will later persuade the Jews to demand his execution! It is hard to imagine that they had anything to teach him, yet Jesus listens to them in order to teach us. One of the biggest roadblocks to sharing our faith effectively with others is that we are far too quick to speak and far too slow to listen. Yet James 1:19 commands us, *"My dear brothers and*

---

[1] It was easier for Mary to mislay the Messiah than we imagine. First-century pilgrims would often travel in extended communities, and Jesus was the most trustworthy 12-year-old ever! Note the follow-on, however, from "Right Under Our Noses". Even those who know Jesus well can lose sight of him and not notice.

[2] Jesus also expresses his love through his patient gift of time. He sits with them for three consecutive days.

sisters, take note of this: everyone should be quick to listen, slow to speak." God has given us two ears and one mouth so that we might use them in proper proportion.

When Jesus wants to share the Gospel with people, he therefore starts by *asking questions*. However little the teachers of the law might be able to teach him, he understands that asking questions is the easiest way to start a spiritual conversation and to keep it going. Many Christians go into lecture mode whenever they have a chance to talk about Jesus with an unbeliever. They are like my little son, who ate six pieces of chocolate cake at a party and looked surprised when he vomited it all back up again when he got home. However sweet the Gospel may be to us, we need to serve the right-sized slices to people. Otherwise they will change the subject and the next time around will run and hide.

Questions also help us to find out what is really going on in a person's heart. We often launch into a one-size-fits-all presentation of the Gospel, Jesus remembers Proverbs 20:5: *"The purposes of a person's heart are deep waters, but one who has insight draws them out."* Jesus recognizes that questions are like the bucket in a well. They will help him to find out what is troubling these particular teachers of the law and what God has been saying to them already. There is no point in telling someone how to get somewhere from a different place from the one where they are standing. Jesus therefore asks questions to discover how he can show each individual that the Gospel is good news for them personally. Francis Schaeffer taught this as a vital principle: *"Give me an hour with an unbeliever and I will listen for the first 55 minutes, and then in the last 5 minutes I will have something to say."*

When Jesus wants to share the Gospel with people, therefore, he *is successful*. It takes Mary and Joseph three days to find Jesus. This surprises him, not because they ought to have come to the Temple earlier to lodge a prayer, but because they know that Joseph isn't really his father: *"Didn't you know I had to be in my Father's house?"*[3] Luke says that Mary and Joseph are astonished, not by his precocious self-awareness, but by his fruit in just three days: all of the teachers of the law are now listening to him! Jesus started out by sitting and listening and asking questions, but his approach quickly turned the tables. *"Everyone who heard him was amazed at his understanding and his answers."* How many times that year do you think the rabbis stopped talking and started listening to the wisdom of a twelve-year-old? That's right, just the one. It's why we so badly need to learn to share the Gospel like Jesus ourselves.

When Jesus wants to share the Gospel with people, he *leaves the outcome to his Father.* Yet again he and I would differ here. Knowing that I was about to enter a further eighteen years of obscurity, I would have made a strong-armed appeal for salvation then and there. But Jesus doesn't. He sees saving a soul as something that only his Father can do. His words have been a link in the chain of what God is doing in these people's lives, and that is all they are. Jesus leaves the Temple with Mary and Joseph, entrusting the next steps to his Father.

It is good that you want to share the Gospel with people. Luke 1:2 affirms that we are all *"servants of the word"*. But it's not enough to share it. We need to share it in a manner that ensures a hearing. That's why we need to learn these lessons from a twelve-year-old.

---

[3] Luke happily refers to Mary and Joseph as the parents of Jesus in 2:27, 41, 43 and 48. However, when Mary complains to Jesus that "your father and I have been anxious," he insists firmly, "No, God is my Father."

Mind the Gap (2:51–52)

Jesus grew in wisdom and stature, and in favour with God and man.

(Luke 2:52)

Every time I use the London Underground, I hear the station announcement: *Please mind the gap.* It's good advice if you don't want to get your foot stuck in the space between the train and the platform edge, but it's also good advice if you want to understand the message of Luke's gospel. He leaves several gaps in his story and he wants us to notice them. They teach us something of what it means to follow Jesus.

In 2:51, Luke tells us that Jesus spent the next eighteen years in obedience. He says nothing else about what Jesus did in his teens and in his twenties.[1] All he says is that, while most teenagers believe that they know better than their parents, Jesus obeyed Mary and Joseph completely despite the fact that he actually did! Luke also emphasizes that Jesus obeyed every detail of the Jewish Law. He was only able to die as a sacrifice for our sins because he was free from sin himself. In that sense, we are saved by works: by **his** works. It is only through the perfect life of Jesus that we can be declared innocent. The apostle Paul explains:

---

[1] By recording what happened to Jesus as a 12-year-old, Luke actually gives us less of a gap than the other gospel writers. He does not mention the Magi, Herod's attempts to kill Jesus and his time as a refugee in Egypt (Matthew 2) because he doesn't want to suggest to Theophilus that Roman officials are anti-Jesus.

"God sent his Son, born of a woman, born under the law, to redeem those under the law, that we might receive adoption to sonship."[2]

In 2:52, Luke tells us that Jesus spent the next eighteen years *growing*. It's important that we notice this, because many Christians act as if Jesus was already the finished article when he was born. Luke has no time for the foolish kind of thinking that inspired the carol "Away in a Manger" to claim that *"little Lord Jesus, no crying he makes"*. In both 2:40 and 52, he deliberately echoes the accounts of the childhood of Samson and Samuel in order to emphasize the humanity of Jesus.[3] He wasn't like Keanu Reeves in *The Matrix*, receiving an instant download of everything he needed from heaven. He became one of us, so he had to grow in everything like one of us.

Luke tells us that Jesus had to *grow in wisdom*. That's the background to his insightful teaching in the Temple courtyards as a twelve-year-old. Since he was born without original sin, as a child he enjoyed a level of communication with his Father which had been unknown since the Garden of Eden.[4] Grasping in his infancy that he was the promised Messiah, he devoted himself to such diligent study of the Scriptures that the teachers of the law were able to learn from him before he celebrated his bar mitzvah. If we are followers of Jesus, we must therefore become students of the Bible too. The Greek word for disciple simply means *learner*. Jesus was only able to use the Old Testament in chapter 4 to resist the Devil, to launch his ministry and to define his calling because he carefully studied the Scriptures during the 11,000 days between his birth and his baptism.

Luke also tells us that Jesus had to *grow in stature*. I find

---

[2] Galatians 4:4–5. Luke emphasizes that Jesus obeyed the Jewish Law in 2:21, 22–24, 27 and 39. In the best Greek manuscripts of 2:22, he even writes about **"their** *purification"* – that is, of both Mary and her child.

[3] Compare Luke 2:40 and 52 with Judges 13:24–25 and with 1 Samuel 2:26 and 3:19–21.

[4] Luke 1:35 seems to link the fact that Jesus was not born of a man to his identity as the Holy One.

that helpful, because Christians are often tempted to think neglecting their bodies is a mark of godliness. I remember being hugely impressed, shortly after my conversion, by the way that the hard-working George Whitefield declared to his friends, *"I would rather wear out than rust out!"* It was only later that I stopped to consider whether this might have contributed to the fact that he died aged only fifty-five! Jesus believed that he had been given a human body to steward it carefully. He didn't starve it or neglect it or damage it needlessly in his work as a carpenter. If you are a follower of Jesus, it really matters that you watch your weight and your health and your fitness levels. To neglect your body in the service of God is to be as foolish as a cavalryman who neglects his horse before he rides into battle.

Luke also tells us that Jesus had to *grow in favour with God*. That's his most surprising statement so far, because surely Jesus had his Father's complete favour from day one! Well, evidently not. He knew God better than any other toddler but he needed to cultivate that relationship as he grew older. He needed to get to know God as his Father: no other Jew at the time would have ever dared to say what he said in verse 49.[5] He needed to develop such a solid friendship with his Father in his teens and twenties that he was able to resist the Devil's temptations in chapter 4. No, he would not turn stones into bread because he trusted his Father to provide. No, he would not cut a deal with the Devil because he loved his Father more than this world's splendour. No, he would not abuse his position as the Son of God because he cherished his friendship with his Father.

Lastly, Luke tells us that Jesus had to *grow in favour with man.* He had to overcome the strong temptation to become a loner. Every Christian faces this temptation early on in their walk with Jesus. Will they allow their godly hatred of sin to morph into an ungodly disdain towards sinners? Luke says that

---

[5] There are only 14 direct references to God as Father in the whole of the Old Testament. Jesus calls God his Father more times than that in Luke's gospel alone.

Jesus passed the test. He developed strong friendships with his neighbours and with his carpentry customers in Nazareth.[6] He learned a lifestyle that would be vital later, since he had not been sent to earth to write books or to found a university, but to call and mentor a group of friends. That's our calling too. Bill Hybels reminds us that

> *People were Jesus' One Thing. And they still are. People who are sick. People who are lonely. People who are wandering, depressed, and hopeless. People who have got themselves tangled up in suffocating habits and destructive relationships... As you love people, serve people, point people toward faith in Christ, redirect wayward people, restore broken people, and develop people into the peak of their spiritual potential, you reaffirm your understanding of your primary mission in the world.[7]*

To be a Christian is to be a friend.

Luke is about to fast-forward eighteen years to the start of Jesus' public ministry. Before he does that, however, he wants us to slow down and mind the gap. He wants us to feel encouraged that even Jesus had to learn to become the kind of person his Father could use. He wants us to feel challenged that there is therefore no shortcut to fruitfulness. We need to devote ourselves to Bible study and to exercise and to prayer and to deep friendship with others. We need to mind the gap between Luke 2 and Luke 3, recognizing the importance of the simple lessons that God teaches us in our daily lives.

---

[6] We are told about his carpentry business in Mark 6:3. Luke gives a more generic account so that we can all follow the example of Jesus in our own professions.

[7] Bill Hybels in *Just Walk Across the Room* (2006).

Spot the Difference (3:1–38)

Now Jesus himself was about thirty years old when
he began his ministry.

(Luke 3:23)

If you want to understand the message of Luke's gospel, all you
need to do is compare a chapter like this one with the parallel
passages in the other gospels. There are a lot of similarities
here, particularly with Matthew and Mark, but there are also
some glaring differences. Let's look at a few of them to help us
understand Luke's purpose in writing.

The first big difference is *Luke's attention to history*. Once
again he helps us to pinpoint dates more clearly than any other
gospel writer. He tells us that we are now in the fifteenth year
of the Emperor Tiberius, long after the death of Herod the Great
and the division of his kingdom among his four sons (tetrarch
is Greek for *quarter-ruler*). Luke explains that by now one of
the tetrarchs has been deposed and replaced by the Roman
governor Pontius Pilate, while another tetrarchy is under the
rule of Lysanias. Herod's children still rule over the other two
tetrarchies and, although the Romans have deposed Annas as
high priest in Jerusalem, he still operates as the true leader
of the Jewish Sanhedrin through his son-in-law Caiaphas.[1] All
this detail reflects Luke's self-perception as a classical Greek
historian. It dates the action in this chapter to 28 AD, which

---

[1] The Romans deposed Annas as high priest in 15 AD, but he was succeeded
by five sons and one son-in-law. Caiaphas was the greatest of these, serving
as high priest from 18 to 36 AD.

concurs with Luke's statement in 3:23 that by now Jesus is aged about thirty.[2]

The second big difference is *Luke's insistence that Christianity is true Judaism*. The other gospel writers say this but none of them underlines it quite as forcefully as Luke. None of them needed to, because they were not writing to secure the official legal status of Christianity through the apostle Paul's test case in Rome. Religious sects were viewed as dangerous threats to the cohesion of the Roman Empire, but Julius Caesar had granted the Jews an important concession after the conquest of their land. The worship of Yahweh had been formally recognized as a *religio licita*, a *permitted religion* with legal protection alongside the Roman gods.[3] It was therefore of paramount importance to Luke and his friends that Judge Theophilus should see the Christian faith as a subset of Judaism. If he did, the Church could claim legal protection from the emperor. If he didn't, Christianity was a cult and the Church was a community of outlaws.[4]

We have already noted that Luke begins his gospel in the Jewish Temple and that the songs of Mary and Zechariah proclaim that Jesus is the hope of Israel. We have also noted the way that Luke mentions the circumcision of Jesus and his careful obedience to the Jewish Law. We have heard what devout Jews such as Simeon and Anna said about him, and we have watched him take his place among the Jewish rabbis at the Temple, even as a child. So don't miss the way Luke begins his account of John the Baptist's ministry in the same way that the Old Testament begins its account of the Jewish prophets.[5] Don't miss the way he quotes from Isaiah 40:3–5 in verses 4–6 to declare that the

---

[2] Tiberius ruled from 14 to 37 AD. Since part years were counted as whole years, his 15th year was 28 AD.

[3] Josephus records Caesar's landmark concession in his *Antiquities of the Jews* (14.10.17–26).

[4] See Acts 13:32–33; 24:5, 14–21; 26:4–7; 28:20–22.

[5] *"The word of God came to John"* in Luke 3:2 is meant to echo 1 Kings 17:2, Jeremiah 1:2, Ezekiel 1:3, Hosea 1:1, Jonah 1:1, Micah 1:1 and Zephaniah 1:1.

arrival of Jesus represented the culmination of the ancient faith of the Jews.

The third big difference is *Luke's inclusion of non-Jews from the very outset*. The other gospel writers record John's insistence that Jews be baptized, a ritual normally reserved for Gentiles converting to Judaism as a sign that they were washing away the filth of their pagan past, because Jews need to repent and be cleansed of their own sin too. Matthew adds that John the Baptist offended the rabbis by insisting that their Jewish ancestry did not make them true children of Abraham unless their lives showed that they shared Abraham's faith in God.[6] But Luke goes further here than any of the other gospel writers by telling us that John addressed this challenge, not just to the rabbis, but to the Jewish nation as a whole. He also lengthens the quotation from Isaiah in Matthew and Mark so that it includes a promise that "**all people** *will see God's salvation.*" Luke declares from the outset that the Jewish Messiah is the Saviour of all nations.[7]

A fourth big difference is *Luke's application of the Gospel to a Roman context*. Like Matthew, he records John's teaching that genuine repentance is proved not by our words but by our actions, yet in 3:10–14 he alone spells out in detail what this means for the citizens of Rome. Only Luke records John's teaching that the rich must share what they have with the poor, that imperial officials must not abuse their positions of power and that Roman soldiers must be scrupulously honest and content with their pay.[8] This would be music to the ears of Theophilus, as one of many leaders in the capital who tore their hair out over the petty abuses of their agents in the provinces.

---

[6] See also Acts 26:20. It was in this sense that John the Baptist *"prepared the way"* for the arrival of Jesus (1:17, 76; 3:4). The Jews had to recognize how lost they were before they would lay hold of their Saviour.

[7] The trees that are in danger of being axed in 3:9 are the Jews. See the parable, unique to Luke, in 13:6–9.

[8] John does not tell them to leave the civil service and the military, but to be godly witnesses within them.

But it also serves a far higher purpose. Luke wants to convict and convert his Roman readers by connecting John's world to their own, because all of this happened for them.[9]

A fifth big difference is *Luke's presentation of Jesus as Adam's greater son*. Matthew is the only other gospel writer to give us the family tree of Jesus. It is different, not just because Matthew gives us Joseph's ancestry and Luke gives us Mary's ancestry, but because Matthew only takes us back as far as Abraham.[10] He wants to show us that Jesus is the hope of the Jewish nation: the true son of David and the true seed of Abraham. Luke's family tree in 3:23–38 takes us all the way back to Adam because he wants to show that Jesus is the hope of every nation: he is the true son of Adam. He has come to restore what Adam lost for all humanity in the Garden of Eden.[11]

So don't miss these differences between Luke's account of the preaching of John the Baptist and the accounts of the other gospel writers. Don't miss the way he tells us in 3:17–18 that it is *euangelion: Good News* for all nations that there is a God in heaven committed to banishing sinners to hell and admitting the saved to heaven.[12] Don't miss the way he presents it as history that God has ensured both outcomes by sending his Son into the world to live the perfect life we should have lived and to die the guilty death we should have died. And don't miss the way he includes you in the story right from the outset. Don't miss his insistence that all this happened for you.

---

[9] Luke also does this by stating in 3:19–20 that the deeds of the Roman official Herod Antipas were evil. Although the Roman law courts had permitted his brother's wife a divorce so that he could run off with her, Luke warns that in God's sight she remained Philip's wife.

[10] Since Joseph was the son of Jacob (Matthew 1:16), the phrase *"so it was thought"* alerts us to the fact that the family tree that follows is his biological ancestry through Mary, not his legal ancestry through Joseph.

[11] Luke 19:10. Remember, Luke travelled with the man who wrote Romans 5:12–19 and 1 Corinthians 15:21–22.

[12] When John talks about Jesus burning chaff on a threshing-floor fire, he is linking back to Malachi 4:1.

I'll Have What He's Having
(3:15–4:19)

Jesus, full of the Holy Spirit... was led by the Spirit into the wilderness.

(Luke 4:1)

Ancient historians didn't just deal in facts. They dealt in examples. One leading scholar explains: *"What history the Roman student got was typically in the form of **exempla** – pre-digested anecdotes about famous historical personages... The Roman educated class wanted not a balanced and thorough understanding of the past, but exempla."*

As for moral teaching, he continues:

*How was this attempted? Through philosophers' precepts? Hardly. Philosophy, obviously out of the question for the poor, was the pursuit of the bookish few and generally considered an eccentricity unsuitable for Romans intent on a publicly useful career. Through religious instruction? No. Roman paganism had no bible, no memorized creed, no list of commandments, even if the gods were felt to expect and reward honesty and virtue. The primary Roman vehicle of moral teaching was the **exemplum**, a concrete instance or story taken from history... that shows a vice to be avoided or a virtue to be emulated.*[1]

---

[1] Christopher Francese in *Ancient Rome in So Many Words* (2007).

Given this background, it shouldn't surprise us that one of the distinctive features of Luke's gospel is that he presents Jesus as our great Example. He doesn't play down the divinity of Jesus. Far from it. Knowing full well that one of the Roman emperor's favourite titles was *divi filius* – Latin for *the son of a god* – he states firmly in 1:35 and 3:22 that Jesus is the true Son of God. Everywhere you look in Luke's gospel, Jesus is presented as divine, but everywhere you look he is also presented as human. Luke won't allow us to say anything as foolish as "Of course Jesus did that, he is God; but we can't do that." On the contrary, in everything he presents Jesus as the one who leads the way for us to follow. Jesus didn't just come to be our Saviour. He also came to be our Example.

One difference that we didn't spot in the previous chapter is that Luke is the only gospel writer to tell us that Jesus was anointed with the Holy Spirit *"as he was praying"*. That's significant in 3:21–22 because Luke speaks about the prayer life of Jesus eleven times, seven of which are unique to his gospel. He wants us to see this as the secret behind all that Jesus said and did: *"Jesus often withdrew to lonely places and prayed."*[2] Luke emphasizes that Jesus performed miracles, not because he was God, but because he was a prayerful man full of the Holy Spirit.[3] He limited his actions only to those that could be copied by his followers. The Emperor Augustus boasted that *"I have provided future generations with many **exempla** for their imitation,"* but Luke says that Jesus actually did so.[4] He even tells us in 5:17 that healing didn't happen unless *"the power of the Lord was with Jesus to heal those who were ill."*[5]

[2] Luke 3:21; 5:16; 6:12; 9:18; 11:1; 23:34, 46.

[3] This remains a big theme in the book of Acts too. *"Jesus of Nazareth was a man accredited by God to you by miracles, wonders and signs, **which God did among you through him**"* (Acts 2:22).

[4] Augustus writes this in his not very humbly entitled *Deeds of the Divine Augustus* (8.5).

[5] Luke says something similar in Acts 10:38: *"God anointed Jesus of Nazareth with the Holy Spirit and power... He went around doing good and healing all who were under the power of the devil, because God was with him."*

We need to understand this as we read Luke's third and fourth chapters. In 3:15-18, he wants to us to grasp that the arrival of the Messiah marked a new type of partnership between God's Spirit and human flesh and blood.[6] John the Baptist tells the adoring crowds at the River Jordan that his baptism in water is nothing compared to what is about to be unleashed by the Messiah's baptism in the Holy Spirit.[7] The arrival of Jesus will catapult people one of two ways: they will either rebel so defiantly that God makes their home hellfire or they will repent so utterly that God makes them home to the heavenly fire of the Holy Spirit. The Messiah's arrival will force humanity to pick a side.[8]

In 3:21-22, Jesus serves as an example of what this means. He has waited in obscurity for the Father's appointed moment to anoint him publicly with the Holy Spirit, and as he prays in the water at his baptism in the River Jordan the moment finally arrives. The crowds know that Jesus is human, but they can see the Holy Spirit descending upon him in the form of a dove. As they watch in wonder, a voice booms from heaven: *"You are my Son, whom I love; with you I am well pleased."*[9] As we witness this public partnership between the members of the Trinity – the Spirit anointing the Son as the Father roars out his approval – Luke wants us to see it as a milestone for us too. The Hebrew word Messiah means *Anointed One*. A new era of Spirit-Filled Humanity has now begun.[10]

---

[6] This wasn't news. Many Old Testament prophecies linked the arrival of the Messiah to the coming of the Holy Spirit. See Joel 2:28-29; Isaiah 32:15; 44:3; Ezekiel 36:26-27; 39:29; Zechariah 12:10-13:1.

[7] The phrase "baptism in the Holy Spirit" is only used seven times in Scripture, and six of them contrast it with John's water baptism. "Baptism" here therefore means the same thing as "filling", "outpouring" or "receiving".

[8] It is naive to insist that God's Spirit always brings unity. John says he often brings righteous disunity.

[9] Note the echo here of Psalm 2:7 and Isaiah 42:1. To the children of vipers comes God's Son (3:7).

[10] All four gospel writers mention this event and all four of them mention that the Spirit looked like a dove. To receive forgiveness from Jesus without the

In 4:1-13, Jesus provides an example of this new partnership in action. Luke says that *"full of the Holy Spirit"* he was *"led by the Spirit"* into the wilderness for forty days.[11] If you know your Old Testament, this will instantly remind you of the forty years that the Israelites spent in the wilderness. They died in the wilderness because they sinned, so Luke shows us Spirit-Filled Humanity succeeding where those who only had the Law of Sinai failed. The Devil's three temptations each try to seduce Jesus into ministering out of his own inherent divinity instead of partnering with his Father through the Holy Spirit.[12] Will he provide for his own physical needs? Will he chart his own path to glory?[13] Will he try to manipulate his Father into doing things his own way? Three times Jesus quotes from Deuteronomy 6 and 8, the two great chapters in which Moses gives a potted history of Israel's forty years in the desert. Eventually the Devil gives up in disgust. Jesus has succeeded where Israel failed, as the great Example of a Spirit-filled believer.

In 4:14-19, Jesus goes on the offensive. He returns to Nazareth *"in the power of the Spirit"* and stands up in the synagogue to read one of the greatest Old Testament prophecies about what partnership with God's Spirit means. *"The Spirit of the Lord is on me, because he has anointed me,"* Jesus reads from Isaiah 61, before explaining that the partnership which helps us to resist the Devil also helps us to rout his crumbling kingdom. It empowers us to proclaim and prove the Gospel of forgiveness, freedom and favour.

Pliny's complaint about the teenagers of Rome was that

---

fullness of the Spirit is to enter into only half his story.

[11] The Spirit-filled life isn't necessarily easy. For Jesus it meant terrible hunger and thirst in the desert.

[12] *The Devil* is Greek for *the Liar*. Unless we pursue active partnership with God's Spirit, the Devil will even misuse Scriptures such as Psalm 91:11-12 to deceive us into resisting God's plan (2 Thessalonians 2:13).

[13] Luke's account is similar to Matthew 4:1-11 but it emphasizes that this was about *authority* as well as glory. Satan had genuine authority through Adam's sin, but Jesus chose to retrieve it the Father's way (19:10).

*"They think they already know everything. They don't want to copy someone better than them. They act as their own **exempla**."*[14] The same thing could be said of many Christians today. We have grown so used to a bastardized, Spiritless form of Christianity that we barely notice we are not partnering with the Father in the way that Jesus modelled for us. We barely notice that being filled with the Spirit has become a footnote instead of the main event in our lives. So don't read any further in Luke's gospel until you have reread these verses slowly and told Jesus that you accept him as your great Example. Then as you read on, tell the Father how much you like what you see in Jesus and that you want to have what he is having.

---

[14] Pliny the Younger voices this complaint to Marcellinus in his *Letters* (8.23).

929 Chapters (4:14–44)

Today this scripture is fulfilled in your hearing.

(Luke 4:21)

The Old Testament contains a very long story. It takes 39 books or 929 chapters or 23,145 verses to tell it. It took more than thirty authors more than a thousand years to write it, so it was quite a pronouncement when Jesus declared that the entire story was being fulfilled at that very moment through what was happening to him.

In 4:14, Jesus returns in triumph from his forty days in the desert, having succeeded where Israel failed.[1] Ever since his baptism, he has been so full of *"the power of the Spirit"* that every synagogue in Galilee wants him as a visiting speaker.[2] Eventually the leaders of the synagogue in Nazareth decide that they ought to invite him to speak in his home town too.[3] They look at the man who not so long ago was working as their local carpenter and they hand him an Old Testament scroll. Jesus turns to one of the passages that he studied during his years of obscurity. It is the great promise in Isaiah 61 that the Messiah will model a new partnership between God's Spirit and our humanity. He reads:

---

[1] Israel is God's son in Exodus 4:22–23, Deuteronomy 32:6 and Hosea 11:1. Matthew's gospel makes much of this, explaining that, as the true and better Son of God, Jesus also came to be the true and better Israel.

[2] Luke and Acts mention Jewish synagogues almost 40 times and these local worship communities provided a model for the first churches. If Jesus made it his habit to attend "church" weekly then so ought we (4:16).

[3] Luke misses out the early ministry of Jesus in Galilee and Judea (John 1:35–4:54). He takes us straight to this event, unique to his gospel, so that he can underline the strong link between God's Messiah and God's Spirit.

The Spirit of the Lord is on me, because he has anointed me to proclaim good news to the poor. He has sent me to proclaim freedom for the prisoners and recovery of sight for the blind, to set the oppressed free, to proclaim the year of the Lord's favour.

The people at the synagogue in Nazareth know the passage well. They know that these are the words of the Messiah, God's *Anointed One*, in one of the greatest Old Testament summaries of the *euangelion*, the Good News of God's salvation. Since Jewish rabbis normally preached seated, Jesus is not signifying that he has finished when he hands the scroll back to the synagogue official and sits down. He is just getting started. He starts his sermon with an astonishing claim: *"Today this scripture is fulfilled in your hearing."*

It is easy for us to judge the people of Nazareth harshly for their reaction to this claim. That's because we fail to grasp what it actually means. We imagine that Jesus is using the passage in Isaiah to announce his mission statement, but his sermon is as much about his own identity and place in history as it is about his plan. It is a claim that he is the long-awaited Messiah whose coming is predicted throughout the Old Testament – all 929 chapters of it – from the start of Genesis until the final words of Malachi. To emphasize this, the passage in Isaiah predicts that the Messiah will fulfil what was foreshadowed by the Year of Jubilee and the rest of the Jewish Law.[4] Jesus is proclaiming that he is more than just an anointed man. He is the Anointed One who embodies every Old Testament promise and who is fulfilling them all one by one.

When we understand this, it isn't so hard to see why the people of Nazareth are outraged. They have nothing but good to say about the character and speech of Jesus, but they struggle

---

[4] Leviticus 25. Isaiah 61:1 repeats the unusual Hebrew phrase *qārā' derōr* (*proclaim freedom*) in Leviticus 25:10.

to believe that Joseph's boy can truly be the fulfilment of all 929 chapters of the Jewish Scriptures. Jesus knows they are demanding a miracle to prove it, like the ones that they have heard about in the other towns of Galilee, but he hasn't finished his sermon yet. They didn't notice that he stopped reading Isaiah 61 mid-sentence, just before a reference to *"the day of vengeance of our God"*.

First-century Jews expected the Messiah to come and take their side against the pagan nations, and especially the Romans. That's one of the reasons Luke records this confrontation. Jesus finishes his sermon by drawing their attention to the fact that he missed out those words. He will fulfil them in due time, but not before he has fulfilled all the Old Testament warnings that if Israel refuses to receive its Messiah, the pagan nations will gladly receive him instead. Jesus reminds them that, when their Jewish ancestors refused to listen to Elijah and Elisha, a foreign widow and an enemy general received God's saving power instead. Their nation is therefore now at a crossroads: if the whole of the Old Testament is bound up in a single person then how Israel responds to him is absolutely crucial.[5]

The people in the synagogue have heard enough. They are fond of their 39 books, their 929 chapters and their 23,145 verses. They would rather get lost among their scrolls than be found by a Messiah who favours filthy pagans. They force Jesus out of the building and then drive him to a cliff edge outside the town. How many times has Jesus gone there over the years when seeking solitude to pray? Enough times to ensure that nobody can harm a hair on his head until the Father decrees that the moment for his crucifixion has finally come. As Jesus walks through the crowd and says goodbye to his home town, he is not the only one that Nazareth has rejected. It has turned

---

[5] Jesus uses a play on words to warn them. Having proclaimed the year of God's *favour* (*dektos*) in 4:19, he observes that no prophet is *accepted* (*dektos*) in his home town in 4:24. His neighbours are too angry to notice.

its back on the Old Testament faith of Israel. It has reduced 929 chapters to a lifeless shadow.[6]

Jesus takes another preaching invitation at the synagogue in nearby Capernaum. The sight of one so evidently full of the Holy Spirit causes quite a stir among the evil spirits in the town. One demonized man in the congregation can take it no longer. He cries out that Jesus is *"the Holy One of God"*. If you know your Old Testament, you will recognize this as an echo of one of the great descriptions of Yahweh in the book of Isaiah. The prophet refers twenty-six times to *"the Holy One of Israel"* and it almost certainly inspired the angel's words in Luke 1:35. The demon is so panicked to see all 929 chapters of the Old Testament personified before him that it blurts out a startling confession. It asks Jesus, *"Have you come to destroy us?"* – a frank admission that even the demons know there is only one way that their battle against the promises of God can go.[7]

Later that evening, Jesus continues to partner with the Holy Spirit long after the synagogue has closed its doors. The evil spirits tormenting people in the area cannot help but recognize that the Old Testament is being fulfilled right before their eyes. They hail Jesus as *"the Son of God"* and as *"the Messiah"*. Luke wants this to challenge you, so don't miss that what he is saying has now taken place in history: one man has become the living, breathing fulfilment of the ancient Jewish Scriptures – all 929 chapters of them. Don't be stubborn like the people of Nazareth. Accept it with gladness that the arrival of Jesus has changed everything. Celebrate the fact that all this happened for you.

---

[6] Matthew 4:13 says that from this moment on he relocated his home from Nazareth to Capernaum.

[7] See also Matthew 8:29; Luke 8:31; Revelation 12:12. Demons recognize who Jesus is, even if we don't.

What Are You Doing Here?
(4:41–44)

He said, "I must proclaim the good news of the kingdom of God to the other towns also, because that is why I was sent."

(Luke 4:43)

I have to confess that I wasn't excited when I was offered an old church building in the London borough of Kingston. I was already leading a church in nearby Wimbledon and it was growing fast. It had doubled in size in two years and I felt completely exhausted. I was full of excuses. What if this offer of a building is a tactic of the Devil to distract us? What if planting out some of our best leaders into the adjoining borough scuppers some of the amazing things that God is doing in Wimbledon?

I got up early in the morning to pray about it. To be more honest, I got up early in the morning to pray *against* it. I told the Lord that I was tired and wanted his permission to say no. Then my Bible reading took me to the events recorded here, in 4:41–44. *"At daybreak, Jesus went out to a solitary place."* So far, so good. That was precisely what I was doing. *"The people were looking for him and when they came to where he was, they tried to keep him from leaving them."* Right on that score too. Every day brought a mountain of emails, wall-to-wall meetings and the phone non-stop ringing. It was comforting to read that Jesus knows exactly how it feels. Then I read the next line and experienced what I can only describe as a violent inner prompting from the Holy Spirit. I felt like I had just been punched in the stomach. I was so far from where God wanted me to be in that moment that I'm sure anything less would have failed to register. *"But he said, 'I must proclaim the good news of the kingdom of God to the other towns also, because that is why I was sent.'"*

That was the beginning of Everyday Church, a movement that would plant a number of new church congregations across London. When I look back on that moment, I give glory to God because I very nearly missed what he was trying to do right under my nose. It makes me wonder how much the failure of the Western Church is caused by people like me forgetting why we are here in the first place. So before we leave chapter 4 and the heady days of the Messiah's early ministry, let's take a moment to ponder. What do these verses tell us our true priorities ought to be? What on earth are we doing here?

Verse 43 says that we are to keep on moving with the Gospel. Years of studying the Scriptures had given Jesus a razor-sharp awareness of why he came from heaven. He was to preach good news to every community in Galilee and then to head south and do the same thing in every community in Judea.[1] There is a place for stability (Jesus says yes to a similar request to stay in a Samaritan village in John 4:40), but even when we stay in one place it should only be to gather strength so that our mission can stretch further. In practice, church leaders and missionaries tend to prize stability over extension.[2] Vincent Donovan discovered this as a missionary in East Africa:

> *I can remember an old missionary telling me that he had spent his life under the snows of Kilimanjaro, and his dream was to die and be buried under the snows of Kilimanjaro. I was deeply impressed at the time. It was*

---

[1] We would have expected Luke to say *Galilee* rather than *Judea* in 4:44. Either he is referring generically to the land of the Jews for the sake of his Roman readers (as in 7:17) or he is saying Jesus just kept on going!

[2] Luke deliberately contrasts an *open heaven* in 3:21 with a *closed heaven* in 4:25. If we fail to respond to the open heaven that God has given us, we must not be surprised that our churches experience a closed one.

a beautiful thought, but looking back on it now I do not think it was a particularly missionary thought... There is something definitely temporary about Paul's missionary stay in any one place. There is something of a deadly permanence in ours... I discovered that the whole area could be divided into twenty-six sections. A different section could be reached every day if one moved out of the mission house and lived in a Landrover and a tent. Instructions in the Christian message would take about a year in any one section visited once a week. Realistically, six sections could be reached in a year. So, the whole Loliondo area of twenty-six sections could be evangelized in five years; less, if others joined me in the task. This struck me as of extreme importance and significance. It would mean I could leave that particular mission after five years, having completed my work.[3]

But verse 43 also reminds us that going isn't everything. What matters is what we do in the places where we go. The Great Commission in Matthew 28 reads literally in Greek, *"Going, therefore, disciple all nations."* In other words, the focus isn't on the going (a Greek participle) but on the command to make disciples as we go (the main Greek imperative). Verse 43 tells us how to do this. Jesus tells us to *"proclaim the good news of the kingdom of God"*. We are to share the *euangelion* that the Messiah has come from heaven and defeated the Devil's reign of sin and misery on the earth. God the Father has entrusted him with the authority and power of his heavenly Kingdom. Faith in him sends the Devil packing and it unlocks the promises of Isaiah 61: freedom, forgiveness and favour.

Most of the time the Devil knows what we are here for better than we do, so don't miss the panic in the voices of the demons when they see Jesus in the synagogue at Capernaum and outside Simon Peter's home. They know that distraction

---

[3] Vincent Donovan in *Christianity Rediscovered* (1978).

tactics are their only last-ditch weapon. The missionary James Fraser warns us how much they use them:

> *Interruptions, visits, and attention to details absorb a good deal of my time... The enemy is delighted to have us so occupied incessantly with secondary and trivial concerns, as to keep us from attacking and resisting in the true spirit of the conflict... It is all IF and WHEN. I believe the devil is fond of those conjunctions... Satan suggests, wait until a good opportunity for working, watching, and praying presents itself – and needless to say, this opportunity is always in the future... I can imagine Satan laughing up his sleeve.[4]*

Note what this chapter promises us will happen whenever a person filled with God's Spirit remembers what they are here for.[5] The Lord will empower us to speak with his own authority (verse 32) and to issue orders to demons that force them to submit and flee (verse 36).[6] He will enable us to heal illnesses through similar commands (verse 39) and through laying our hands on people so that the Spirit can flow out of us and into them (verse 40). As we follow him as our great Example, we will discover that the partnership he began in Galilee is still active within us.

So ask yourself, where are you going? What are you saying and doing as you go? What on earth are you doing here?

---

[4] Excerpts from his journal, recorded in his biography *Mountain Rain* by Eileen Crossman (1982).

[5] Luke emphasizes in 4:18–19 that God fills us with the Spirit, not just so that we can enjoy a personal discipleship experience, but so that he can send us out to make more disciples! One reason many Christians fail to experience the power described in Luke 4 is that they care little for the Holy Spirit's agenda.

[6] Jesus talks to the demon like a dog in 4:35, commanding it literally to *"Be muzzled!"* Luke is a trained doctor, yet he does not deny that many sicknesses are caused by demons. Far from downplaying the supernatural, he mentions demons more than any other gospel writer and says dislodging them is normal Christianity.

Partners (5:1–11)

Don't be afraid; from now on you will fish for people.

(Luke 5:10)

Simon Peter wasn't an obvious choice to be one of the twelve disciples of Jesus. He doesn't even appear to have been a very good fisherman. He caught so few fish that, had he not been self-employed, he would have lost his job a long time ago.

Yet Jesus chose him for a reason. If you have read the other gospels, you will notice that Luke tells the story of his calling rather differently. The key word in Luke's account is *partners* in 5:10. It hints that Jesus is looking for ordinary people with whom he can share his own experience of God's extraordinary power.

Peter co-owned a fishing business on Lake Galilee with the brothers James and John.[1] Luke describes them in 5:10 as his *koinōnoi*, which is related to one of the most important Greek words in the New Testament. The apostle Paul says in 2 Corinthians 13:14 that the Christian life requires us to respond to the Trinity in three distinct ways. We need to grasp *"the love of God"*, since salvation is all about the Father's longing to adopt us as his children. We need to grasp *"the grace of the Lord Jesus Christ"*, since this adoption is only made possible through what he has done for us. We also need to grasp *"the partnership with the Holy Spirit"* – the Greek word is *koinōnia* – because this is a key aspect of what our adoption means. We are to become partners in God's family business.

Luke omits much of the background to the moment when

---

[1] *Gennesaret* is the Greek form of the official Hebrew name for the lake. It literally means *Harp-Shaped*.

Jesus calls Peter to choose a new partner. We know from John's gospel that Peter had already started spending less time fishing and more time listening to Jesus. He had seen him turn water into wine at a wedding in Cana, and Luke tells us at the end of chapter 4 that he was also there to witness the Messiah's miracles in Capernaum.[2] Since he lived in the town, he took Jesus home from the synagogue to heal his mother-in-law from a serious fever.[3] When Jesus healed her instantly, Peter's house became his base for ministering to the whole town. It was everything that Peter had ever wanted. The Messiah was performing miracles in his home while he played host and his mother-in-law made the tea.[4] But Jesus says that it is now time to move on from Capernaum. One-man ministry in one town has to be eclipsed by something better: a whole team of partners who will reach the whole world.

Jesus steps into Peter's story in order to call him to step into his. He asks to use his fishing boat as a floating pulpit so that after he has finished preaching to the crowds on the beach he can demonstrate what partnership with God's Spirit truly means.[5] Peter and his fishing partners wash their nets while Jesus preaches, since they have caught nothing all night and are longing

---

[2] Luke 6:14 tells us that Jesus gave Simon the new name Peter, meaning *Rock*. Always a stickler for exact chronology, Luke calls him Simon up until 6:14 and then Peter thereafter. This also explains why the order of events is different in Luke from Matthew and Mark. Their main concern is theme, while his is chronology.

[3] Matthew and Mark tell us that she had *a fever*. As a doctor, Luke gives a more thorough diagnosis of it as *a high fever*. Mark 1:29 says that the house also belonged to Peter's brother Andrew. First-century Jews would often live as extended families – brothers, wives, children, parents and in-laws all under one roof.

[4] Mark 1:33 tells us that *"the whole town gathered at the door"*. Peter's house was suddenly very busy.

[5] Preaching from a boat across the water made his voice carry to a larger crowd, but it also served another purpose. So many people were pushing through the crowd to be healed through touching him that it was a necessary measure to avoid constant interruption (Luke 6:19; 8:43–48; Mark 3:9–10).

for bed.[6] Jesus suddenly commands them to *"Put out into deep water, and let down the nets for a catch."* In other words, to do what he told them in 4:43 – go somewhere new and see what God can do through you. Peter protests. If they throw their nets back into the water, they will have to clean them all over again. Still, he has seen enough to trust that Jesus knows a whole lot more than your average carpenter. When Peter obeys, he is rewarded. He nets the largest haul of fish that he has ever seen.

Luke wants us to notice all the little details in this story. Peter signals to his *partners*, so we are to see this miracle as a call to partner with the Holy Spirit. Working with James and John, all of Peter's efforts couldn't even net him a single fish, but working with God's Spirit delivers instant breakthrough. Now Luke zooms in on our own role in the partnership. He tells us that *"they caught such a large number of fish that **their nets began to break**"* and *"filled both boats so full that **they began to sink**"*. In other words, Jesus could only give them what their nets could hold without bursting and their boats could carry without sinking. Stronger nets or bigger boats would have enabled Jesus to give Peter even more. Luke wants us to grasp that there are no limits to the work of God's Spirit in the world except for those he finds in us. We need to play an active role in this partnership. That's why Jesus calls Peter to leave his boats behind to learn how to follow his example.

We have as much to learn as Peter. We need to start by confessing that we need to partner with God's Spirit, not just to catch a massive crowd of converts, but to catch any converts at all. We also need to confess that our own half-heartedness is often the main thing stopping the Holy Spirit from doing everything he wants throughout the world. We are told in 2 Chronicles 16:9 that *"The eyes of the Lord range throughout the earth to strengthen those whose hearts are fully committed*

---

[6] Fishing was best at night-time because boats cast no shadow to warn the fish, as in the daytime.

to him." If we are unwilling to commit ourselves entirely to the Spirit's agenda, we should not be surprised that we experience so little of him. If we fail to do the hard work of preparing our churches to receive an avalanche of new converts, we should not argue that God has reneged on his half of the deal.[7] He cares too much about lost people and about our churches to save people into nets that will tear and into boats that will sink under them.

Peter understands this. He does not respond, as we might have expected, by requesting time to sell the fish before he follows or to chat things over with his wife before he closes down the family business. Instead, he recognizes the enormity of being invited into partnership with God. *"Go away from me, Lord; I am a sinful man!"* is an unusual response to a miraculous catch of fish unless we grasp what Peter grasped, that Jesus is telling him that he can follow his example and become a Spirit-filled man too. In verse 5 Peter addressed Jesus as *epistatēs*, meaning *master*, but now he addresses him as *kurios*, the Greek word for *the Lord*, as a way of protesting that Jesus is different. He is holy, whereas Peter is a sinner. Jesus smiles at him. He still has so many things to learn. He reassures him, *"Don't be afraid; from now on you will fish for people."*

There is a brilliant epilogue to these verses in the final chapter of John's gospel. Once again Peter fishes all night and catches nothing. Once again Jesus arrives on the shore and calls him to partner with the Holy Spirit. This time, however, we see what Jesus managed to achieve in Peter's heart through two years together. This time the nets hold firm, with no signs of breaking, because when Jesus calls us he also enables us. If he calls you to partner with his Spirit, he also commits to teaching you how to do so. That's good news, because this story isn't just about Peter. Luke says Jesus is also calling you.

---

[7] This is a principle throughout the whole Bible. Isaiah 54:2–3 reminds us that readiness precedes revival.

Power Supply (5:12–32)

I have not come to call the righteous, but sinners to repentance.

(Luke 5:32)

There is a really old joke about a vacuum-cleaner salesman who tried to sell his product door-to-door. When the lady in the first house answered his knock, he bounded into her hallway and emptied the contents of a plastic bag all over her floor. *"Do you see all this filth on your carpet?"* he boasted. *"If my new vacuum cleaner fails to suck it up without a trace then I will lick it up myself."* The woman looked at him and pointed to the floor. *"Well you had better get down on your knees, then, because you've come right in the middle of a power cut!"*

Jesus had arrived during a power cut for Israel. Hardly anybody actually expected the Lord to perform miracles for his people any more. The Sadducees and Herodians believed that power now belonged to Rome, so they cut a deal with Caesar's governors in return for control of the Temple. The Pharisees believed instead that power lay with the people. Their name means "separatists" in Hebrew and they attracted many people with their radical modernization of the Law of Moses into 248 commands, 365 prohibitions and 1,521 amendments. These groups had different solutions to the problem, but all of them agreed on what it was: there was a power cut in Israel.[1]

In 5:12–14, Luke illustrates the problem through an

---

[1] Luke mentions the Pharisees for the first of many times in 5:17. He also mentions the group that the Jews called "scribes" but that Luke refers to as *"teachers of the law"* in order to explain their role to Theophilus.

encounter with a leper. Now that the disease is curable and less contagious, it is hard to imagine just how much it terrified people in the ancient world. For them, it was like HIV, cancer and the Ebola virus all wrapped into one. Those who had it were ostracized even by their families and friends.[2] They lived in communities of their own on the edges of towns, while the disease disfigured and destroyed them. A doctor describes its horror: *"The disease attacked the ears and nose, causing them to enlarge. Cartilage in the nose then collapsed. The eyes became inflamed and began to tear. Eyelids, lips and chin distended enormously... The whole face has a horrid appearance... The skin becomes gangrenous... by the slow progress of this terrible disease."*[3]

The leper that Jesus meets on the outskirts of one of the towns he visits must be in an advanced stage of the disease because he is alone. Even other lepers don't want him to be with them now. In the days of Moses or Elisha the Lord had healed lepers, so he refuses to accept that Israel is in a power cut now.[4] He believes what he has heard about the Spirit-filled man before whom he bows down and begs, *"Lord, if you are willing, you can make me clean."* One simple touch and a brief command – *"I am willing. Be clean!"* – is all it takes to remove all trace of the disease from his body. Jesus tells him to go to the priests at the Temple as *"a testimony to them"* that God's power supply is back on.

In 5:15–16, Luke explains what is going on. "Is God willing?" is now a redundant question because the Messiah's arrival has brought the long power cut to an end.[5] Of course God is willing,

---

[2] In Jewish society lepers were also ostracized for religious reasons (Leviticus 13; Numbers 5:1–4). Jesus demonstrates that leprosy cannot pollute the power of God's Spirit. Instead the leper is cleansed.

[3] This was written in 1866 by Dr Edward Hoffman, as quoted by John Tayman in *The Colony* (2006).

[4] Exodus 4:6–7; Numbers 12:10–16; 2 Kings 5.

[5] This does not mean that healing is automatic (Galatians 4:13–15; Philippians 2:25–27; 2 Timothy 4:20), but it does mean that we ought to see it as the new normal. God doesn't expect us to glorify him by wallowing in our sickness. Luke 5:25–26 insists that he wants to be glorified through our healing.

because Jesus came to pioneer a new partnership between human flesh and God's Spirit. Luke reminds us that *"Jesus often withdrew to lonely places and prayed."* He tells us that the leper asks to be made "clean" and not just healthy, because sin and sickness are part of the same toxic venom that the Devil injected into the veins of the human race through Adam's sin. Jesus came into the world to suck that venom out.

In 5:17–26, Luke explains this further. He says that *"the power of the Lord was with Jesus to heal those who were ill"* – in other words, he didn't heal people through his own inherent divinity but as a man filled with the Spirit of God.[6] A group of men are so desperate to plug their paralysed friend into God's power supply that they tear off the roof of the house where Jesus is ministering in order to leapfrog the rest of the crowd, and Jesus loves their reckless faith.[7] He declares that their friend's sins are forgiven, which surprises them because they were actually asking for healing. Jesus explains that sin and sickness are all part of the same package that he has come to remove from the earth. The Pharisees are horrified at this, accusing him of blasphemy since forgiving sin is God's prerogative alone. In response to their outrage, Jesus ups the ante by healing the man to prove his authority to forgive sins, then declares that he is the one that Daniel saw in his great vision of a King who would wield far greater power than the Roman Empire:

> *One like a Son of Man... was given authority, glory and sovereign power; all nations and peoples of every language worshipped him. His dominion is an everlasting dominion that will not pass away, and his kingdom is one that will never be destroyed.*[8]

---

[6] Paul expects us to see this as our own model for ministry too. He tells us to be aware of times when *"the power of our Lord Jesus is present"* (1 Corinthians 5:4).

[7] The accounts in Matthew, Mark and Luke all emphasize that Jesus responded to *their* faith, not just his.

[8] Daniel 7:13–14. Jesus calls himself "the Son of Man" 25 times in Luke's gospel. It was code to the Jews that he was the God-Man prophesied by

In 5:27–32, Luke shows that this unveiling of God's power supply means that he has all the strength he needs to complete his work of salvation. Jesus spots one of the most hated men in the region sitting at his tax-collecting booth beside the road. It is Levi, one of the human parasites who sucked money from hard-working Galileans like a mosquito sucking blood from its prey. When Jesus calls Levi to *"Follow me"*, it is a bold declaration that God's power is enough to overcome the very worst human weakness.[9] When the Pharisees see that Jesus and his disciples are willing to eat and drink with Levi's tax-collecting friends, it offends every separatist bone in their bodies.[10] Jesus warns that they have forgotten that God's power is enough to transform anybody. Our biggest danger isn't being too weak, but thinking that we are too strong. *"It is not the healthy who need a doctor, but those who are ill. I have not come to call the righteous, but sinners to repentance."*

The good news of the Kingdom of God is that he is most glorified when he displays his power through the weak and undeserving. He is calling us to partner with him, but it is not a partnership of equals. He is looking for lepers, for cripples, for tax collectors and sinners – weak people through whom he can display his mighty power.

John Piper explains: *"The gospel is not a help-wanted ad. It is a help-available ad. God is not looking for people to work for Him but people who let Him work mightily in and through them... How do we serve so God is glorified? We serve by the strength He supplies."*[11]

Daniel, without sounding seditious to Roman ears.

[9] Matthew 9:9–13 says that this man Levi went on to become the gospel writer Matthew.

[10] Unlike Matthew and Mark, Luke tells us that the Pharisees were disgusted, not just that Jesus ate with sinners, but that his disciples did so too. This is to be the model for all of our Christian ministry.

[11] John Piper in *Brothers, We Are Not Professionals* (2003).

Second Half (5:33–6:16)

New wine must be poured into new wineskins.

(Luke 5:38)

As a soccer fan, I have seen a lot of great second halves over the years but none of them can compare with the European Champions League Final in 2005. If you don't know much about football, all you need to know is that this is the greatest club tournament in the world. Every footballer dreams of winning it, and after the first half of the game the AC Milan players must have thought they had. From the moment they scored in the first minute of the game, they looked like a team of champions. The Liverpool players limped into their dressing room for their half-time team talk an unassailable 3–0 down.

But someone had forgotten to tell them that the game was as good as over. When they came back onto the pitch for the second half, they produced one of the greatest turnarounds in sporting history. In what many still refer to as the "Miracle of Istanbul", the Liverpool players scored three times in six short minutes to take the match to a penalty shoot-out, which they duly won. I still get goosebumps remembering it now.

I don't know what the manager said to his players during his half-time team talk, but Luke gives us a ringside seat on what Jesus said in his half-time talk to Israel. In 5:33–39, we see him clashing with a group of religious Jews who are upset that he does not appear to be following in the footsteps of Moses, Samuel, David and the other Old Testament heroes by teaching his disciples to fast.[1] If he must go and eat with tax collectors, can't he at least abstain from food with the Pharisees too? Won't he at least play his part in attracting God's attention and dragging salvation down from heaven?[2]

Jesus uses his half-time talk to point out that the Messiah has come to earth as a bridegroom looking for a bride, so Israel already has the Lord's undivided attention! Fasting is a helpful way of expressing that we are hungrier for God's Spirit than for food, but the Pharisees had turned it into a kind of hunger strike that sought to wrestle blessings from the hands of a reluctant God. Their first-half attempts to earn God's favour might be superficially attractive – *"No one after drinking old wine wants the new, for they say, 'The old is better'"* – but they are incompatible with life in the Spirit.[3] Jesus illustrates this by telling the first of many parables in Luke's gospel.[4] Responding to God's offer of his Spirit with first-half striving would be like cutting a hole in a new coat to patch an old one, like putting this year's wine in old and leaky bottles, or like weeping at a wedding reception![5] It would be to reject God's second-half turnaround for Israel.

In 6:1–11, we see Jesus clashing with the Pharisees over

---

[1] Fasting is something positive in 1 Samuel 7:6, 2 Samuel 12:16, 1 Kings 21:27–29, Ezra 8:21–23, Nehemiah 1:4 and Esther 4:16, but not in Luke 18:12. Jesus brings Israel back in Matthew 6:16–18 and Mark 9:29 to what fasting was meant to be.

[2] Matthew 9:14 tells us that this question was posed by John the Baptist's disciples. Luke leaves it ambiguous who *"they"* might be so that this can act as a clash between Jesus and first-century Judaism as a whole.

[3] These words do not appear in the parallel passages in Matthew and Mark. Luke knows full well that our instinct is to cling to our old ways, yet partnership with the Spirit is far better and has to change everything (7:28; Hebrews 8:6–13).

[4] Our word parable comes from the Greek word *parabolē*, meaning *something thrown alongside* or *a comparison*.

[5] New wine would ferment and burst old leather bottles, ruining both the wineskins and the wine. In the parallel accounts in Matthew 9:14–17 and Mark 2:18–22, Jesus points out that a patch from a new coat will shrink and tear the old coat. Here he emphasizes that, even if it doesn't, the two coats still won't match!

the Sabbath. Here they feel on safer ground because God's command to down tools and rest on the seventh day was one of the Ten Commandments. They complain that the disciples are breaking the Sabbath by picking food and eating it (doing the work of a farmer) and so is Jesus by healing people (doing his day job as a miracle worker). Jesus carries on his half-time team talk. Can't they see that their lists of what can and can't be done have made God's day of rest more difficult than a workday? Can't they see that they have made the Sabbath a burden to people instead of a weekly reminder that God wants to set them free?

Jesus explains how things are going to work in the second half for Israel. They are going to rediscover God's heart behind the Law of Sinai, just like David did when he set aside the detailed rules about the Tabernacle in order to revel in the just-in-time provision of God. Jesus knows that he will anger the Pharisees by repeating his claim to be the *Son of Man* that was prophesied by Daniel and *the Lord* who gave the Ten Commandments to Moses, but he wants to provoke them into making a firm choice one way or the other. Unless they agree to play by his second-half rules, he is determined to substitute them from the field.

Luke's account of this confrontation is shorter than Matthew's account for Jewish readers, but it is long enough to make one thing abundantly clear. Jesus is not calling Theophilus and his Roman friends to become like the Pharisees. Far from it. The rabbis have strayed so far from the faith of their fathers that their rules have even turned the great psalmist who sang about his love for the Law into a law-breaker![6] Jesus uses this half-time team talk for Israel to call people back to the God who wants to give them rest and to grant them salvation, not through hunger strikes, but through simple faith in who he is. He reminds the Jews that the Sabbath was never meant to

---

[6] The Pharisees prided themselves on their knowledge of the Scriptures, so Jesus is trying to convict them when he points to a famous passage about David and asks in 6:3, *"Have you never read...?"*

be about working hard to persuade God to bless us, but about resting in the blessings that are already ours.

In 6:12–16, Jesus does something very radical. It demonstrates that he is not abolishing Israel, but resetting its wonky foundations. Have you ever wondered why he chose twelve disciples when he had a much larger crowd in attendance? The rest of the New Testament explains that it was to reforge the twelve tribes of Israel.[7] Luke conveys this by telling us that Jesus prayed all night about who the Father wanted him to designate *apostles*. These twelve would be the second-half leaders of Israel, restoring God's people to the faith of Abraham, Moses and David that its first-half leaders had thrown away.[8]

This is a big moment in the story. It marks a crossroads both for the Jewish nation and for the Christian Church. Jesus has affirmed his commitment to the Old Testament story of Israel, but he has warned the Israelites that they are wandering away from the faith of their fathers and in danger of leaving their own story behind. He has chosen twelve of his followers to serve as apostles, the leaders of his reconstituted Israel.[9] As a result, for the first time the Jewish leaders start to discuss with one another how they might do away with their nation's Messiah. They reject his half-time team talk and his second-half ideas. They prefer their first-half way of viewing the world. Jesus and the Jewish leaders are now set on a collision course, but God's new Israel has begun.

---

[7] Matthew 19:28; Luke 22:29–30; Revelation 21:12–14.

[8] *Iscariot* is a Greek transliteration of the Hebrew *Ish Kerīōth*, meaning *Man of Kerioth*, a town in Judea. As the sole Judean disciple, Judas ought to have proved more devoted than the other 11 who were Galileans.

[9] Luke reinforces this message by starting his gospel with a priest in the Temple waiting for the Messiah (1:5–10) and by ending it with the apostles waiting in the Temple courtyards for the Holy Spirit (24:49–53).

Character Witness (6:17–49)

Everyone who is fully trained will be like their teacher.

(Luke 6:40)

It is still one of the most famous court cases in history. A judge like Theophilus must have known it well. Nobody expected Cicero to convict Verres of embezzlement during his time as governor of Sicily. Cicero was relatively unknown, and Verres had many rich and powerful friends. They had already asserted their influence to postpone the trial for long enough to ensure that Cicero had no time to secure a guilty verdict.

But this was the court case that revealed Cicero's genius to the world. Since he had no time to convict Verres the conventional way, he announced to the court that he would not be making any speech for the prosecution at all. Instead, he would rely on character witnesses alone. Nine days and dozens of character statements later, he was able to turn to the court and simply declare, *"Behold! All the world knows that Verres is distinguished by nothing except his monstrous offences and his immense wealth!"*[1] Cicero's surprise victory made legal history. It proved to the world that clear character witnesses are everything.

Luke knows that the Christian faith is on trial before Theophilus. He also knows that his best defence is that of Cicero. The best way to prove that Christians are the true heirs of the ancient faith of the Jews is to contrast their character with that of the rabbis. The best way to reassure the imperial government

---

[1] For a brilliant modern paraphrase of *Against Verres* (70 BC), see the Robert Harris novel *Imperium* (2006).

that they are not dangerous troublemakers is to contrast their character with that of their accusers. The best way to convince Theophilus and his friends that they ought to follow Jesus is to contrast the character of those who say yes to his message with those who say yes to the low morality of Rome.

In 6:17–26, Luke recounts the teaching that is known as the Beatitudes. If it sounds different from the more famous version in Matthew 5:3–12, that's because Jesus gave it on a separate occasion. That was the "Sermon on the Mount", whereas this is the "Sermon on the Plain".[2] This time around, Jesus replaces his eight or nine blessings with four blessings and four woes. The poor are blessed and the rich are cursed.[3] The hungry are blessed and the satisfied are cursed. Those who weep over their sin and weakness are blessed and those who laugh at God's Word are cursed. Those who are hated for their faith in Jesus are blessed and those who enjoy the world's approval are cursed. The new era of human partnership with the Holy Spirit has turned the old world order on its head. It's those who recognize how much they need God's power who are now the lucky ones.[4] It's those who succeed in the eyes of this fallen age who are to be pitied above all.

In 6:27–36, Luke records how Jesus says his followers must reflect his love to others. The Stoic philosophers of Rome told their disciples to avoid doing evil things to others unless they wanted the same things to be done back to them, but Jesus goes much further when he states that principle positively: *"Do to others as you would have them do to you."*[5] Don't just avoid

---

[2] Matthew 5–7 describes teaching given *"on a mountainside"* and Luke 6:17 teaching given *"on a level place"*. Other echoes of the sermon in Matthew 5–7 can be found in Luke 11:2–4, 9–13, 34–36 and 12:58–59.

[3] The Greek word *ptōchos* in 6:20 means *reduced to beggary*. Blessed are those who know they need God.

[4] We must not over-spiritualize the word *makarios*, or *blessed*. It simply means *happy* or *lucky*.

[5] Jesus says in Matthew 7:12 that this serves as a summary of the entire Jewish moral Law.

doing evil; be eager to do good! Don't just love, bless and pray for your friends; be a blessing towards those who wrong you, lend generously to those who swindle you and be kind to all those who abuse you. Become a character witness to the Spirit that is within you. Show everybody that you are a true child of the One who showers his grace on ungrateful and rebellious human beings every day.[6]

In 6:37–42, Luke recounts what Jesus taught about not judging one another. Human discernment is a good thing, but usurping God's role as Judge makes us far guiltier than the objects of our displeasure. Jesus warns us that he will judge us according to the way that we judge others. If we forgive and excuse people, he will forgive and excuse us. If we judge and condemn people, he will judge and condemn us. Every time we point at someone else, we have three fingers pointing back at ourselves, so we ought to complete our own sanctification before we start to point out the sins of others. Discern as a human and speak as witnesses, but don't play at being God and speak as Judge.

In 6:43–49, Luke records two of the parables that Jesus told to demand an active response from his listeners. The first points out that trees are known as good or rotten, not by what people claim they are, but by what fruit they bear. If we guard the sap inside us by feasting our eyes and ears on God's Word, we will bear good fruit, but if we allow our hearts to be corrupted by sinful words, we never will. Jesus insists that it is an inviolable principle that *"A good man brings good things out of the good stored up in his heart, and an evil man brings evil things out of the evil stored up in his heart. For the mouth speaks what the heart is full of."*[7] Good character witnesses have hearts full of God's Word.

---

[6] Verses 27–36 do not teach us to be passive in the face of evil (James 4:7), but to sacrifice our rights for others.

[7] These words of Jesus echo Proverbs 4:23. To change your actions, you need only change your heart.

The second parable is very similar. It tells us that the true mark of a Christian is not whether they cry *"Lord, Lord"* in church services, but whether they take God's Word to heart and do what it says. Jesus warns that stormy times are coming (it is not a case of *if*, but *when*) that will reveal whether we have dug deep foundations of discipleship or whether we have built quick with phoney faith and shallow words.[8] Sooner or later our true character will be revealed before the jury of the watching world.

Mahatma Gandhi famously challenged British missionaries to India that *"You Christians are so unlike Christ. If Christians would really live according to the teachings of Christ, as found in the Bible, all of India would be Christian today."* When we read these verses, it is easy to believe him. If we were truly to live this way in front of unbelievers, we would convince them speedily that our faith in God is real. Character witnesses always convince a jury.

So here's the massive promise that Jesus gives us in this sermon. It comes in 6:39–40, the only verses in the "Sermon on the Plain" that are not in the "Sermon on the Mount".[9] Jesus says that these commands are not a set of unattainable Christian ideals. They are a description of the character that God pledges to work in our hearts if we say yes to partnership with his Holy Spirit. They are a promise that, if we follow Jesus as our Example, he will teach us to partner with God's Spirit too. If we respond to the message of Luke's gospel, *"Everyone who is fully trained will be like their teacher."*

---

[8] Building without foundations is quicker and looks more impressive, but trouble quickly reveals our faith as shallow. Jesus warns that Satan often leaves phoney faith unchallenged for years to effect maximum damage in the end.

[9] Instead they appear in Matthew 10:24–25 and 15:14. Jesus repeated a lot of his teaching as he travelled.

What Do You Expect?
(7:1–50)

Are you the one who is to come, or should we expect someone else?

(Luke 7:19)

The church I lead in London was planted by the famous nineteenth-century preacher Charles Spurgeon. He entrusted the work of reaching the local community to a man named Tommy Medhurst, an uneducated ropemaker from the London dockyards. Converted only three years earlier, he soon grew despondent and came to see Spurgeon:

> One day, with a very sad countenance, he said to me, "I have been preaching for three months, and I don't know of a single soul having been converted." Meaning to catch him by guile, and at the same time to teach him a lesson he would never forget, I asked, "Do you expect the Lord to save souls every time you open your mouth?" "Oh no, sir!" he replied. "Then," I said, "that is just the reason why you have not had conversions: According to your faith be it unto you."[1]

Tommy Medhurst took the lesson to heart and as a result saw 200 conversions over the next four years. It makes me wonder whether one of the reasons I am seeing fewer conversions than I would like in the same community is that my expectations are

---

[1] Spurgeon records this conversation in his autobiography *The Early Years* (1900).

wrong. Luke's big question to us in chapter 7 is: *What do you expect from the Messiah?*

Expectations are high going into the chapter, because things have just moved up a gear. After naming the twelve apostles, Jesus sees a fresh breakthrough in 6:17–19. He starts gathering large crowds, not just from Jerusalem and Judea, but also *"from the coastal region around Tyre and Sidon"*. Even as the Jewish leaders start plotting how to kill him, the Gentiles from the borderlands of Israel begin to believe. Luke says that Jesus does three things for the crowds: he preaches the Gospel, he heals the sick and he drives out demons. As he does so, he succeeds in *"healing them all"*. That should challenge our expectations before we even start chapter 7. I know that I slip far too readily into thinking that I'm called to share the Gospel verbally but not to demonstrate it practically by being God's instrument to heal people and drive out demons. Even when I remember all three of the things that Jesus did for the crowds, I very often don't expect to see many people healed or delivered. I think Charles Spurgeon was right. My expectation, or my frequent lack of it, tends to dictate what I see.[2]

In 7:1–10, Luke responds to this by raising our expectations.[3] Most Jews assumed that the Messiah would lead an armed insurrection against the Romans. The Jewish leaders clearly expect this too, because they come to him with a list of mitigating reasons why they think he ought to help a hated Roman officer.[4] Jesus doesn't actually need their persuasion, and when the centurion sends messengers to intercept him he exclaims that this Roman grasps the Gospel better than the Jews.

[2] Spurgeon was not making it up. He was quoting Matthew 9:29. See also Luke 7:50; 8:48; 17:19; 18:42.

[3] This event is similar to the one in John 4:43–54, but spot the difference. This time it is a Gentile, not a Jew.

[4] Their list shows just how far first-century Judaism had become a religion of works. Luke uses the Greek word *axios*, or *worthy*, in both 7:4 and 7:7 to emphasize that the centurion's philanthropy could never earn him a miracle from Jesus. The Gospel is all about grace, never about graft.

Let this shape your expectations the next time you are tempted to assume that there is no point in sharing the good news about Jesus with the Muslim in your office or with the Buddhist who lives next door. The Roman centurion's background actually made it easier for him to grasp the message of God's Kingdom. Jesus declares that *"I have not found such great faith even in Israel."* [5]

In 7:11–16, Jesus raises our expectations again. There are many reasons why he should not intervene to help the widow in the village of Nain at the funeral of her only son. First, nobody has performed a miracle of resurrection since the days of Elijah and Elisha – not even Jesus himself. Second, rabbis were not permitted to touch a corpse or a coffin, since both were viewed as ceremonially unclean. Third, nobody has even asked him to intervene. Despite all this, Jesus defies our preconceived ideas. The son of a widow himself by now, Jesus is filled with compassion and needs no cajoling to intervene. [6] He touches the coffin and speaks a command to the corpse. The boy sits up and calls an end to his own funeral! He won't be put in a box any more than Jesus. [7]

In 7:18–23, Jesus warns us not to let discouragements dilute our expectations of him. John the Baptist's faith starts to wobble when Herod imprisons him and Jesus shows no sign of mounting an armed insurrection in time to rescue him. To his credit, John has the wisdom to bring his doubts to Jesus straightaway. Jesus gently responds by drawing John's attention

---

[5] The fact that Jesus heals the centurion's slave from afar should also raise our expectations for today. Just because Jesus is now in heaven does not make him any less powerful to heal people on earth through us.

[6] This illustrates the principle of 2 Corinthians 1:3–7. Our own sorrows often prepare us to comfort others.

[7] Luke is the only gospel writer to mention this amazing event. He does so to shatter our preconceived ideas. Nain was 12 miles from Capernaum, near to Shunem, where Elisha had performed his resurrection miracle. The phrase *"He gave him back to his mother"* is also a deliberate echo of what Elijah did in 1 Kings 17:23.

to the Messianic prophecies in Isaiah.[8] He is healing those who are ill, delivering those who are demonized, raising those who are dead and rescuing those who are lost. The problem lies with John's expectations, not with the actions of Jesus. He came to do something bigger than defy Caesar. He came to defang and destroy Satan.

In 7:24–35, Jesus turns to the crowd and warns that having too low expectations is a danger for us all. John's disciples are feeling equally discouraged that he is in prison, so Jesus quotes from Malachi 3:1 to remind them that, despite Herod's actions, John is still the one who prepared Israel for the arrival of its Messiah. He is still the greatest first-half prophet, whose ministry was promised in the Old Testament and who has paved the way for every believer to know God better than himself. They must not flag in their faith. Of course John has been imprisoned. If the stubborn Jewish leaders hadn't rejected him for being an ascetic, they would have rejected him for not being ascetic enough! Their problem isn't with the messenger, but with the message. They have *"rejected God's purpose for themselves".*[9]

In 7:36–50, Jesus raises our expectations that, if we persevere through our discouragements, many will be saved through our message. He goes to dinner with a Pharisee, one of the respectable people that we find it easiest to believe we might see saved. Invite Simon to church with us? No problem. Invite the prostitute who sneaks into his dining room?[10] Never in a month of Sundays. Jesus therefore surprises us by rebuking Simon for his self-centredness and by commending

[8] See Isaiah 29:18–19; 32:3–4; 35:5–6; 42:6–7; 61:1–3. John was confused about the "now and not yet" of God's Kingdom. Jesus would fulfil some prophecies now and others at his second coming.

[9] By stressing choice in salvation, Luke tells us to expect many such choices by reminding us that even tax collectors were saved through John. They were made righteous (*dikaioō*) by confessing God is right (*dikaioō*).

[10] *"Sinful woman"* is a euphemism for a prostitute. The traditional view is that this was Mary Magdalene, although Luke does not say so. He only talks about Mary Magdalene two verses later in 8:2.

the prostitute for confessing her sins in floods of tears. Although we might expect her to be hostile to the Gospel, she embodies the Beatitudes here. It's precisely because she isn't respectable that she comes with her perfume and receives forgiveness. Jesus tells her, *"Your faith has saved you; go in peace."*[11]

So Luke asks you at the end of this chapter: *What do you expect from the Messiah?* Do you expect to see people saved when you tell them about him? Do you expect to see illness and demons and even death flee when you issue commands in his name? Do you expect to see the unexpected as you follow him? According to your faith will it be unto you.

---

[11] Simon's friends complain that Jesus has forgiven her (7:48), so he declares unequivocally she is saved (7:50).

Recap: Good News (8:1–21)

Jesus travelled about from one town and village to another, proclaiming the good news of the kingdom of God.

(Luke 8:1)

Every teacher knows how to do it. So does every preacher and every historian. Luke therefore knows exactly what to do as he draws Act 1 of his gospel to a close. He gives us a final recap, a helpful summary of the three big themes in his account so far.[1]

The first big theme is that Jesus has come into the world to proclaim the Good News. Luke says that everywhere the Messiah goes he preaches the same message: *"the good news of the kingdom of God"*. Luke demonstrates how inclusive this Good News is by describing those who are on the road with Jesus. The twelve apostles are there as a reminder that the Good News is first and foremost a message for Israel. The woman who was demonized seven times over and the wife of one of Herod the tetrarch's top officials remind us that the Good News is a message for sinners. A number of wealthy women remind us that the Good News isn't just for down-and-outs. The Messiah delivers forgiveness and healing through the Holy Spirit to anybody who believes.

Jesus tells his famous Parable of the Sower in order to illustrate what the Good News is and how it works in people's

---

[1] The word *kathexēs* in 8:1, which is translated *after this*, means literally *next in order*. It is a historian's word, used only five times in the New Testament, all of which are in Luke or Acts.

lives.[2] He explains that *"the seed is the word of God"*.[3] We are not to share the message stingily, waiting until we are sure we will receive a positive response. We are to share it lavishly and to trust in God that it will do its work in people's hearts. Some people will ignore our words. Satan will swoop down and snatch away the Good News from right under their noses, like the first type of seed that falls on the path. We mustn't be discouraged by this. Keep on sharing. Jesus assures us that three times out of four we can expect the Good News to take root and grow.

Some people will appear to have been instantly converted. Their response to the Good News will be characterized by great joy and lavish affirmations that they believe. However, they are like the man in the earlier parable who tried to build his house without foundations. Their rapid response masks the fact that there is very little going on under the surface. They have not taken time to consider the true cost of following Jesus. They haven't dug deep roots down into what the Gospel means for them at all. As a result, when trouble comes, as it always does, they get offended and fall away. They didn't realize that following Jesus meant turning away from *that* sin. They didn't expect it to mean becoming unpopular with *those* people. They begin to think that it is not good news at all. They have never grasped that the Good News is the announcement of a new King on the throne. It isn't the promise of an easy life, but a command to switch sides.

Other people grow more slowly. In fact, they don't appear to grow much at all. They are all stalk and no ear. They haven't grasped that the Good News is a call to cut things out of their lives as well as a call to allow God's new thing in. They try to follow Jesus *and* pursue their pre-conversion plans. They don't

---

[2] As in Matthew 13:1–23 and Mark 4:1–20, Jesus quotes from Isaiah 6:9 to emphasize that his parables (literally *comparisons*) aim to conceal truth from rebellious hearts as well as illustrate it to honest ones.

[3] It stands to reason, then, that if what we share is not the genuine Gospel then it will not yield genuine fruit.

expect their new-found faith to alter their job, their bank balance and their friends. As a result, they never come to maturity. They bear no fruit because their lives are already too full of other things to be full of the Spirit.

The fourth type of seed falls on good soil. It makes all the disappointments with the other three types of seed feel worth the while. Jesus says that these are people who do three things: they *"hear the word, retain it, and by persevering produce a crop"*. They count the cost of following Jesus and make radical sacrifices to make the Gospel the one thing that matters in their lives. As a result, they yield *"a hundred times more than was sown"* – not just 100 more converts like themselves but 100 times as many as the whole batch of seed that was sown. They more than make up for the apparent wastefulness of sowing the other three types of seed.[4]

The purpose of this recap is partly personal. Before we move on from Act 1 of his gospel, Luke wants us to decide what type of seed we are going to be. Jesus is interrupted in 8:19–21 by Mary.[5] You can't get more Jewish than the woman who gave birth to the Jewish Messiah, yet Jesus turns around and declares that *"My mother and brothers are those who hear God's word and put it into practice."* Christianity isn't about our parents or our nationality. It's about our obedience to God's Word.

The purpose of this recap is also to transition us into the message of Act 2. Jesus is about to call us to do more than respond to the Good News ourselves. He wants to make us messengers of the Good News too. That's why he tells us in 8:16–18 that, if God has lit a lamp of salvation in our own hearts, we need

---

[4] While Matthew and Mark's accounts call us to expect *"thirty, sixty or a hundred times what was sown"*, Luke simply tells us to expect *"a hundred times"*. That said, Luke alone emphasizes that such fruit will only come *"by persevering"*.

[5] Luke never calls her *the Virgin Mary* after chapter 1. She slept with Joseph after their marriage (Matthew 1:25) and had several sons and daughters with him.

to shine that lamp into the hearts of others.[6] It's also why he encourages us that it takes very little for a person to be saved.

Many people read the Parable of the Sower and miss this. They major on the birds and the rocky ground and the thorns. They assume that seeing people saved is hard, the exception to the rule. They miss what Jesus tells us in 8:15, that salvation is God's work and not ours. People don't need to have all their questions answered before they can be saved. They don't need the faith that moves a mountain. What they need is very small. Jesus says that all a person needs to be saved is *"an honest and good heart"* towards God.[7]

Watchman Nee explains:

He is not required – in the first place – to believe, or to repent, or to be conscious of sin, or even to know that Christ died. He is required only to approach the Lord with an honest heart... Of the two thoroughly dishonest thieves crucified with the Lord, there was in the one a little bit of honest desire. The publican who prayed in the temple was a crooked man, but in him too there was that honesty to acknowledge his sinfulness and cry to God for mercy... I affirm once again: all that is needed is an honest heart. If you **want** *God there is no difficulty. But praise God, even if you do* **not** *want Him, He will still hear you if you will come to Him and be honest about it... There is not one other condition necessary to being saved except that of being a sinner and being honest enough to say so to the Lord.*[8]

So spread the Good News. Sow it lavishly. Whenever it finds people who have an honest and good heart, you will see God carry on the Messiah's work of salvation through you.

---

[6] Jesus tells us in 8:18 that how much we share the Good News in this life affects our reward in the next.

[7] In 8:15, *kalē kai agathē* means literally *good and good*. It speaks of our hearts being sincere and open to God.

[8] Watchman Nee says this in his book *What Shall This Man Do?* (1961).

Recap: Authority and Power (8:22–39)

RECAP: AUTHORITY AND POWER (8:22–39)

In fear and amazement they asked one another, "Who is this? He commands even the winds and the water, and they obey him."

(Luke 8:25)

Anyone who has ever watched a Hollywood movie knows which two things an American policeman is given to enable him to do his job. It's a cliché that the hero will lose his badge and gun at the start of the movie, only to have them restored to him in triumph at the end. Cue the music and credits. I'm sure you've seen it countless times.

It makes a good story because the policeman's badge and gun are potent symbols of authority and power. It doesn't matter how small or weak or unarmed a policeman is. When he flashes his badge, most people fall into line. The gun is for people who refuse. The badge speaks of authority, but the gun enforces it with power. If you don't respect Clint Eastwood's badge, you'll do whatever he says when he draws his .44 Magnum.

The second of the three big themes that Luke recaps for us at the end of Act 1 of his gospel is that of authority and power.[1] Verses 22–25 are about authority. They are like the scene where the cop shows his badge and everyone does what he says. Verses 26–39 are about power, like the moment when the bad guys are forced to toe the line. We need to grasp both concepts before we move on, because they will dominate Act 2.

---

[1] Greek has two distinct words for authority (*exousia*) and power (*dunamis*). Both are essential concepts in Luke.

Jesus says to the disciples, *"Let us go over to the other side of the lake."* He promptly falls asleep because he knows his own authority. If he commands something, it is done.[2] He is the man who confronted a fever in 4:39, and it immediately fled. He is the man who commanded a leper to be clean in 5:13, and he immediately was. He is the man who told a lame paralytic to get up and walk and, when he did so, declared in 5:24 that this was proof of his authority to forgive sins. Jesus falls asleep in the boat because he knows that he carries heaven's badge wherever he goes. If he has told the disciples to go over to the other side of the lake, there is no authority on earth or in hell that can stand in their way.

The disciples have not yet fully understood this concept of authority. They are seasoned fishermen, so it must have been quite a storm to spook them on Lake Galilee, but they wake up Jesus in a panic that the boat is going under and that they are all about to die. It's interesting that in their fear they address Jesus twice in 8:24 as *epistatēs*, which means *master* only in the sense that a servant might use the word. It means *boss* rather than *the Lord*. One of the distinctive features of Luke's gospel is that, in contrast, he keeps referring to Jesus as *kurios* – that is, as *the Lord*, Yahweh in human flesh and blood.[3] Jesus rubs his eyes and expresses his surprise that the disciples haven't yet understood this. He gets up and commands the wind and the waves to be still. Instantly they fall into line.

The disciples are amazed and afraid. They can't understand how Jesus just took on the wind and waves and won. They haven't learned the lesson that the Roman centurion tried to teach them in 7:8 when he told them, *"I myself am a man under authority, with soldiers under me. I tell this one, 'Go', and he goes;*

---

[2] This also demonstrates that Jesus chose to minister not out of his inherent divinity, but as a man filled with the Holy Spirit. God does not get tired from working in the world, but Jesus was exhausted.

[3] For examples so far of Luke calling Jesus *ho kurios*, or *the Lord*, in his narrative, see 2:11, 7:13 and 7:19.

and that one, 'Come', and he comes. I say to my servant, 'Do this', and he does it." They have not grasped that a man who wields heaven's badge trumps any earthly authority – even the very elements themselves.

This is how, in 6:10, Jesus could order a man unable to stretch out his hand to stretch it out, knowing that his body would have to fall into line. It is how, when he ordered a corpse to jump to its feet, Luke can say with deliberate irony in 7:15, *"the dead man sat up and began to talk."*[4] It is how the Roman centurion knew that Jesus did not need to come to his home to heal his slave but could simply *"say the word"*. It is why Luke told us literally in 7:21, not that Jesus prayed for his Father to heal blind people, but that he *granted them to see.* This is the Good News of the Kingdom: Jesus carries heaven's badge.

The boat reaches the other side of the lake safely, just as Jesus said it would. In a graveyard in this pagan region lives a man tormented by an army of demons, the perfect candidate to demonstrate the difference between authority and power.[5] We are meant to see him as the toughest villain in a movie – like Jaws in the *James Bond* films or like Lord Voldemort in *Harry Potter*.[6] Luke tells us that *"though he was chained hand and foot and kept under guard, he had broken his chains"*. If anybody is going to try to defy the badge that Jesus carries, it will be this man, who even goes by the name of Legion to boast about the vast number of demons that empower him inside.[7]

But what's this? The army of demons scream at the sight of

---

[4] Note how aware Jesus is of his heavenly authority. His message to the corpse is, *"I say to you..."*

[5] The boat arrives in the mixed-race region of The Decapolis, between the towns of Gerasa and Gadara. Consequently, the gospel writers refer to the region variously as that of the *Gerasenes* or *Gadarenes*.

[6] Matthew 8:28–34 says that there were two men. Luke only mentions one of them in order to present it as a powerful showdown between heaven's man and hell's man.

[7] A Roman legion consisted of over 5,000 soldiers. The demons in this one man filled 2,000 pigs (Mark 5:13).

Jesus and fall down in fear, confessing that he is the *"Son of the Most High God"*. They want to defy heaven's badge of authority, but heaven's power forces them to comply. Speaking through their host, the demons beg Jesus not to torture them or send them packing off to hell before the Final Day of Judgment.[8] Luke says that they beg for *"permission"* to move house from the man to a large herd of pigs on the mountainside. In other words, the struggle is entirely one-sided. Demons that try to argue with the badge that Jesus carries prove no match for the power of his gun. The pigs rush into the water and drown, presumably sending the demons to the Abyss anyway, just as Jesus had planned. When the people of the region panic and ask him to leave, he tells the man he has delivered to go and spread the Good News: Jesus will be back in the area soon, carrying heaven's badge and heaven's gun.

We need to understand these two concepts before we end Act 1 of Luke's gospel, because in Act 2 Jesus hands badges and guns to his followers too. Designating them *apostles* did not just mean that they were his new tribal leaders. The word is Greek for *sent ones*, and Act 2 begins with Jesus sending them out with *"power and authority"* into the world. What's more, in Act 2 it won't just be the apostles. Every follower of Jesus will be invited to play. The amazing events in these verses all happened for you.

---

[8] *Abyss* is Greek for *bottomless*. It refers to hell in Romans 10:7 and in Revelation 9:1–11 and 20:1–3.

Recap: Faith (8:40–56)

Then he said to her, "Daughter, your faith has healed you. Go in peace."

(Luke 8:48)

I can sympathize with people who are offended by the idea that God still gives the same authority and power he gave to Jesus to men and women today. I have been to the shrines in France, Spain and Portugal where crowds queue for hours to lay their hands on relics. I have watched televangelists promise miracles for money. I have seen the things that made Walter Chantry doubt that God empowers people to do miracles at all:

There is no Biblical reason to limit God to performing miracles at certain seasons only... It is plain that God's working of wonders cannot be limited to ages past... The question of our inquiry is not "Should God be working miracles today?" It is rather, "Should men be doing miracles on behalf of God?"... Serious students of God's Word must deny that miracles are being performed today by men who are filled with God's Spirit... Great numbers believe the opinions of those who perform wonders because their "gifts" indicate that they are "filled with the Spirit". The implication of such logic is clear. How can anyone question the doctrines of miracle workers?... "Can a man be teaching false doctrine when he does such mighty things?" ask the captivated.[1]

---

[1] Walter Chantry in his seminal anti-charismatic work *Signs of the Apostles* (1973).

I understand Walter Chantry's concerns. I'm even tempted to go along with them some of the time. Yet in the end I just can't be won over by them because of what Luke says at the end of Act 1 of his gospel. The last of the three big themes that he recaps for us is that God wants us to believe that we can access his power and authority today. He will work with outcast shepherds and lowlife tax collectors. He will work with slow-witted fishermen or penitent prostitutes. He will even work with the flawed theology of a leper. But the one thing he won't work with, it seems, is an emasculated form of Christianity that has stopped expecting to experience heaven's power and authority today.

Luke ends Act 1 of his gospel by introducing us to a woman who has been suffering from non-stop menstruation for the past twelve years. In first-century Jewish culture, that was more than inconvenient. It meant that life was not worth living. Under the Jewish Law, she was ceremonially unclean and liable to be cut off from the nation of Israel if she ever went outside her front door.[2] Naturally she spent all the money she had on doctors in an attempt to find a cure, but after twelve years she was bankrupt and still a shut-in, without any hope in the world.[3] That's where she challenges the view that Christians shouldn't expect to wield the same power and authority as Jesus. Luke reminds us that people still need the hope of heaven. For many, it's the only hope they have.

The woman decides to gamble everything on Jesus. She doesn't question how those who touch him are getting healed. She simply believes that they are, and that she can somehow access heaven's power supply too. She creeps up behind Jesus and touches the edge of his cloak. She can feel in her body that she is instantly healed, but (she hadn't counted on this) Jesus

---

[2] See Leviticus 15:19–31; 20:18; Numbers 19:20. This banished her from the Temple, the synagogue, her friends and any sexual relations with her husband – that is, if her husband still wanted her around at all.

[3] Although not all Greek texts of Luke 8:43 contain the detail about doctors, all the texts of Mark 5:26 do.

can also feel in his body that power has gone out of him to heal her.

The woman is in terrible trouble. She was breaking the Jewish Law by leaving her home. Now she has been caught placing her unclean hands on a rabbi. The only Bible verse that she can point to in her defence is a terrible exegesis of the text.[4] But here's the thing. Jesus isn't angry with her. He is delighted with her faith. Israel may have rejected her, but he receives her as one of his own: *"Daughter, your faith has healed you. Go in peace."*

Luke tells us that a synagogue leader named Jairus is suffering too. His twelve-year-old daughter, his only child, is dying. We can tell how desperate he is, since most of the synagogue leaders were Pharisees. Turning to Jesus for help meant breaking ranks with his friends. His Pharisee textbook tells him that the power of God is no longer available, but his family crisis spurs him to believe that Jesus truly carries heaven's badge and gun.[5] He must have been encouraged to see the woman healed on the way to his home – note the link between twelve years of bleeding and a twelve-year-old daughter – but then a messenger arrives from his home: *"Your daughter is dead. Don't bother the teacher anymore."*[6]

The synagogue leader is devastated, but Jesus tells him to have the same faith as the woman he just healed. *"Don't be afraid; just believe, and she will be healed."* As a student of the Scriptures, that must have offended him straightaway. Healed? I don't need a promise of healing. Can't you see I need a Bible

---

[4] The word for *wings* or *rays* in Malachi 4:2 was also the word used for the *tassels* on a rabbi's prayer shawl. Having heard about what happened in Luke 6:19, she seems to have misunderstood the promise to mean that the Messiah had arisen *"with healing in his tassels"*. Jesus ignores her awful theology to praise her awesome faith.

[5] Mark 5:23 says that, like the woman, he believed that the touch of Jesus conducted heaven's power supply.

[6] The repetition of the number *12* here is to link what happens to the calling and sending out of the Twelve.

verse about resurrection?[7] When they arrive at his home, Jesus offends him further. He tells the mourners who have gathered to *"Stop wailing. She is not dead but asleep."* They sneer at Jesus openly because they know for sure that she is dead. He clearly doesn't have an earthly clue what he is saying.

That's Luke's point. Jesus did not come into the world to abide by Peter's earthly logic (lots of people are touching you) or by earthly facts (the girl is dead) or by earthly expectations (stop bothering the teacher). He came into the world to demonstrate what happens when God's Spirit partners with a perfect human being. He is not denying that the girl is dead. He is simply insisting that earthly facts don't get to speak the final word. He speaks to the corpse and commands the dead girl to get up. Instantly the universe surrenders to heaven's badge and gun. Her spirit returns and she stands up alive![8]

I wish that those who believe that God still gives this same authority and power to people today did so in a less offensive manner. But I can't deny what Luke is saying here as he ends Act 1 of his gospel. If our concerns lead us to create a theology that leaves no room for faith for heaven to break into our world, we have become as blind as the mourners outside the synagogue leader's home. Our churches will become like the synagogue in Nazareth, where Jesus *"did not do many miracles there because of their lack of faith"*.[9] As we end Act 1 of his gospel, Luke urges us to believe that heaven's badge and gun are still available to us today. He shouts above the noise that might tempt us to deny it: *"Don't be afraid; just believe. Your faith has healed you."*

---

[7] The Greek word that Jesus uses in 8:48 and 50 isn't the normal word for *healing*. It is *sōzō*, the normal word for *saving*. Jesus is actually promising that Jairus is about to see heaven's power – the salvation of the Lord.

[8] This is the first of several times that Jesus singles out Peter, James and John as leaders among the Twelve. He tells the girl's parents to keep quiet about the miracle to stop his healings distracting from his teaching.

[9] Matthew 13:58. Contrast this with Luke 7:50; 8:25, 48, 50; 9:41; 17:6, 19; 18:42. See also John 11:40.

Act Two:

He Can Use You

It's Your Turn (9:1–17)

When Jesus had called the Twelve together, he gave
them power and authority.

(Luke 9:1)

Stomp is one of the cleverest shows ever to run in the West End
and on Broadway. Even if you have never seen it, you must at
least have heard about its musicians. They are so talented that
for ninety minutes you watch them making music out of just
about anything. Bin lids, buckets, wet socks, garbage cans, shoes,
pots and pans, brooms, plates, cutlery and keys – you name it,
they play it. Kitchen sinks, blenders, newspapers, drainpipes
and apples – there doesn't appear to be anything they can't play.
If you go to see them, I hope you have a brilliant time and I hope
it reminds you of Act 2 of Luke's gospel. At the start of chapter
9, God starts to reveal his skill as the master musician of the
universe. Jesus suddenly turns to his followers and says: *It's*
your turn.

Given all that Luke has told us about the way that Jesus
wields the power and authority of heaven, it's startling how Act
2 begins: *"When Jesus had called the Twelve together, he gave*
them power and authority."[1] Jesus suddenly informs the Twelve
that he is giving them badges and guns of their own. We saw
throughout Act 1 that Jesus came to be our great Example,
resolving to minister only in ways that his Spirit-filled followers

---

[1] Luke prepared us for this by repeating the number *12* in the final verses of
Act 1. See 8:42, 43.

are able to follow. All the same, this sudden transition into stage two of his plan still comes as an abrupt surprise.[2]

Jesus splits the Twelve into six pairs and sends them out into the towns and villages of Galilee.[3] He does not dumb down the mission as he sends them, since achieving it is all about partnering with God's Spirit and not about any talents of our own. Note how closely the mission Jesus gives them mirrors his own ministry in Act 1: *"He gave them power and authority to drive out all demons and to cure diseases, and he sent them out to proclaim the kingdom of God and to heal those who were ill."*[4]

I don't know which is more surprising – that the Twelve go ahead and attempt the impossible or that verses 6–10 say that they actually succeed. It doesn't matter that they are the human equivalents of wet socks, bin lids and garbage cans. It's the skill of the master musician that counts, not the quality of the instruments he decides to play.[5]

In fact, Jesus assures them, their weakness is their strength. They must burn their bridges with the resources of this world if they want to learn to operate on the resources of heaven. He instructs them to *"Take nothing for the journey – no staff, no bag, no bread, no money, no extra shirt."*[6] To become powerful, they

---

[2] That's why I can't agree with those who view Luke's structure primarily in terms of geography: *Galilee* (1:1–9:50), *Judea* (9:51–13:21), *Perea* (13:22–19:27) and *Jerusalem* (19:28–24:53). The big progression in Luke's gospel isn't about where the action takes place. It's about who lies at the heart of the action!

[3] We are given a much longer record of his instructions in Matthew 10:1–42. Luke keeps it brief for now because he will give us lengthier instructions later on in 10:1–24.

[4] They are even to follow his example by lodging with their own "disciples" in 9:4.

[5] Luke gives a far shorter account of the beheading of John the Baptist than Matthew 14:1–12 or Mark 6:14–29. He is writing for Judge Theophilus, so he does not want to dwell on a Roman official ordering an execution!

[6] This is a great example of a perceived contradiction in the gospels, since Mark 6:8 says only to take one staff, while Matthew 10:10 and Luke say not to take a staff at all. We need to remember that Jesus spoke these words in

need to weaken themselves. To become strong, they need to rid themselves of the things that fool them into thinking they are strong already.[7]

When the Twelve come back to Jesus, they are very excited. They can hardly believe that they have seen so many people healed and delivered and brought to repentance through their own voices and hands. They are pleased when Jesus suggests that they withdraw to a quiet place together for a ministry debrief. When thousands of people gatecrash their little retreat and Jesus starts teaching and healing them, the Twelve want him to send the crowd away.[8] Quite apart from their own desire to continue their debrief undisturbed, there is a practical consideration. They are in a deserted place and there are around 5,000 men in the crowd, not including women and children. Unless Jesus disperses them to the surrounding villages to buy food, they will go hungry.[9]

This was actually why Jesus brought them here, knowing that the crowds would follow. It wasn't just to debrief them on the past few days, but also to give them the next lesson on the syllabus. He wants to teach them that partnership with God's Spirit is not like a labouring job, where you clock in and clock out at fixed hours. It is about watching to see what the Father is doing and then joining in, whatever the time.

Unlike John's gospel, Luke does not mention that the five loaves and two fish were provided by a boy in the crowd, because he wants to use this miracle as a picture of what God can do through the limited resources of the Twelve. Jesus sees that

---

Aramaic. The gospel writers interpret differently his Aramaic command, *"Do not take staffs."*

[7] Churches and missionary organizations tend to work on the opposite principle, but Jesus says that lack of necessary funds is no good reason to postpone obedience. Lack of resources is a key element of his strategy.

[8] Note that Luke says preaching the Kingdom and proving the Kingdom through miracles go hand in hand.

[9] Mark 6:45 explains that they were in the countryside near Bethsaida. The disciples rowed to the town later.

they do not yet have faith to perform this kind of miracle, so he performs it for them. He looks up to his power supply in heaven, speaks a prayer of blessing over the bread and fish, and then lays his hands on them to tear them into pieces for the crowd. He asks the Twelve to do the three things that they at least have faith to do.[10] They are to divide the crowd into groups of fifty, to distribute the food to them and to go round with a basket each in which to gather up all the leftovers.[11] When everyone has eaten, the Twelve look at one another in amazement. Each of their baskets is full (note the number twelve again). They have more food than when they started. It's a promise that God will provide all the resources that they need as they enter this new stage in his plan.

Luke wants you to be excited about this new stage in the story too. Remember, Luke came from the city of Antioch, where the believers were first labelled Christians – a derogatory term which meant *little Christs*. The Antioch believers had gladly accepted the insult, since two Old Testament passages spoke about the Messiah's army of little messiahs.[12] They were happy to be known as a band of Christians, and so must we be. The message of Act 2 of Luke's gospel is that Jesus is calling you to be a little Christ. Jesus is your Example and he is able to use you.

---

[10] If Jesus could multiply the food without them, he didn't need their help to distribute it! This miracle aimed to teach them how to partner with God.

[11] Good church administrative structures aren't unspiritual. They are often key to partnership with the Spirit.

[12] 1 Chronicles 16:22; Psalm 105:15; Acts 11:26; 26:28; 1 Peter 4:16. See also John 14:12.

How to Share the Gospel
(9:18–26)

Who do the crowds say I am?... Who do you say I am?

(Luke 9:18, 20)

According to World War Two folklore, the Nazi tanks that invaded Poland in September 1939 were met by Polish cavalrymen wielding lances. Their courage was as great as the carnage that followed. Napoleonic weaponry was no match for the Nazi Wehrmacht.

Jesus was determined that the mission of the Twelve would not be like the one-sided Battle of Krojanty. He gave his followers all the weaponry they needed. He taught them the secret of how to share the Gospel. We need to read these verses very slowly.

In 9:18, Jesus demonstrates to his disciples that successful Gospel-sharing always starts with prayer. In case we are in any doubt how his dirty dozen disciples were able to heal the sick and cast out demons and distribute five loaves and two fish to 5,000 people, Luke reminds us that Jesus constantly withdrew to a place of prayer. He tells us literally that *"Jesus was praying on his own"*, not because private prayer is more powerful than corporate prayer, but to prevent us from saying anything as foolish as *I'm more of a pray-all-the-time kind of person.* Jesus was fruitful because he recognized that people are only saved when the Holy Spirit brings them to new birth and that he therefore needed to root his Gospel-sharing in partnership with his Father through prayer.[1]

In 9:18–20, Jesus teaches the disciples that successful Gospel-sharing always involves asking people questions. He showed us as a twelve-year-old that we need to follow the wisdom of Proverbs 20:5: *"The purposes of a person's heart are deep waters, but one who has insight draws them out."* He does so again here by the way he tells the Twelve that he is the Messiah. Instead of blurting out the truth, he asks them a third-person question – *"Who do **the crowds** say I am?"* – because questions about what other people believe are far less threatening than questions about our own beliefs. A general conversation about Elijah, John the Baptist and the other prophets leads very naturally on to a tougher, more personal question: *"But what about **you**? Who do **you** say I am?"*

I have had to learn this lesson the hard way. I am a preacher, so my preferred method of evangelism is to lecture unbelievers. Trust me, it doesn't work. I have had to learn to copy Jesus as a twelve-year-old by sitting, listening and asking questions, because nobody wants to be lectured. They want somebody who can help them to process what they already see. Instead of telling people that they ought to go to church, I have found it far more profitable to ask them why they think most of their neighbours have given up on church and whether those third-person reasons are also why church never makes it into their own diary. After half an hour of listening to their complaints about religious hypocrisy, empty formalism and perceived irrelevance, I find I have a much better hearing when I tell them about the real Jesus – the one who clashed with the Pharisees over their religious hypocrisy, their empty formalism and their majoring on minors. If your own Gospel-sharing feels a bit like

---

[1] Jesus prays hard in Luke 5:16, 9:18, 28 and 11:1 because of what he teaches in John 3:3–8.

Polish lancers fighting German tanks, perhaps Luke wrote these verses for you.

Too many Christians conclude that God has not gifted them to share the Gospel with unbelievers, when in reality they have simply missed the fact that these verses are God's gift to them. Between the sending out of the Twelve (9:1–6) and the sending out of the Seventy-Two (10:1–24) Luke gives us verses that equip us to join them in their mission.[2] If we hurry through them, it shouldn't surprise us that Gospel-sharing feels very hard. Just look at what happens in 9:21–26 when Jesus prays and then starts asking questions. He is able to communicate some incredibly unpalatable truths to the Twelve. He tells them that he is about to be crucified in Jerusalem, and that they must also walk the death-and-resurrection road themselves if they truly wish to be his disciples.[3] When we pray and ask questions, it's amazing what it enables us to share. It permits us to challenge people gently yet forcefully that they need to submit to Jesus Christ as King.

This is not a one-off strategy for Jesus. It's what he did when he was a guest at the home of Simon the Pharisee at the end of chapter 7. When his host reacted angrily to a prostitute anointing his feet with perfume, Jesus could have gone for the jugular by listing Simon's own sins back to him. Instead, he asks for Simon's permission to tell a story about two debtors and ends it with a question: *"Now which of them will love him more?"* In 2 Samuel 12, the prophet Nathan uses a story and question to trick King David in the same way into passing sentence on himself for his sin. We don't ask questions because we fear telling the truth, but to ensure that the truth hits home.

---

[2] The whole of Matthew 14:22–16:12 and Mark 6:45–8:26 takes place between Luke 9:17 and 9:18. Luke omits those events from his gospel to keep us focused on the practical training that we need for the task in hand.

[3] Jesus predicts his death earlier in the other gospels, but this is the first occasion in Luke's gospel. Even as he equips the Twelve to carry on his mission, Jesus warns them that he will hand it over to them very soon.

Jesus does the same thing in 10:25–37. When a Jewish rabbi asks him what he needs to do to inherit eternal life, Jesus does not launch into a thirty-minute sermon. He asks him a question: *"What is written in the Law? How do you read it?"* When the rabbi replies but misses the point, Jesus tells him the famous story about a Good Samaritan. At the end of the story, he asks the rabbi again, *"Which of these three do you think was a neighbour to the man who fell into the hands of robbers?"* Don't miss how important this is. Jesus was wiser than any man on earth, yet in his wisdom he asked lots of questions.

Jesus does it again at the start and end of chapter 20, when he issues two last Gospel challenges to the Jewish leaders. First he asks them, *"Tell me: John's baptism – was it from heaven, or of human origin?"*, knowing that it will force them to confess that their rejection of John the Baptist is entirely irrational. Next he asks them to explain how Psalm 110 fits within their world view – *"David calls him 'Lord'. How then can he be his son?"* – knowing full well that it cannot. Again and again, Jesus shows us that questions ought to be our weapon of choice whenever we try to share the Gospel. Follow the wisdom of Proverbs 18:17: *"The first to present his case seems right, till another comes forward and questions him."*

I am not claiming that asking questions is a silver bullet when it comes to sharing the Gospel. I am simply pointing out that it works far better than the lances we tend to use. Questions help people to clarify what they believe and to see where they are wrong. They help people to see the wisdom of the Gospel. If we ask questions like Jesus in these verses, we will enjoy a far better response when we repeat his challenge in verse 25: *"What good is it for someone to gain the whole world, and yet lose or forfeit their very self?"*

How to Heal People
(9:27–43)

Jesus rebuked the impure spirit, healed the boy and gave him back to his father.

(Luke 9:42)

I can see why many people deny that God still heals today. We have all prayed for people to be healed and seen nothing happen. One of my friends sees extraordinary miracles – the blind seeing, the deaf hearing and more – yet even he confesses that he leaves more people unhealed than he sees healed. Bad experiences hinder many of us from believing that God still wants to heal people through us today. That's why it's vital that we understand the two events that happen in quick succession here.

Jesus is transfigured at the top of a mountain – in other words, he appears to Peter, John and James in his heavenly glory.[1] They are so stunned by this, and by the sight of Moses and Elijah descending from heaven to talk with Jesus, that Peter asks for permission to build three tabernacles to set up permanent residency on the mountain.[2] Suddenly the cloud of God's presence that filled the Tabernacle built by Moses in the desert descends on the mountaintop. Peter, John and James witness the interaction of the Trinity in the same way that the Trinity interacted when Jesus was baptized in the River Jordan.

---

[1] Yet again Luke reminds us that we need to find a quiet time and place to pray. Jesus could pray anywhere, but he models for us here that we need to get alone if we want to meet powerfully with God (Matthew 6:6).

[2] The Greek word *skēnē* in 9:33 is the normal word for the *tabernacle* in the Greek Old and New Testaments.

As God the Holy Spirit descends on God the Son in the form of a cloud, God the Father booms out from heaven, *"This is my Son, whom I have chosen; listen to him."*

When Jesus and the three disciples descend from the mountaintop, they come back down to earth with a bump. The other nine disciples have failed in their attempts to deliver an epileptic boy from a demon.[3] Here are nine apostles, all with power and authority to heal, and all with a track record of fruitful healing ministry during their tour of Galilee. The fact that they have failed to heal the boy appears at first glance to be an open-and-shut case of God being unwilling to heal – that is, until Jesus takes one look at the boy and heals him in a moment! Luke wants to use this event to convince us that God is more than willing to heal people through us. He wants to teach us how to do so.

Luke shows us that healing comes through *listening to the words of Jesus*. We need to confess that we know less about the Kingdom of God than we ought. Luke emphasizes this in 9:27 by recording a cryptic prophecy from Jesus that some of his disciples would witness the Kingdom of God before they died.[4] He wants us to grasp that God's Kingdom is not just something "out there" in the future. Peter, John and James saw a vision on the mountain of who Jesus is in heaven, right here and right now.[5] At his baptism, the Father emphasized his *love* for Jesus, but here he emphasizes that he has *chosen* him to be the greatest Prophet and that his words deserve our rapt attention.[6]

---

[3] Luke is the only gospel writer to tell us that this was the man's *only* son. He wants to stir our compassion.

[4] The cryptic prophecy refers to the transfiguration. Matthew 17:1 and Mark 9:2 say it was fulfilled *six* days later, but Luke makes it *eight* days because he includes the day that Jesus prophesied and the day they spent climbing the mountain.

[5] Jesus insists in Luke 11:20 that *"The kingdom of God **has come** upon you."* We mustn't believe any less.

[6] At his baptism, the Father emphasized that Jesus is the Son he *loves*. Here, he emphasizes that Jesus is the Son he has *chosen*. He is the promised

If we want to see more people healed, we need to listen to the promises of Jesus.

Luke shows us that healing comes through *listening to what Jesus says about the Devil*. It can't have been easy for a professionally trained doctor like Luke to confess that the root cause of the boy's epilepsy was not physical but demonic. He was just as tempted as we are to view ill people as victims of biological forces rather than as victims of a spiritual foe. Nevertheless, he instructs us that demons can be at work behind epilepsy (9:39), muteness (11:14), excruciating back pain (13:11) and mental health issues (8:27, 35).[7] He is not claiming that this is always the case, but he is insisting that if we want to see more people healed we need to believe what Jesus says about the Devil's role in illness. If it is the Devil's work, we need not ask whether it is God's will to heal it. Jesus came into the world to destroy illness as one of the ways Satan imprisons people (13:16).[8]

Luke shows us that healing comes through *listening to what Jesus says about partnership with the Holy Spirit.* Jesus tells the nine disciples in verse 41 that their failure stems from thinking like their *"unbelieving and perverse generation"* instead of thinking as the agents of God's Kingdom.[9] In many manuscripts of Matthew 17:21 and Mark 9:29, he identifies their problem as a lack of *"prayer and fasting"*. In other words, the more time we spend partnering with God in prayer the more we can get up off our knees to partner with him in healing ministry.

The gospel writers emphasize this by the way they describe

Messiah, the one about whom Deuteronomy 18:15 says: *"Listen to him"*.

[7] Luke uses the Greek word *therapeuō*, or *to heal*, to describe the driving out of demons as well as the healing of illness in 6:18, 7:21 and 8:2. Even as a doctor, he believed what Jesus said about the Devil and diseases.

[8] Since illness is part of the Devil's work in the world (Acts 10:38), we need be in no doubt that it is God's will to reverse it through Jesus (1 John 3:8). That is why Jesus corrects the leper so firmly in 5:12–13.

[9] The Greek word *genea* means more than *generation*. We can tell from its use in 17:25 and 21:32 that Jesus is expressing his frustration here with the Jewish *race* for failing to grasp its calling to partner with God.

the healing miracles of Jesus. If we only had Mark's account of Jesus healing Peter's mother-in-law, we would assume that the key factor was helping her to her feet; if we only had Matthew's that it was the laying on of hands; and if we only had Luke's that it was rebuking her fever. If we only had Mark's account of Jesus healing a blind beggar, we would assume that the key factor was proclaiming over him that *"Your faith has healed you"*; if we only had Matthew's that it was the laying on of hands; and if we only had Luke's that it was the command to *"Receive your sight!"*[10] Healing people is never about following a formula, but about being full of God's Spirit.[11] We need to grasp this if we want to see more people healed ourselves.

Finally, Luke shows us that healing comes through *listening to what Jesus says about ourselves*. Peter mistakenly assumes that Christianity consists of static marvelling at Jesus, not realizing that our mountaintop experiences are meant to send us back down the mountain to partner with Jesus in the world. Luke emphasizes this by using the Greek word *exodos* in verse 31. Those who follow Jesus are on a new and better exodus, actively confronting Satan's power with the blood of Jesus. Jesus has sent us into the world to perform signs and wonders, just like Moses before Pharaoh, to convince many sceptics to join us in our exodus. We may feel weak like Moses at the burning bush, but Luke reminds us in verse 43 that it is not about us. It is all about *"the greatness of God"*.

Luke is not claiming that we will see everybody healed. Paul is honest in his letters that he and Luke saw a few failures along the way.[12] But Luke is promising that if we listen to the words of Jesus then we will see miracles beyond our wildest dreams. These verses were written for you, because you have been called to heal people in the name of Jesus.

[10] Matthew 20:29–34; Mark 10:46–52; Luke 18:35–43. Matthew 8:14–15; Mark 1:29–31; Luke 4:38–39.

[11] The father says literally in 9:40 that they *did not have the power* to heal his son (*ēdunēthēsan*). See Acts 1:8.

[12] Galatians 4:13–15; Philippians 2:25–27; 2 Timothy 4:20.

How to Follow Jesus
(9:43–62)

No one who puts a hand to the plough and looks
back is fit for service in the kingdom of God.

(Luke 9:62)

When we talk about following in the footsteps of Jesus, it's easy to forget what his footsteps look like. They have nail-holes in the middle. They speak of sacrifice and pain. Before Jesus sends the Twelve out on their second preaching tour, he therefore gives them some sobering instructions about what following in his footsteps truly means.

In 9:43–45, Jesus bursts the bubble of excitement around his ministry. Luke says that it was *"while everyone was marvelling at all that Jesus did"* that he chose to prophesy his imminent execution in Jerusalem. The twelve apostles do not understand what he is saying, even the second time around.[1] Three of them have just seen a vision of his heavenly glory, and all of them have just witnessed his power over demons, so they are starting to get excited that now might be the moment when he will attack the Romans and turn its empire over to Israel.[2] They are in for a surprise. Instead of declaring war on Rome, the Messiah announces that he is about to allow himself to be executed by Rome.

---

[1] He prophesied this for the first time in 9:22, and now he says literally in 9:44, *"Take these words into your ears."* The disciples cannot understand why God's Victor would ever choose to become Rome's victim.

[2] They still expected this in Acts 1:6. Our wrong views of the Messiah are very hard to shake off.

The twelve disciples do not understand the death-and-resurrection road. In 9:46–48, they start to argue about which of them is the Messiah's right-hand man.[3] Peter, John and James are able to point out that Jesus clearly sees them as his special Three. They alone were invited to watch him raise the daughter of Jairus from the dead and to glimpse his heavenly glory on the mountaintop. They had been with Moses and Elijah while the other nine disciples struggled to drive out a single demon. Peter can go one further and claim to be the Special One. After all, Jesus chose to turn his boat into a floating pulpit and his house into a healing centre for Capernaum, not those of John and James. Whatever the detail, it's a pretty ugly conversation.

Jesus doesn't need to overhear their conversation to know what they are thinking.[4] He rebukes them by calling over a little child and by insisting that humility is the currency of God's Kingdom. Greatness is measured by how much we are willing to walk in his footsteps and by how much we are willing to stoop down to serve others, just as he stoops down to us.[5] Those who jostle for position instead of revelling in the fact that they are children of God will not even enter the Kingdom, let alone be great in it.[6]

In 9:49–50, John tries to resist this teaching.[7] He points out that, while on the road, they spotted somebody driving out demons in the name of Jesus and tried to stop him because

[3] Luke says literally that *"an argument entered in among them."* He seems to be implying that this kind of rivalry within the Church is often inspired by demons. See James 3:14–15.

[4] When Luke tells us that Jesus replied, *"knowing their thoughts"*, he seems to imply that Jesus received some kind of supernatural insight through the Holy Spirit. See also 5:21–22; 7:39–40; 1 Corinthians 12:8.

[5] Jesus does not say that it is wrong for us to desire to be great in the Kingdom of God. He simply says that we should seek to be great by following his example, not by mimicking the world.

[6] Jesus says this even more clearly in the longer account of his teaching in Matthew 18:1–14. He prepares the disciples to partner with God's Spirit by teaching them to humble themselves as children of God.

[7] Luke tells us literally in 9:49 that John said these words in reply to Jesus.

he was not one of them. Surely Jesus doesn't mean that he is willing to do through other people what he is doing through the Twelve? Jesus echoes Moses in Numbers 11:29 when he tells John to believe that *"Whoever is not against you is for you."*[8] Following Jesus means refusing to treat other believers and churches as our rivals. Jesus says that there is more than enough God-glorifying ministry to go around for us all, so rivalry is a telltale sign that we are in fact ministering in order to glorify ourselves.

In 9:51–56, Jesus raises the stakes. Up until now, he has been leading his disciples on a road trip back to Galilee from Caesarea Philippi in the far north of Israel.[9] Instead of stopping in Galilee, however, he surprises them by setting his face towards Jerusalem and heading south on the road through Samaria.[10] The Jews and Samaritans hated one another and, sure enough, as soon as they see that the rabbi is heading for Jerusalem, a group of Samaritans make it clear he is not welcome in their village. James and John are furious.[11] Taking a leaf out of Elijah's book in 2 Kings 1:9–12, they ask Jesus for permission to call fire down from heaven to destroy them. Jesus has to rebuke them and to offer a more compassionate solution: *"he and his disciples went to another village"*! Don't miss the irony when Luke tells us later, in Acts 8:14–17, that God used John to baptize the Samaritans with the fire of the Holy Spirit. Following Jesus means practising

---

[8] This does not contradict what Jesus goes on to say in 11:23. John's complaint is literally *"he is not following with us."* Jesus' later statement refers to people who are not following him at all.

[9] Matthew 16:13; Mark 8:27. This means that the Mount of Transfiguration was probably Mount Hermon, the great mountain that overshadowed Caesarea Philippi.

[10] This is an important moment in Jesus' ministry. He leaves Galilee to locate its final nine months in the south.

[11] Mark 3:17 tells us that their fiery tempers caused Jesus to nickname them the *"Sons of Thunder"*.

what Jesus preaches: dying to our own self-centred passions by returning good for evil every time.[12]

In 9:57–62, Jesus makes this clear through his reaction to some of the people that he meets along the road.[13] He tells one would-be follower that he can only be his student if he is willing to become a homeless wanderer, like his Teacher. He challenges two more would-be followers that to follow him they must love him more than they love their family.[14] Jesus would rather have a small band of dedicated followers than a large congregation that is only willing to follow him on its own terms. Nobody can follow him and, like Lot's wife in Genesis 19, look back longingly at the world. Nobody can embrace his message of resurrection and still cling to the dead priorities of this world.[15]

Jesus is not talking here about an elite group of committed followers. He is repeating what he told us in 9:23–26, that we must follow him this way or else we can't follow at all. His definition of what it means to follow him reminds me of a famous creed that someone gave me on the day that I surrendered my life to him. It changed everything for me:

The die has been cast. The decision has been made. I have stepped over the line. I won't look back, let up, slow down, back away or be still... I no longer need pre-eminence, prosperity, position, promotions, plaudits or popularity.

---

[12] Later, less accurate Greek manuscripts contain the extra line: *"And he said, 'You do not know of what manner of spirit you are, for the Son of Man did not come to destroy men's lives but to save them.'"*

[13] Matthew 8:19–22 recounts these conversations out of chronological order for the sake of theme. It says that the first man was a teacher of the law and that the second man was part of Jesus' larger entourage.

[14] In the first-century Middle East, corpses were buried within hours of death. The second man is therefore not requesting a few hours to attend a funeral, but putting off God's call on his life until after his father dies.

[15] In order to plough a straight furrow, ancient ploughmen needed to remain focused on an object in the distance. So do we. Jesus tells us what that object is in 9:60: *going and proclaiming the Kingdom of God.*

I don't have to be right, first, top, recognized, praised, regarded or rewarded... My face is set, my gait is fast, my goal is heaven, my road is narrow, my way is rough, my companions are few, my Guide is reliable, and my vision is clear. I cannot be bought, compromised, detoured, lured away, turned back, deluded or delayed. I will not flinch in the face of sacrifice, hesitate in the presence of adversity, negotiate at the table of the enemy, ponder at the pool of popularity or meander in the maze of mediocrity. I won't give up, shut up, let up or slow up until I have stayed up, stored up, prayed up, paid up and spoken up for the cause of Christ. I am a disciple of Jesus.[16]

---

[16] These words come from an anonymous work entitled *The Fellowship of the Unashamed*.

Back to School (10:1–24)

*After this the Lord appointed seventy-two others and
sent them two by two ahead of him to every town
and place where he was about to go.*

(Luke 10:1)

At the start of chapter 10, Jesus sends the twelve apostles back
to school. You can't fail to notice how similar these verses are to
the start of chapter 9, but make sure you also spot how different
things are this second time around. The disciples have learned a
lot in the past few verses about how to share the Gospel, how to
heal people and how to follow Jesus. Now they are able to take
things to a whole new level.

The most obvious difference is that the Twelve have now
become the Seventy-Two. If you are good at your times tables,
you will quickly see why. At the start of chapter 9, Jesus sent the
Twelve out two by two to cut their teeth at partnering with the
Holy Spirit. Now he tells each pair of disciples to train up a dozen
more disciples like themselves. This is not just the Twelve plus
sixty more. It is six new groups of twelve, each under the tuition
of two of the original Twelve.[1] Jesus shows them how to train up
the first new recruits in an army that will take the Gospel to the
entire world, partnering with the Holy Spirit in the same way as
them. Here we see the constant principle of Christian ministry
that Paul teaches in 2 Timothy 2:2: *"The things you have heard*

---

[1] Luke tells us in the Greek text of 10:1 that the 72 were *heteroi*, meaning
others. There is nothing in the Greek text that precludes some of these 72
being women, just like the 120 believers in Acts 1:14–15.

me say in the presence of many witnesses entrust to reliable people who will also be qualified to teach others."[2]

Another big difference is that the mission field has become greater. The Twelve could only reach the villages of Galilee, but the Seventy-Two can go ahead of Jesus to every town and village in the southern regions of Judea and Perea. The larger the team, the larger the mission field, and this is only the beginning. Jesus points out that *"The harvest is plentiful, but the workers are few. Ask the Lord of the harvest, therefore, to send out workers into his harvest field."* When churches forget how to partner with the Holy Spirit, they tend to assume that the harvest is meagre and the workers sufficient, but Jesus says that this will never be the case until he returns. God's very name is *"the Lord of the Harvest"*! Yes, the fields are full of rocks and rats and rubbish, but they are also full of people that the Holy Spirit wants to save through us as we go.

Those are two big differences, but the message has not changed. It is still a proclamation that *"the kingdom of God has come near."* It still provokes such a strong reaction, one way or the other, that Jesus has to warn us, *"Go! I am sending you out like lambs among wolves."*[3] Nor has the method changed. It is still to go out in pairs and express our reliance on the Holy Spirit by not waiting for sufficient funds before we go. The strategy also remains the same: find an individual who is sufficiently receptive to the Gospel that they will offer board and lodgings to the missionary and allow their house to become a local mission centre. Jesus is interested in making new disciples, not just filling the air with Christian words, so he commands the

---

[2] Reproduction lies at the heart of Christian ministry. Matthew 28:19 echoes Genesis 1:28.

[3] Remember, this is spoken by the Lamb of God. Following Jesus means walking the same path as him.

Seventy-Two, *"Do not move around from house to house."*[4] Long-term stability is crucial.

If we expected the authority and power that Jesus gives to the wider group of Seventy-Two to be diluted from that of the original Twelve, we are in for a surprise. The badge and the gun that they carry are exactly the same. They can speak on behalf of the Father and the Son with just as much authority: *"Whoever listens to you listens to me; whoever rejects you rejects me; but whoever rejects me rejects him who sent me."* They can lay hands on people with just as much power from God's Spirit: *"Heal those there who are ill."* This is a vital principle for us, a great many generations down this recruitment line. We are still entrusted with precisely the same badge and gun as the original Twelve.[5]

Another thing that has not changed is the urgency of the message. Jesus repeats his command for his messengers to brush the dust off their feet in any town that rejects them, as a warning that those associated with that town are hurtling towards hell.[6] If anything, Jesus steps up the urgency this second time around by commanding the Seventy-Two in verse 4 not to stop and chat on their journey, and by calling down curses on the Galilean towns that rejected the earlier mission of the Twelve. He shocks the Seventy-Two by telling them that the towns of Chorazin, Bethsaida and Capernaum will be judged more severely than pagan Tyre and Sidon and the notoriously wicked Sodom because they received more revelation of the

---

[4] Acts 16:15 gives us an example of this in action. If the Hebrew phrase *"son of peace"* in Luke 10:6 means the same thing as *"man of peace"* in Psalm 41:9 and Jeremiah 20:10 then it simply means to look for "a key ally".

[5] Although we are permitted to deviate from these principles in certain circumstances (22:35–38), the fact that Paul quotes from 10:7 in 1 Timothy 5:18 demonstrates that they still generally apply to us today.

[6] Paul also shows that this command still applies to us in Acts 13:51 and 18:6. Sharing the Gospel is not just about offering forgiveness. It is also about proclaiming God's judgment over those who reject the offer.

Gospel.[7] This is not just a training assignment for the Seventy-Two. Their mission will spell life or death for many Jews. The same is true of the unbelievers around us every day.[8]

When the Seventy-Two return from their mission, they are excited that the demons recognize that they carry the same badge and gun as Jesus and the Twelve. Jesus is excited too, although for different reasons. He is overjoyed to see that his Father is truly willing to entrust his ministry to a ragtag bunch of nobodies. God has made good on his promise to inaugurate a new kind of partnership between the Holy Spirit and ordinary, everyday believers. Jesus tells the Seventy-Two that he saw Satan fall from heaven before the first humans sinned and that he is delighted to see the human race back on the spiritual offensive.[9] However, their primary focus ought to be that God has saved them.[10] Their primary business isn't to be shouting at hell, but delighting in heaven.

As he feasts his eyes on this growing army of believers, Jesus bursts out his thanks *"full of joy through the Holy Spirit"*.[11] Don't end this chapter without praying a similar prayer of joyful thanks yourself. If you are a follower of Jesus, these verses describe your own marching orders. The joy of Jesus and of the

---

[7] Luke uses the pagan word *Hades* for hell in 10:15 because he is reaching out to Theophilus and his Roman friends. One of their biggest objections to the Gospel was that it meant that their ancestors were in hell, so Luke replies that they can trust God to judge them fairly based on the amount of revelation they received.

[8] The children of Christians cannot be saved through their parents' faith any more than Jews can be saved without faith in the Messiah. The greater revelation that church children have received makes them guiltier.

[9] Isaiah 14:12–15; Revelation 12:7–9. Jesus uses a Greek perfect tense in 10:19 to emphasize that he has given us lasting authority (*exousia*) and power (*dunamis*) to defeat Satan and his demons in every generation.

[10] The *Book of Life*, recording the names of all those who are saved, is mentioned in Exodus 32:32–33, Psalm 69:28, Isaiah 4:3, Ezekiel 13:9, Daniel 12:1, Philippians 4:3 and Revelation 3:5, 13:8, 17:8, 20:12, 15 and 21:27.

[11] The Greek word *agalliaō* in 10:21 does not simply mean to smile happily. It means *to jump for joy*.

Seventy-Two is to be your daily delight too. Jesus turns to you and invites you to worship alongside him: *"Blessed are the eyes that see what you see. For I tell you that many prophets and kings wanted to see what you see but did not see it, and to hear what you hear but did not hear it."*

In other words, you are now living in a new era of history. All of this happened for you.

Lesson One: Love
(10:25–37)

"Love the Lord your God with all your heart and with all your soul and with all your strength and with all your mind"; and, "Love your neighbour as yourself."

(Luke 10:27)

It's amazing how much people are willing to pay for a lesson from a teacher they admire. Tony Blair earned £400,000 for delivering two speeches in the Philippines, each of them only half an hour long. If you think that's a bit pricey, it's a bargain compared to the £500,000 that Bill Clinton charged for a single speech in Hong Kong.[1] People pay enormous sums of money for the right teacher because, deep down, they know that what Jesus says in Luke 6:40 is true: *"Everyone who is fully trained will be like their teacher."*

So here's the good news: Luke says that Jesus is willing to become your teacher completely free of charge. He explains in 10:21–24 that God takes such great pleasure in revealing his secrets to the weak and ordinary that he wants even you and me to take our place alongside the Seventy-Two. Jesus offers to teach us mysteries that eluded the Old Testament prophets and kings so, in 10:25–14:35, Luke records eight important lessons that he taught his disciples during the final nine months of his earthly ministry in Judea and Perea. None of the other gospel writers includes this teaching, but Luke does so because he

---

[1] These huge fees were reported in the London newspaper *City AM* on 31st July 2015.

believes that Jesus taught these eight lessons for you and for me.[2]

The first lesson is all about love. It had to be, not just for the Jews who crowded around Jesus, but also for Theophilus and his Roman friends. Rome was fiercely anti-Semitic. The great statesman Cicero declared that Jewish culture was *"at variance with the glory of our empire, the dignity of our name and the customs of our ancestors"*, and Seneca taught Romans to despise *"the customs of that most accursed nation"*.[3] Although this racism was indefensible, it was still a major obstacle to faith for Theophilus and his Roman friends. Luke therefore needed to show them that conversion to Christ did not mean embracing the smug self-righteousness and barefaced hypocrisy which were prevalent among the Jews. Following Jesus is first and foremost about love.

A leading Jewish rabbi tries to trick Jesus in 10:25. His question about how to obtain eternal life sounds dreadfully sincere, fawning over Jesus as his *teacher*, but Jesus spots straightaway that he is not looking for teaching. He is looking to accuse Jesus of teaching something wrong. Jesus turns the question back on him by asking him to summarize the Law in just two verses.[4] The rabbi's answer is faultless, quoting the same two Old Testament verses about loving God and others that Jesus also uses to summarize the Jewish Law in Matthew 22:35–40.[5] But Jesus isn't satisfied with mere head knowledge. He reminds the rabbi that it has to be lived out: *"Do this and you will live."*

---

[2] All of the events recorded in Luke 9:51–18:14 are passed over very briefly in Matthew 19:1–2 and Mark 10:1.

[3] Marcus Tullius Cicero in *For Flaccus* (69). Augustine quotes Seneca's words in *The City of God* (6.11).

[4] The rabbi is asking how to go to heaven when he dies, but when Jesus talks about *eternal life* he is always keen to emphasize that it means more than life beyond the grave. It means knowing God today (John 17:3).

[5] Deuteronomy 6:5; Leviticus 19:18. Since the rabbi adds the words *"and with all your mind"* to the quotation, just as Jesus does elsewhere, he may have been repeating words from one of Jesus' early sermons.

Luke exposes the shortcomings of first-century Judaism by telling Theophilus in 10:29 that the rabbi actually *"wanted to justify himself"*.[6] He was not interested in love, but in earning salvation on his own terms and at bargain-basement prices. But following Jesus does not mean exchanging our pagan gods for the dead religion of the Jews. It means exchanging self-salvation through rule-keeping for a lifestyle that is all about partnering with the Holy Spirit to express God's love towards a dying world.[7]

Jesus illustrates this by telling the famous Parable of the Good Samaritan. A Jewish traveller falls into trouble on the road from Jerusalem to Jericho. Although the two cities are only seventeen miles apart on the map, the journey involved a steep descent on twisting mountain roads with many places for ruthless highwaymen to hide.[8] Solo travel was foolish and, sure enough, the man is robbed of all he has and left for dead by the roadside.[9] Cue the music for a hero to step onto the stage and save the day. A priest from the Temple in Jerusalem demonstrates much of what was wrong in first-century Judaism when he decides not to risk becoming ceremonially unclean through contact with a dying man. He crosses the road and chooses ritual purity instead of love.[10]

But all is not lost. The hero music starts playing again. This

---

[6] The Greek word *dikaioō* can also be translated that the rabbi *"wanted to make himself righteous"*. A more natural response to the rabbi's question would have been to talk about Jews needing to help Samaritans. Jesus reverses the emphasis in the rabbi's question to expose the dead hypocrisy of first-century Judaism.

[7] Romans 5:5, Galatians 5:22 and Philippians 1:8 all say that true love is the work of God's Spirit within us.

[8] Jerusalem is 765 metres above sea level. Jericho is 258 metres below sea level.

[9] The man's folly teaches us not to differentiate between the "deserving" and "undeserving" poor. The fact that the man had acted foolishly did not make him any less deserving of help as an expression of God's love.

[10] Since the priest was travelling *down* the road rather than up it (*katabainō*, as opposed to *anabainō*, in 10:31), he was not even on his way to the Temple. Fear of ritual impurity had simply become a way of life for him.

time it is a Levite, a busy Temple official from the same tribe as Moses and Aaron. The Levites were more practical than the priests, so we expect him to help, but Jesus shocks us by saying that he is too busy with his religious duties to stop in the name of love. No doubt he prays for the dying traveller as he crosses the road. No doubt he tells his friends in Jericho that someone really ought to start a project to help the victims of violent crime. But he does nothing. His religion is all about meetings and busy programmes. Twenty-first-century Christians can fall into this trap just as easily as first-century Jews, so Jesus insists that faith in God that doesn't inspire love is not faith in God at all.[11]

Now the music changes to the tune that is played when a villain steps onto the stage during a pantomime. A Samaritan is passing by – one of those mixed-race interlopers who populated the Promised Land while the Jews were away in exile. Jesus shocks us by insisting that, for all his confused doctrine, he understands the way of love better than the priest and Levite put together.[12] He risks his life to stoop down and lift the man onto his donkey. He gets his hands dirty to clean the man's wounds. He forfeits his money to save the man's life.[13] Jesus ends the parable by turning to the rabbi, to Theophilus and to us, and explaining what it means to follow him: *"Go and do likewise."*

This is lesson one in Jesus' school of ministry. Unless we love those around us, we have not grasped what it means for us to partner with the Holy Spirit. On the other hand, if we ask God's Spirit to stir the love of Jesus in our hearts, the

[11] Jesus is *not* saying that the Jewish Law is wrong (Matthew 5:17–20), but that it has been corrupted. The rabbi confesses that love lies at the heart of the Law, but he fails to turn head knowledge into action.

[12] Luke accentuates this sense of shock by making *passed by on the other side* the last Greek word of 10:31 and 32 (*antiparēlthen*), and by making *took pity on him* the last Greek word of 10:33 (*esplagchnisthē*).

[13] Some readers see the *oil* and *wine* as a picture of the saving work of the Holy Spirit and the blood of Jesus. *Two denarii* was around £300 in today's money, yet the Samaritan is willing to pay more. He has the opposite attitude to the one that confronts need with the excuse that "I already gave at the office".

unbelieving world will soon surrender to the Gospel. The final pagan emperor of Rome complained that the rise of Christianity was unstoppable on account of the love of Christians towards everyone: *"It is disgraceful that... while the impious Galileans support both their own poor and ours as well, everyone sees that our people lack aid from us!"*[14]

Following Jesus is not about rule-keeping or busy activity. It is all about loving like Jesus.

---

[14] Emperor Julian the Apostate in a letter to the pagan high priest of Galatia in 362 AD.

Lesson Two: Prayer (10:38–11:13)

"Martha, Martha," the Lord answered, "you are worried and upset about many things, but only one thing is needed."

(Luke 10:41–42)

Have you ever seen the black-and-white footage of birdmen strapping wings onto their arms and attempting to fly? It is tragic to watch brave men throw away their lives on film. The look on Franz Reichelt's face as he jumps from the Eiffel Tower in 1912 is enough to move a grown man to tears. His wings look like an overcoat designed for an elephant and they help him fly about as well as an elephant too. There's a lot of flapping and a huge amount of courage, but the flight is over very quickly. Franz Reichelt plummets to the ground and is instantly killed, while the cameras continue to roll.

Luke doesn't want our churches to be full of birdmen. He predicts that they will become what so many of them are – communities of courage and of frenzied flapping but of very little fruitfulness. That's why he records for us lesson two in Jesus' school of ministry, reminding us that partnership with the Holy Spirit is first and foremost about prayer.

In 10:38–42, Luke introduces us to two sisters named Martha and Mary.[1] Martha appears to be the elder of the two and her name is Aramaic for *the person in charge*. She takes her leadership

---

[1] Bethany was a village less than two miles from Jerusalem. These two sisters and their brother Lazarus are also mentioned in John 11:1–12:11. Martha is distracted in 10:40 by *pollē diakonia* – literally by *much ministry*.

responsibility very seriously, and very soon she is flapping in the kitchen like a birdman in free fall. Nobody can fault her love for Jesus or her diligence in serving him, but she is stressed out and increasingly resentful towards him. She is a picture of any believer who attempts to serve Jesus in their own strength instead of learning how to partner with the Holy Spirit. Eventually she snaps when she sees her younger sister relaxing at the feet of Jesus. She blurts out, *"Lord, don't you care?... Tell her to help me!"*

Mary is not flapping around like a birdman. She is more like a Boeing 747. She understands that partnering with Jesus is about receiving jet propulsion from God's Spirit, not about pursuing busy projects of our own. She keeps her eyes fixed on Jesus because she firmly believes that relationship matters far more than rushing around. Jesus defends her with a gentle rebuke to Martha: *"You are worried and upset about many things, but only one thing is needed. Mary has chosen what is better, and it will not be taken away from her."* If you feel like a birdman yourself, these words were written for you.

In 11:1, Jesus demonstrates for us what this means in practice. Nobody was busier than Jesus. He had so many people clamouring for his attention that he often had no time to eat and had to jump into a boat to get away. We have tasks crying out for our attention and emails clogging up our inboxes, but he had people crying out for healing and demons addressing him by name. Even when the crowds went away, he was still surrounded by his disciples. If anybody might have been expected to flap around like a birdman then it was Jesus, but he chose the same "one thing" as Mary. Luke tells us that Jesus kept withdrawing to quiet places to enjoy unhurried prayer time with his Father.[2]

Jesus spent his prayer time listening to his Father. Luke tells us literally in 10:39 that *"Mary sat at the Lord's feet listening to his Word"*, because prayer is always meant to be a conversation.

---

[2] Mark 6:31–34 describes the constant pressure that Jesus was under. Nevertheless, Luke says he constantly chose the same "one thing" as Mary (3:21; 5:16; 6:12; 9:18, 28–29; 11:1; 22:32, 41–44).

Jesus also spent his prayer time receiving power from his Father for ministry. The Greek word *sunantilambanomai* is only used twice in the Bible: once when Martha demands that Mary *help* her in 10:40 and once when Paul promises that God's Spirit will *help* us in Romans 8:26. Don't miss this. Luke is sharing with us the secrets of Jesus' ministry. Because he spent time each day receiving the Spirit from his Father, he was able to say in 8:46, *"Someone touched me; I know that power has gone out from me."*[3]

Jesus also spent his prayer time talking to his Father. In 11:1–4, he teaches us the kind of words that we are to pray as we follow his example. We are to begin with confidence that we are partners in God's family business (*"our Father"*) and that he has appointed us to be the earthly agents of his heavenly Kingdom (*"your kingdom come, your will be done on earth as it is in heaven"*).[4] We are to pray for God's great purposes to be fulfilled in the world (*"hallowed be your name"*) and to ask for our own more mundane needs to be met through his love and power too (*"give us each day our daily bread"*). We are to ask for forgiveness for our continued sin (*"forgive us our sins, for we also forgive everyone who sins against us"*) and for strength to sin less and less as we grow (*"lead us not into temptation"*).[5] Jesus provides us with these headings in order to help us group our thoughts together as we pray. God wants to hear you voice these items to him.

In 11:5–13, Jesus emphasizes that this is how we develop a relationship with God. He warns us up front that the Father will not answer all our prayers straightaway because prayer is as

---

[3] 1 Corinthians 1:9, 2 Corinthians 13:14, Philippians 2:1 and 1 John 1:3 all tell us that Christian ministry means learning to partner with God's Spirit in precisely the same way as Jesus.

[4] The whole of the Old Testament only refers to God as *Father* 14 times. It is therefore nothing short of revolutionary when Jesus tells us that we can each address God as our Father, just like him.

[5] Jesus places confession of sin towards the end of the prayer because he wants us to approach God with confidence as our Father and not with cringing fear as our Judge. See Psalm 100:4 and Hebrews 10:19–22.

much about the journey as it is about the destination. We need to pray each day for our daily bread because, if God granted us a stockpile, it would make us neglect our relationship with him. Instead, our need forces us to partner with him daily in our sowing and reaping. Since even bad friends say yes eventually for the sake of a quiet life, we need not worry when God withholds an answer to detain us longer in the place of prayer. If we *keep on asking* and *keep on seeking* and *keep on knocking*, we will get far more than what we ask for. We will also get to know God as our closest friend and Father.[6]

In 11:13, Jesus says that the aim of all this teaching on prayer is to equip us to partner with God's Spirit. He leaves mention of the Holy Spirit to the very last verse for the sake of emphasis, because our daily walk with God's Spirit matters even more than our daily bread. Knowing that many Christians fear what might happen if they surrender themselves completely to God, Jesus reassures us that our Father only gives good gifts to his children. The Holy Spirit is no exception. Knowing that other Christians browbeat themselves into thinking they are not good enough to partner with God, Jesus emphasizes that the promise of the Spirit belongs to every believer who asks.

So don't flap about like a birdman, attempting to serve God through your busy activities and your frenzied list of jobs to do. He isn't asking you to stress out, but to stretch out your arms in prayer.[7] Jesus assures you that only one thing is needed. All you need to do is to follow his example and partner with the Holy Spirit through prayer.

---

[6] These are Greek present imperatives, speaking of continued action, but Jesus is not saying God is like the lazy man in the parable. He is contrasting the lazy man with God's willingness to say yes! We are to keep on asking for more of God's Spirit every day, persevering in our call to partner with him (Hebrews 6:12).

[7] The Greek word *anaideia* in 11:8 means *shameless audacity*. Jesus says that we can never ask too much of God in prayer. Massive prayers express a massive view of God, whereas tiny prayers insult him.

Lesson Three: Scripture (11:14-36)

Blessed rather are those who hear the word of God and obey it.

(Luke 11:28)

It's amazing how rapidly the Gospel has spread across China in the past forty years. The wife of Mao Zedong boasted that *"Christianity in China has been confined to the history section of the museum; it is dead and buried,"* but she was wrong. There are now more Chinese Christians than there are Chinese members of the Communist Party.[1]

When the leaders of the Chinese church are asked to give a reason for this phenomenon, their explanations are disarmingly simple. Brother Yun insists that *"There were no networks or organizations, just groups of passionate believers who came together to worship and study God's Word... If you truly want to see God move, the two main things you must do is learn the Word of God and have the obedience to do what God tells you to do."*[2]

This is lesson three in Jesus' school of ministry. These verses hinge on the reply that he gives to a heckler in the crowd in 11:27-28. The woman who shouts out is like any Catholic who honours a lifeless icon of Mary more than God's call to partner with the Holy Spirit, or like any Protestant who is more interested in the books of dead Reformers than in the Spirit's work today. When she cries out, *"Blessed is the mother who*

---

[1] This was reported by *The Economist* on 1st November 2014.

[2] Brother Yun says this in his excellent book *The Heavenly Man* (2002).

gave you birth and nursed you," Jesus corrects her very firmly: *"Blessed rather are those who hear the word of God and obey it."*[3]

Those two pivotal verses shed light on what Jesus wants to teach us in 11:14–20. The crowd have just witnessed him drive out a demon to heal a mute man. They are confused. Does this mean that all physical illness is a work of the Devil?[4] Does this mean that Jesus is God's Messiah or that he is doing a doubleact with the Devil? They demand a miracle from heaven in order to prove that he is not in cahoots with hell.[5]

Jesus warns them that they are being foolish. They accept plenty of other exorcists, so their objections are clearly a smokescreen for their hatred of his words.[6] He has just given them a miracle, so why demand another? They can't truly believe that demons are helping him to drive out demons. That would mean that Satan's kingdom is at civil war! He takes them back to Exodus 8:19, where Pharaoh's obstinate officials describe the Holy Spirit as *"the finger of God".*[7] They are as blind as Pharaoh unless they are willing to admit the obvious: the Scriptures are being fulfilled because God's Kingdom has come.[8]

In 11:21–26, Jesus teaches us that those who truly know

---

[3] Luke is not denying that Mary was blessed (1:42). He is saying that we are even more blessed if we obey.

[4] *"Mute demon"* does not mean that the demon was mute, since Jesus converses with a *"deaf and mute spirit"* in Mark 9:25. Luke means that this was a demon that afflicted people with muteness.

[5] *Beelzebul* was the name of a Canaanite god (2 Kings 1:2) and first-century Jews used it as a name for the Devil. Jesus endured this same accusation in Matthew 9:34, 10:25 and 12:22–37, and in John 7:20, 8:48 and 10:19–21.

[6] The same is true of the objections of many sceptics today. Even Jesus' enemies did not attempt to deny that his miracles really happened. It requires 2,000 years of distance to be able to do that.

[7] Matthew 12:28. The phrase is also used to describe God's Spirit in Exodus 31:18 and Deuteronomy 9:10. Yet again, Luke emphasizes that Jesus performed miracles as a human being who partnered with God's Spirit.

[8] Up until now, John the Baptist and Jesus have only preached that God's Kingdom is *near* (10:9). As Jesus heads south to be crucified in Jerusalem, he says a new day is dawning. Now God's Kingdom *has come*.

the Scriptures will perform the same miracles as him. If it was ludicrous for the Jewish crowds to witness miracles yet resist the fact that God's Kingdom had come, it is just as ludicrous for us to read that Jesus has defeated Satan yet resist his call to rise up and plunder Satan's possessions! Jesus warns us in verse 23 that, if we fail to partner with God's Spirit to bring his Kingdom to bear in the world, we are tacitly in partnership with Satan.[9] There is no neutral ground. We are called to perform miracles which prove that Jesus is stronger than the Devil.[10] We are to drive out demons, just as he did, to make disciples who are so full of the Spirit that there is no place left in their lives for the Devil.[11]

In 11:29–32, Jesus tells us that a generation which doubts the Word of God is not wise or sophisticated. It is *"a wicked generation"*. Jonah only needed to preach five words in Hebrew to bring the pagan Ninevites to repentance, so we dare not resist the 800,000 words in the Bible.[12] The Queen of Sheba travelled many miles in response to Solomon's proverbs, so we must not remain unmoved by all sixty-six books of the Bible. If we want to partner fruitfully with God's Spirit we need to take our lead, not from the sceptical seminaries of the West, but from the revival fields of China.[13] In a throwaway statement, Brother Yun challenges us,

---

[9] Jesus is not contradicting his words in 9:50. One statement addresses rivalry, the other passivity.

[10] Prayer for miracles brings great glory to God because it shows that we believe he is far stronger than Satan.

[11] 11:24–26 is a specific warning for the Jews not to accept John the Baptist yet reject the Messiah. However, it also contains general truth for us today. Those who aren't full of the Spirit will soon be full of something else.

[12] Jonah 3:4. When Matthew 12:38–42 describes a similar confrontation in Galilee, it says that Jesus performed a better miracle than Jonah. Luke does that too (11:16), but he also highlights Jesus' better teaching (11:31–32).

[13] The Greek word *genea* in 11:29 refers to the Jewish *race*, which was too proud to learn from Gentile Nineveh and Sheba (1 Kings 10:1–9). Western Christians are just as foolish to ignore lessons from the East.

I have learned that when the Lord tells us to do something there is no time for discussion or rationale, regardless of the situation we face. When we are sure God has told us to act, as I was on this occasion, blind obedience is called for. Not to obey God implies that we are wiser than him, and that we know better how to run our lives than he does.[14]

In 11:33–36, Jesus therefore urges us to study the Bible in order to partner with God's Spirit. He points out that what we look at dictates what we think and do.[15] Our eyes are "the lamps of our bodies" – in other words, if we feast them on the Scriptures then we enlighten all our thoughts and deeds, but if we feast them on the Devil's lies in the world around us then we plunge our whole lives into utter darkness. In verse 36, Jesus particularly puts his finger on the Scripture verses that we find the hardest to accept. He tells us that we need to let God's Word correct even our most entrenched ways of thinking instead of thinking that our culture can ever bring correction to God's Word.

Brother Yun challenges us one final time that this is what it truly means for us to partner with the Holy Spirit:

The first thing needed for revival to return to your churches is the Word of the Lord. God's Word is missing. Sure, there are many preachers and thousands of tapes and videos of Bible teaching, but so little contains the sharp truth of God's Word. It's the truth that will set you free. Not only is knowledge of God's Word missing, but obedience to that Word... You can never really know the Scriptures until you're willing to be changed by them.

Read it, believe it, submit to it and apply it. That's lesson three in what it means for us to partner with the Holy Spirit.

---

[14] Brother Yun says this in *The Heavenly Man* while describing his miraculous escape from jail.

[15] The Bible repeatedly teaches this. See Proverbs 4:23; 2 Samuel 11:1–5; Matthew 6:22–23; Philippians 4:8–9.

Lesson Four: Courage
(11:37–12:12)

*I tell you, my friends, do not be afraid of those who
kill the body and after that can do no more.*

(Luke 12:4)

Many Christians long for spiritual revival to sweep their nation,
but few understand what it would actually mean. We tend
to assume that it would make church life a whole lot easier,
but that wasn't the experience of George Whitefield in the
eighteenth century. Overseeing a great revival that transformed
Britain and America cost him everything. He was insulted
in the newspapers, lampooned in song and ridiculed in plays
performed at every theatre. He was pelted with mud and rotten
vegetables and excrement. He survived assassination attempts.
He told his followers that this is always the price that has to be
paid to advance the Gospel rapidly in a world that hates God:
*"Unless your hearts are free from worldly hopes and worldly
fears, you will never speak boldly, as you ought... You will never
preach with the same demonstration of the Spirit, and of power."*[1]

That's why the fourth lesson that Jesus teaches us is that
anyone who wishes to partner with the Holy Spirit needs a
healthy dose of courage. He does not merely tell us this in theory.
He leads the way by accepting a dinner invitation from one of
the separatist synagogue rulers who plotted his murder back in
6:11. This invitation from a Pharisee might be a trap. He might

---

[1] Whitefield wrote this in a letter to friends on 10th November 1739.

be poisoned or set upon behind closed doors. Nevertheless, Jesus embraces risk for the sake of a Gospel opportunity.[2]

In 11:37–44, Jesus models how to share the Gospel courageously. He doesn't pussyfoot around the Pharisee, but seizes the first opportunity to challenge his host about his lifeless religion. He has not forgotten what he taught us as a twelve-year-old. He sits and listens because he isn't out to score points. He is out to win souls. He loves the Pharisee but he also knows that to win a convert he must risk losing a friend. When his host expresses surprise that he does not wash his hands like a Pharisee, Jesus turns on him with a searing exposé of the flawed thinking behind first-century Judaism.[3]

Jesus points out that, for all their clean hands and crockery, the Pharisees are filthy on the inside. They are so meticulous about giving God a tenth of all their earnings that they even tithe the plants in their back garden, but they are utterly tight-fisted when it comes to sharing what they have with the poor. They fool themselves that they can buy off God with the first tenth of their earnings so that he will turn a blind eye to the unjust manner in which they hoard the remaining nine tenths for themselves.[4] They are professional pretenders, like a grave masquerading as a flower bed.[5] They love to be honoured but they do not honour the love that lies right at the heart of the Jewish Law.[6]

In 11:45–54, Jesus demonstrates that Christians are not

---

[2] This is important. The fact that the Pharisees rejected Jesus did not make him reject them.

[3] Jesus is not overreacting here. 11:37 says that this meal took place straight after the Jewish leaders accused him of partnering with Satan, and 14:1 says that Pharisees only invited him to dinner in order to trap him.

[4] Jesus endorses tithing in 11:42 but says that it is merely one of many expressions of God's love within us.

[5] Graves were marked to prevent people becoming unclean by touching one inadvertently (Numbers 19:16).

[6] Jesus still hates it when church leaders use their position to glorify themselves. All of this happened for us.

to keep silent out of political expediency. A leading rabbi is a fellow dinner guest and points out to Jesus that, although he is not a Pharisee, he too feels insulted by this attack on first-century Judaism. If we expected Jesus to shrink back from declaring a war on two fronts, we are in for a surprise. Having hurled three woes at the Pharisees, he launches into three more for the teachers of the law.[7] Far from apologizing to the dinner guest, Jesus says he is no better than his host. His Bible teaching makes it harder for people to obey God by adding lots of extra rules to the Law, yet it teaches nothing about how the Holy Spirit empowers people to obey. He pretends to take the side of the martyred prophets by building them fancy tombs, but he simply proves that he is on the same side as the rabbis who murdered them.[8] For all their spiritual bluster, he and his friends are not saved at all. They are hell-bound and their religion drags people down to hell with them.[9]

The host and the dinner guests are united in their fury towards Jesus, but instead of backpedalling he carries on. He waits for an occasion when a crowd of many thousand people has gathered around him, then warns his disciples loudly in 12:1–3 that the Pharisees are hypocrites. He picks a further fight with the crowd by pointing out that the secrets of their own hearts will be revealed on the Day of Judgment too. Every military rulebook warns the reader never to wage war on two fronts, but Jesus has the courage here to open up three fronts in only twenty verses.

---

[7] These "Six Woes" are not the same as those he spoke over the Pharisees on a separate occasion (20:45–47; Matthew 23:1–39). They echo the "Six Woes" that the Lord spoke against Jerusalem in Isaiah 5:8–30, and they show Theophilus and his Roman friends that converting to Christ would not mean embracing Judaism.

[8] Since 2 Chronicles is the last book of the Hebrew Old Testament, the Zechariah mentioned here may well be the one martyred in 2 Chronicles 24:20–22 rather than the one who has a book named after him.

[9] Theology is a wonderful thing but this is a sober warning to theologians. This teaching was given for us.

This is raw courage, but it is not courage for its own sake. Jesus is not gung-ho about risk, like Steve Jobs when he declared that *"Remembering that I'll be dead soon is the most important tool I've ever encountered to help me make the big choices in life."*[10] Jesus has weighed the cost and has recognized that nobody gets saved when we stress common ground, but only when we foist our Christian difference in their faces. He teaches his disciples in 12:4–12 that courage must therefore also mark our own partnership with the Holy Spirit. We must not fear the threats of men against our mortal bodies more than we fear the God who will one day judge our eternal souls. We must not shrink from standing up to rabbis and imams and corrupt church leaders, nor fear the angry threats of governors and judges. If we partner with God's Spirit, we need not worry about what to say. He will inspire us to lead our persecutors to Christ, even as they watch us die.[11]

This is how the Gospel spread so rapidly across the Roman Empire. Michael Green observes that

> *Here were men and women of every rank and station in life, of every country in the known world, so convinced that they had discovered the riddle of the universe, so sure of the one true God whom they had come to know, that nothing must stand in the way of their passing on this good news to others... They might be slighted, laughed at, disenfranchised, robbed of their possessions, their homes, even their families, but this would not stop them. They might be reported to the authorities as dangerous atheists, and required to sacrifice to the imperial gods: but they refused to comply. In Christianity they had*

---

[10] Steve Jobs said this in his commencement address at Stanford University on 12th June 2005.

[11] This is not an excuse for sloppy sermon preparation. It is a promise that Paul's conversion through the death of Stephen is not a one-off (Acts 8:1; 26:14). It also warns Theophilus that Paul is not afraid to die.

found something utterly new, authentic and satisfying. They were not prepared to deny Christ even in order to preserve their own lives; and in the manner of their dying they made converts to their faith.[12]

This is also how the Gospel advanced rapidly in the days of George Whitefield. It is how the Gospel is advancing rapidly in China today through Brother Yun and his friends. Whenever Christians disown Jesus before men and women, they are disowned by God, but whenever they have the courage to side with Jesus against the world, they enjoy a mighty partnership with God's Spirit.[13] So take courage. It's what revival really means.

---

[12] Michael Green in his book *Evangelism in the Early Church* (1970).

[13] Jesus cannot be saying in 12:10 that badmouthing the Holy Spirit places us beyond the reach of God's forgiveness (1 John 1:9), but he is definitely saying that our partnership with him is not to be treated lightly.

Lesson Five: Money
(12:13–48)

Where your treasure is, there your heart will be also.

(Luke 12:34)

I will never forget the time that my wife and I visited the Forbidden City in Beijing. The former home of the Chinese emperors boasts 9,000 rooms festooned with gold and marble and precious stones, yet the feeling I experienced was not of opulence but of fear and claustrophobia. The emperors were too scared to step outside. The fifty-metre-wide moat and eight-metre-high walls betrayed that it was for them a gold-plated prison.

Money doesn't just do that to Chinese emperors. If we're not careful, our possessions quickly begin to possess us too. That's why the fifth lesson in Jesus' school of ministry teaches us how to break free from the world's imprisonment to money.

In 12:13–21, a heckler in the crowd attempts to change the subject. He doesn't want to talk about courage and about what God will have to say to us on Judgment Day. Instead, he asks Jesus to take his side in a quarrel with his brother about their dead parents' possessions. Jesus refuses to be sidetracked from his focus on eternity.[1] He asks the man why he wants him to act as judge. Is it because he knows, deep down, that he will call the shots on Judgment Day?[2] Jesus tells a parable about a

---

[1] The Greek word *pleonexia* in 12:15 means literally *a greedy desire to have more*. Jesus warns the man that he can see right through him. He is not interested in justice but in accumulating earthly treasure.

[2] Jesus echoes Exodus 2:14 as a warning. Like the Hebrew slave, this man is saying far more than he knows.

rich farmer who builds big barns to stockpile food so that he can live the life of Riley. In the eyes of his contemporaries he is wise to have achieved both wealth and work–life balance, but in God's eyes he is a madman. *"You fool! This very night your life will be demanded from you. Then who will get what you have prepared for yourself?"*[3] Winning the rat race means losing at life if it causes us to forget that we were created for a better world to come.

In 12:22–34, Jesus tells his disciples that their attitude to money is a mighty witness to the world. Unbelievers worry because their hopes are placed in a most unstable idol. That's why worry isn't just an unfortunate character trait, but a deadly sin. It reveals that we have not truly put our faith in God. Those who trust in money always find that it is like a toy gun on a battlefield: it makes us overconfident until we need it, and then it never fails to let us down. Worry is the worship of Mammon, which is why those who partner with the Holy Spirit are so conspicuously different from the world.[4]

Jesus points out that birds do not build barns yet never lack food from God's hand. He points out that flowers never go clothes shopping yet look more beautiful than kings.[5] Worrying about money is therefore self-defeating. It does not give us strength for tomorrow. It merely saps us of our strength for today. Let unbelievers run after food and drink and clothes. Our hope is not to be in finance, but in our Father.

Theophilus and his Roman friends knew full well that this was one of the big differences between the Christians and

---

[3] God emphasizes his folly by repeating the same Greek word *psychē*, or *soul*, that the rich man uses twice in 12:19 to say literally, *"I will say to my soul, 'Soul, you have many goods laid up for many years!'"*

[4] Jesus describes money as a god named *Mammon* in 16:9, 11 and 13. The name means *Confidence* in Aramaic, since the love of money springs from a desire to trust in ourselves instead of in God (Hebrews 13:5–6).

[5] The Bible does not nullify general revelation. God speaks through his world as well as through his Word.

the pagans.[6] It was a major reason why so many people in Jerusalem had become convinced that God's Kingdom had finally come. It was why the Christians had made such shockwaves right across the money-obsessed Roman Empire.[7] One early observer explains:

They love one another... He that has shares generously what he has with him that has not. If they see a stranger they bring him under their roof, and rejoice over him as if he were their own brother... If they hear that any of their number is imprisoned or oppressed for the name of their Messiah, all of them provide for his needs... If there is among them any man who is poor and needy, and they have not an abundance of necessaries, they fast two or three days so that they may supply the needy with the food they need.[8]

Luke therefore explains to Theophilus in 12:31–34 why Christians act so differently. They believe that God has given them his Kingdom. They are no longer attached to their earthly possessions because such trinkets have been eclipsed by their treasure in heaven. They do not worry because it would disprove their claim to trust in God. Instead, they trust the words of Jesus: *"Seek his kingdom, and these things will be given to you as well."[9]*

In 12:35–48, Jesus therefore warns us that he will judge us based on how we use our money. It is a foolproof test of whether we are living for this life or for the age to come.[10] He says that

---

[6] This is one reason why Luke writes more about economic justice than the other gospel writers. For example, only he records the Parables of the Rich Fool (12:16–21) and of the Rich Man and Lazarus (16:19–31).

[7] Acts 2:44–45; 4:32–37; Hebrews 10:34.

[8] Aristides of Athens wrote this in c. 125 AD in his *Apology* (chapter 15).

[9] God is not reluctant to help us. Jesus says in 12:32 that it is God's *"good pleasure"* to assert his Kingdom rule for us. The return on investment when we give to help the poor is therefore literally out of this world.

[10] Jesus repeats the Greek verb *perizōnnumi*, meaning *to gird up one's loins*, in 12:35 and 37. Astonishingly, he promises that if we live in readiness for his

God entrusts us with money in order to reveal the true state of our hearts and whether we are ready to handle the true riches of heaven. It is like children's pocket money. If we steward it wisely, Jesus will entrust us with far more when he returns suddenly from heaven, but if we squander it on ourselves, like the pagans, he will consign us to hell along with anyone else who pretends to honour God while secretly serving Mammon. Jesus warns that we will be judged even more severely than the pagans, since those who receive more revelation of God are judged more strictly than those who receive little revelation.[11] If we get our attitude to money straight, it straightens out the whole of our discipleship by shifting our gaze from earth to heaven.

Lesson five in Jesus' school of ministry would be sobering enough were it not for the presence of Judas Iscariot among the Twelve. The fact that he heard these words yet still decided to betray Jesus for thirty silver coins reminds us how vital it is that we take these words to heart and willingly obey. Basil of Caesarea preached from these verses during a terrible famine in 368 AD:

> *When someone steals a man's clothes, we call him a thief, so shouldn't we give the same name to one who could clothe the naked and does not? The bread in your cupboard belongs to the hungry, the coat in your wardrobe belongs to the naked, the shoes you let rot belong to the barefoot, the money in your vaults belongs to the poor. You do wrong to all those you could help but do not.*[12]

Jesus warns us that money really matters. There is no truer statement of our faith in God than our bank statements. *"For where your treasure is, there your heart will be also."*

---

coming then he will be ready to serve us when he arrives.

[11] This answers the question "What will happen to people who have never heard the Gospel?" Just as there are differing levels of rewards in heaven (12:44; 19:15–26), so there are differing levels of punishment in hell (12:47–48; 20:47).

[12] Basil preached this in a sermon "On the Rich Fool" from Luke 12:13–21.

Lesson Six: Eyesight
(12:49–13:21)

Hypocrites! You know how to interpret the appearance of the earth and the sky. How is it that you don't know how to interpret this present time?

(Luke 12:56)

Eugene Peterson believes that many Christians have lost their ability to see clearly:

The gospel of Jesus Christ is profoundly countercultural. "I came to cast fire upon the earth," said Jesus; "and would that it were already kindled!" (Luke 12:49)... The Christian is a witness to a new reality that is entirely counter to the culture. The Christian faith is a proclamation that God's kingdom has arrived in Jesus, a proclamation that puts the world at risk. What Jesus himself proclaimed and we bear witness to is the truth that the sin-soaked, self-centred world is doomed... But it isn't easy. Powerful forces, both subtle and obvious, attempt either to domesticate pastors to serve the culture as it is or to seduce us into using our position to become powerful and important on the world's terms... Our culture doesn't lock us up; it simply and nicely castrates us, neuters us, and replaces our vital parts with a nice and smiling face... We've been treated nicely for so long that we've forgotten that we are in enemy territory.[1]

---

[1] He says this in *The Unnecessary Pastor: Rediscovering the Call* (2000).

Lesson six in Jesus' school of ministry therefore takes the form of an eye test. We need to have clear eyesight if we want to partner with the Holy Spirit, so Jesus checks that we see things as they really are. In 12:49–53, he checks that we can see that the Gospel is a declaration of war. *"Do you think I came to bring peace on earth? No, I tell you, but division."* The Kingdom of God has declared war on the kingdom of Satan, so if we want an easy ride then we had better get off the troop transporter now. Jesus is about to be "baptized" – that is, he is about to allow Satan's forces to kill him in order to destroy them by rising from the dead.[2] This will enable him to pour out the "fire" of his Holy Spirit on all who follow him, forcing people to choose whether or not to partner with God against a world that has been ruined by Satan.[3] It's a choice that polarizes opinion. Clear eyesight recognizes that it is not a one-off when John 7:43 says that *"The people were divided because of Jesus."* The Gospel always divides. It is a call to switch sides in a war.

In 12:54–59, Jesus checks that we can see that the Day of Judgment is on its way. He does not want us to be like the Jewish crowd that knew how to read tomorrow's weather in the skies but was illiterate when it came to reading the signs of the times.[4] He points out that a wise man does not wait until he faces his opponent in a courtroom before trying to broker a settlement. When Jesus comes back from heaven to judge the world, it will be too late to accept the terms he has laid down in the Gospel. Anyone who fails to renounce Satan's kingdom before Jesus returns will be consigned to hell alongside Satan forever.[5]

In 13:1–9, Jesus checks that we can see the urgency of this

[2] Mark 10:38–39; Romans 6:3–5. Jesus says something similar in Matthew 10:34–37.

[3] Make sure you see this choice clearly. Jesus is echoing Micah 7:5–6 and Luke 3:16.

[4] Jesus' teaching in Judea strongly echoes his earlier teaching in Galilee. See Matthew 5:25–26; 16:2–3.

[5] We will look more closely at Jesus' teaching about this in the chapter entitled "Hellfire".

call to choose sides. When some people in the crowd give him a newsflash that the Roman governor has just killed a group of Galileans, he warns them not to think that this means those particular Galileans were guiltier before God than the ones who survived.[6] He reminds them of another news story about a tower that collapsed in Jerusalem, killing eighteen people, to state this as a general principle. Disaster victims are seldom guiltier before God than the survivors. Rather than reflecting God's judgment on particular individuals, such news stories normally serve as general warnings that a greater disaster is about to unfold.[7]

The word Jesus uses for guilty in 13:4 is *opheiletai*, meaning *debtors*. We are all creatures who owe a debt of obedience and worship to our Creator. We are therefore all guilty of robbing God of the glory he deserves. Jesus tells the Parable of the Fig-Tree in 13:6–9 to show that this urgent message applies to nations as well as to individuals. Since Jeremiah 24:1–10 pictures the Jews as either good figs or rotten figs, Jesus describes the whole nation of Israel as a fig-tree. He is nearing the end of his three years of public ministry, and as he looks around he warns the crowd that he sees no figs growing at all.[8] Israel is wasting precious soil, taking up space in which Gentile believers could grow.[9] Jesus therefore warns his Jewish hearers that their nation's days are numbered. In less than a year his earthly

---

[6] We have no further detail about this event. All we know is that these verses and John 9:1–3 warn us not to treat news stories as acts of individual judgment, but as general warnings that God's judgment is coming.

[7] Sinful people are always amazed that God should allow suffering in the world. God permits such disasters in order to convict us that our true surprise should be that he has held off the Day of Judgment for so long.

[8] Nobody ate figs until a tree was five years old (Leviticus 19:23–25), so these timescales reflect the public ministry of Jesus. He also uses a fig-tree to describe unfruitful Israel in Matthew 21:18–22 and Mark 11:12–26.

[9] Don't grieve when lifeless churches close. This is why Jesus closes churches down (Revelation 2:5).

ministry will end. Unless they surrender to him urgently, God's judgment is about to come crashing down.

In 13:10–17, Jesus checks that we can see the work of the Devil in the world. In one of the synagogues, he meets a woman with a deformity who has been bent over double in pain for eighteen years. The Jewish leaders think she needs a doctor and, since it is the Sabbath, they want her to wait for the surgeries to reopen.[10] Jesus warns that such appearances can be deceiving. She is *"a daughter of Abraham, whom Satan has kept bound for eighteen long years"*.[11] Luke the doctor echoes this: the woman *"had been crippled **by a spirit"***. He tells us that we need to gain the same perspective as Jesus if we want to partner with God's Spirit against the Devil's work in the world. The toxic symptoms of his rule often include illness, fear, depression, mental health issues and a whole lot more. We need to see this spiritual dimension if we are to carry on the mission begun in Acts 10:38: *"God anointed Jesus of Nazareth with the Holy Spirit and power... He went around doing good and healing all who were under the power of the devil, because God was with him."*[12]

In 13:18–21, Jesus checks that we can see that we are on the winning team. We may seem very small compared to the host of hell that stands before us, but so are the mustard seed that grows into a tree and the yeast that leavens a large batch of dough.[13] We may look weak and feeble, but God's Spirit inside us endues us with mighty power.

---

[10] This miracle is only recorded in Luke's gospel. He wants to show Theophilus and his Roman friends how different the message of God's Kingdom is from the heartless legalism of first-century Judaism.

[11] By declaring that she is a *"daughter of Abraham"* – in other words, a true believer – Jesus teaches us that Christians are not immune to demonic oppression. Spiritual ignorance has very real consequences.

[12] Luke is not saying that all illness is demonic (it definitely isn't in 22:50!), but that it is all part of Satan's sinful regime. Jesus heals her, not by shouting at the demon, but by touching her to impart something of the Holy Spirit to her.

[13] The mustard plant grows up to three metres tall in the Middle East, since it does not die back in winter. Note the way that Jesus links back to the prophecies about his Kingdom in Daniel 4:12 and Ezekiel 31:6.

So open your eyes. Expect conflict but also expect to come out on the winning team in the end. Expect advance to take time, like seed sown in the garden or bread baked in the oven, but expect massive advance to be the norm. Don't view illness as a way of glorifying God. Jesus calls it Satan's prison, and Luke says in verses 13 and 17 that we glorify God by driving it out of the world.[14] If we want to partner with the Holy Spirit, we need to view the world with the clear eyesight of Jesus.

---

[14] While it's possible to glorify God in our sickness, 19:37 echoes 13:13 and 17 that he is even more glorified when we ask him to heal us.

Lesson Seven: Language (13:17–21)

Then Jesus asked, "What is the kingdom of God like? What shall I compare it to?"

(Luke 13:18)

Language matters. Luke knew that all too well as he attempted to communicate the Aramaic words of Jesus to a Latin speaker using Greek, the international language of his day. Luke's gospel therefore offers us a masterclass in smart communication. We need to learn this lesson from him if we want to become skilful Gospel messengers ourselves.

First, we need to learn from Luke's *style*. There is nothing boring about this history book. He constantly piques the reader's curiosity. Knowing that we all hate hypocrisy, he repeatedly presents Jesus as by far the biggest enemy of the puffed-up Jewish leaders. He tries to win over Theophilus here by telling him in 13:17 that *"When he said this, all his opponents were humiliated, but the people were delighted with all the wonderful things he was doing."* Luke tells more parables than Matthew, and three times as many parables as Mark and John put together, to slip past the Roman judge's defences, going straight to the heart with his Gospel challenge.

We also need to learn from Luke's *illustrations*. He reports that Jesus taught fishermen using fishing jargon (5:10) and shoppers in the marketplace using the songs that children were singing nearby (7:32). He records the down-to-earth parables that Jesus used to explain the Gospel to a crowd of rural Jews, and he changes those parables so that they connect just as forcefully with people in Rome. Look very carefully at his account of the Parable of the Mustard Seed in these verses. When Mark tells it, he translates the Aramaic word that Jesus used with the Greek word *gē*, which simply means *ground*. When Matthew records the same parable for rural Jews, he translates the word as *agros*, since they farmed their mustard in the *field*. But when Luke recounts the parable to a city-dwelling judge in Rome, he translates the Aramaic word as *kēpos*, meaning *garden*.[1] Don't miss this, because it illustrates a very important principle for sharing the Gospel. Luke took the trouble to discover that Romans grew mustard in their back gardens instead of farming it like Jews, then he adapted the parable to give it a more immediate impact on his readers. This is called contextualization. Tim Keller explains:

> *Contextualization is not – as is often argued – "giving people what they want to hear." Rather, it is giving people the Bible's answers, which they may not at all want to hear, to questions about life that people in their particular time and place are asking, in language and forms they can comprehend, and through appeals and arguments with force they can feel, even if they reject them. Sound contextualization means translating and adapting the communication and ministry of the gospel to a particular culture without compromising the essence and particulars of the gospel itself... As soon as you express the gospel, you are unavoidably doing it in a way that is more understandable and accessible for people in some cultures and less so for others... If you forget the first truth – that there is no culture-less presentation of the gospel – you will think there is only one true way to communicate it, and you are on your way to a rigid, culturally bound conservatism. If you forget the second truth – that there is only one true gospel – you*

---

[1] Matthew 13:31; Mark 4:31; Luke 13:19.

may fall into relativism, which will lead to a rudderless liberalism. Either way, you will be less faithful and less fruitful in ministry.[2]

We can also learn this lesson from Luke's *choice of words*. The other three gospel writers use the word "rabbi" sixteen times between them. Luke never uses it, because he isn't sure that Theophilus will know that it is Hebrew for "my teacher". Matthew and Mark refer to the Jewish "scribes" almost fifty times, but Luke does so less often and only after he has first explained their role in Jewish society by introducing them as "lawyers" and as "experts in the Jewish Law".[3] Similarly, Matthew and Mark frequently record the exact Aramaic phrases that are used in conversation, but Luke never does so because they won't mean anything to Theophilus.[4] His primary concern is always clear communication. He reminds me of Denzel Washington in the movie *Philadelphia*, when he asks the clients in his legal practice, *"Now explain it to me like I'm a six-year-old."*

We also need to learn from Luke's *brevity*. He is not the type of raconteur who bores his listeners with excessive detail or with a self-indulgent disregard for time. He knows that he can fit fewer than 20,000 words on a scroll, so he chooses very carefully what to say.[5] A classic example is here in 13:22, where he tells us that *"Jesus went through the towns and villages, teaching as he made his way to Jerusalem."* We know from John 7:10–10:42 that Jesus actually took a very roundabout route to Jerusalem, crossing the River Jordan from Judea to spend three months in the region of Perea before retracing his steps to reach his rendezvous with death in the city. Luke does not bother his readers with all this

---

[2] Timothy Keller in *Center Church* (2012).

[3] He calls them *nomikoi* or *nomodidaskaloi* in 5:17, 7:30, 10:25, 11:45, 46, 52 and 14:3.

[4] See Mark 3:17; 5:41; 7:11, 34; 10:46; 14:36; 15:22, 34.

[5] Luke and Acts are the two longest books in the New Testament, filling both scrolls with 19,482 and 18,451 Greek words. For perspective, Matthew, Mark and John are each 18,345, 11,304 and 15,635 Greek words long.

detail because he knows that most of them are unfamiliar with the geography of Israel. We need to learn from this. Effective communication is always short, punchy and clear.

We also need to learn from Luke's *emphasis*. He uses the space that he has saved on the scroll through his brevity to share events that are most likely to connect with Theophilus. It seems pretty clear to me that he had Matthew and Mark's gospels open in front of him while he was writing, not just because he alludes to them in 1:1, but because 570 of his 1,149 verses appear to have been imported with little change from one of those gospels.[6] Having used up half of his scroll echoing their words as the backbone of his story, he then uses the 579 verses that are unique to his gospel to target the message of Jesus particularly towards Theophilus and his Roman friends. They are wondering whether Christianity ought to be a "permitted religion" under Roman law, so he adds lots of new material that takes place in the Temple.[7] They are not Jews, so he adds lots of new events that emphasize that Jesus came into the world to save Samaritans and pagans too.[8] Luke fills the book of Acts with many more examples of how to share the Gospel effectively with different groups of people, but don't miss the fact that here we have the greatest example of them all. Luke's gospel is a masterclass in contextualization.

Pique people's curiosity in Jesus. Use vivid illustrations that go straight to people's hearts with a Gospel challenge. Use punchy language that communicates clearly, and answer the specific questions that particular people are asking. That's how Luke partnered with the Holy Spirit and it's how he teaches us to do the same.

---

[6] Another clue is in 3:4, when he quotes from Isaiah 40:3, since he tweaks the Greek Old Testament text in exactly the same way as Matthew 3:3 and Mark 1:3.

[7] For example, Luke 1:21–22; 2:21–22, 46; 18:10; 21:37–38; 22:53; 24:53.

[8] For example, Luke 2:32; 7:1–10; 9:52–56; 10:30–37; 13:28–30; 17:11–19; 24:45–47.

Lesson Eight: Humility (13:22–14:24)

All those who exalt themselves will be humbled, and those who humble themselves will be exalted.

(Luke 14:11)

Humility was in pretty short supply across the Roman Empire. The poet Horace boasted that *"I shun the common people and always keep them at a distance."* The astronomer Manilius went one step further by claiming that the different sizes of the stars and planets expressed divine approval for the strict class divisions that dominated life in Rome: *"Just as in great cities the populace is divided up into senators, who hold first place, then the equestrians who come second, then the common people, then you see the idle mob and then the nameless crowd, so too there is also a kind of Republic in the great universe, made by nature."*[1]

Luke has therefore saved the hardest lesson till last. The eighth lesson in Jesus' school of ministry is all about humility. It has to be, since the Spirit with whom we are called to partner is the same God who cries out in Isaiah 42:8, *"I am the Lord; that is my name! I will not yield my glory to another."* There is only room for one person to take the credit in this partnership, so the extent of our teamwork with God's Spirit is largely dictated by our willingness to allow all the glory to go to him. There are also plenty of clues in these verses to show us that Luke wants to use this lesson to challenge his aristocratic Roman readers that they

---

[1] Horace in c. 23 BC in his *Odes* (3.1.1). Manilius in c. 15 AD in his *Astronomica* (5.734–739).

are proud sinners in need of a Saviour. He doesn't contextualize the Gospel to avoid offending them. Far from it. He does so in order to issue such a clear call to follow Jesus that they will either be roundly offended or soundly saved.

In 13:22–30, someone asks Jesus whether only an elite group of people will be saved. This is more than a general question about the final number of the redeemed. In a first-century Jewish context it is all about divisions in society. The questioner wants to know whether only the Pharisees or only the priests or only the Sadducees or only the members of a particular synagogue have divine approval. Jesus replies that the door of salvation is indeed narrow.[2] Unless the people in all those groups humble themselves, they will be shut out of God's Kingdom on the Day of Judgment. They will watch in horror as the patriarchs and prophets welcome Gentiles from the north, south, west and east of Israel to the Messianic Banquet through their humble surrender to Jesus.[3] So much for elitism. *"There are those who are last who will be first, and first who will be last."*[4]

In 13:31–35, Jesus drives a further nail into the coffin of human pride. When he arrives in Perea, the Pharisees try to scare him back across the River Jordan by threatening him with the local ruler's power.[5] Herod is a client of the Roman emperor and he speaks for the Senate, but Jesus isn't interested in what authority has been given by the Roman ruling classes. Jesus is a prophet sent by God, who has authority over every demon

---

[2] Jesus actually avoids giving a final number. We should expect it to be large (13:18–21; Romans 5:15; Revelation 21:16), but we should also expect the Gospel's narrow doorway to exclude many who are proud.

[3] This reply deliberately echoes Psalm 6:8 and Isaiah 25:6–10. See also Matthew 22:1–14; Revelation 19:7–9.

[4] Jesus teaches us how to tackle apologetic questions. Always grasp the momentum of general objections to the Gospel and use it to make a specific, personal challenge for the questioner to submit their life to God.

[5] Herod Antipas ruled Galilee and Perea, whereas Pontius Pilate was governor of Judea. This ruse echoes Nehemiah 6:10–13. They were planning to stone Jesus to death once he arrived back in Judea (John 11:7–8).

and each illness. He does not need to run from a trumped-up fox like Herod. Nobody can thwart his destiny to be crucified in Jerusalem. As he weeps over what this will mean for his beloved city, Jesus brings us back to his warning about the narrow doorway to salvation: *"How often I have longed to gather your children... and you were not willing."* Pride destroys people by convincing them that they do not need a Saviour.[6]

In 14:1–11, Jesus braves another dinner party at the house of a leading Pharisee. He knows that he has only been invited so that they can find a reason to accuse him of doing something wrong so, since it is the Sabbath day, he heals a dinner guest who is suffering from a severe inflammation. The Pharisees are furious, but Jesus points out that they drag their cattle out of ditches on the Sabbath. They pretend to honour God with their long list of Sabbath rules, but in reality they just want honour for themselves.[7]

Looking around, Jesus can see that the Jewish leaders are all elbowing each other for the best places at the table. He points out the obvious: they are setting themselves up for humiliation. If somebody important arrives late, they will be relegated to the least important place at the table in full view of everyone. Worse than that, they will miss out on the Messianic Banquet, a picture of the age to come in Isaiah 25:6–8, since *"all those who exalt themselves will be humbled, and those who humble themselves will be exalted"*.[8]

In 14:12–14, Jesus goes on the offensive. He accuses his host of being just as self-promoting as his dinner guests by only inviting the rich and influential to dine with him. He isn't so

---

[6] Jesus would weep again like this later in 19:41–44. He quotes from Psalm 118:26 to warn the Pharisees that he is the Messiah. He still loves them but they have blocked him out with their pride.

[7] The Pharisees are silent in 14:4 because they know that Jesus is right. They are just too proud to admit it.

[8] This was one of the great themes of the Old Testament (1 Samuel 2:7–10; Proverbs 3:34). It is also one of the great themes of Jesus' ministry (18:14; Matthew 23:12; John 13:1–17; Philippians 2:5–11).

much sharing his food as trying to buy himself a place of honour at somebody else's dinner party in the future. Jesus subverts worldly class systems by commanding his followers to invite the destitute, disabled and dishonoured to dine in their homes. That kind of humility won't earn a swanky return invitation, but it trains us to stoop down low enough to enter in through the narrow doorway of salvation.

All of this happened for us. It isn't just Pharisees and Roman judges who are susceptible to pride. Although we talk much about Christian hospitality, what it often tends to look like in practice is entertaining our friends. John Newton, who wrote the hymn "Amazing Grace", exclaimed that

> *One would almost think that Luke 14:12–14 was not considered part of God's Word; at least I believe there is no one passage so generally neglected by God's people. I do not think it unlawful to entertain our friends; but if these words do not teach us that it is in some respects our duty to give a preference to the poor, I am at a loss to understand them.*[9]

In 14:15–24, Jesus therefore teaches us that humility is the currency of God's Kingdom. When one of the dinner guests mentions the Messianic Banquet, Jesus tells a parable which points out that God alone can save.[10] Only he can declare, *"Come, for everything is now ready."* The Gospel is such a one-sided invitation that it offends our sinful pride. Jesus warns the dinner guests that they are like people who offer lame excuses to a dinner invitation.[11] Since they are too proud to accept God's

---

[9] *The Works of John Newton* (1824), in a letter entitled "On Trust in the Providence of God".

[10] The dinner guest is hoping to win a compliment in 14:15 by latching on to Jesus' mention of *"the resurrection of the righteous"*. Jesus warns him that he must stop trying to earn his salvation if he wants to be saved.

[11] Their excuses are ridiculous. Nobody buys a field or a yoke of oxen without viewing them first.

invitation to partner with him in his Kingdom, they will be shut out of the Messianic Banquet. Their places will go to humble and repentant pagans instead.

Luke offends Theophilus and his other Roman readers at the end of this eighth lesson by telling them that Jesus views them as *"the poor, the crippled, the blind and the lame"*. He is not interested in pampering their Roman egos, any more than he is our own. If we want God to fill us with his Spirit, we need to learn lesson eight: empty yourself of all pride.

Graduation Day (14:25–35)

Those of you who do not give up everything you have cannot be my disciples.

(Luke 14:33)

Not everybody who starts out in Jesus' school of ministry is willing to stay the course all the way to graduation day. Augustine of Hippo was a very insightful church leader who understood that *"Pride is the beginning of all sin,"* yet even he struggled to renounce this world's weapons to partner with the Holy Spirit.[1] He tried to use Luke 14:23 to justify the forced conversion of people who disagreed with him:

> *It was originally my opinion that nobody should be coerced into the unity of Christ, that we must act only by words... but this opinion of mine was overcome... He said to them, "Go out into the highways and hedges, and compel them to come in"... Therefore if the church uses the power it has received from God at this time, through the religious piety and faith of kings, against those who are found in the highways and hedges – that is, in heresies and schisms – in order to compel them to come in, then let them not find fault with being compelled.*[2]

Jesus therefore closes off these eight lessons in his school of ministry with a graduation speech which emphasizes that we must be willing to go the whole distance if we want to partner with the Holy Spirit. The only way to go up is to bow down. The

---

[1] Augustine wrote this in *Our Lord's Sermon on the Mount* (1.1).

[2] These words are taken from his letters to a bishop named Vincentius in 408 AD and to a tribune named Boniface in 416 AD.

only way to know peace is to embrace conflict. The only way to find life is to die. The only way to gain the riches of God's Kingdom is to renounce everything that this world holds dear.

In 14:25–27, Jesus warns us that these eight lessons in his school of ministry are not intended for a group of super-keen Christians, but for us all. It's like the scene in the movie *A Few Good Men* where Tom Cruise asks if a soldier was in grave danger, and Jack Nicholson shoots back a baffled question: *"Is there any other kind?"* Jesus says that true Christianity is always about radical partnership with the Holy Spirit. It's either that or it's rebellion against God. There is no compromise option which allows us to offer Jesus a lukewarm love that does not make our love for friends and family and for our hopes and dreams pale into hatred in comparison. He warns us that *"Whoever does not carry their cross and follow me cannot be my disciple."*[3]

The crowd are appalled, but Jesus refuses to backpedal. It is now January 30 AD, and his crucifixion is only three months away. He doesn't want the Church's mission to flounder in its early days through its having to carry the deadweight of false disciples. In 14:28–33, he therefore demands that they count the cost of following him before they go a step further. A man becomes a laughing stock if he fails to check that he can afford to construct a tower before he starts to build and has to stop work halfway through after running out of funds.[4] A king is stripped of his crown on the battlefield if he fails to calculate the odds of victory before he gives up on diplomacy and marches out to war. In the same way, people who set out to follow Jesus without first facing up to how much it will cost them are even bigger fools than out-and-out unbelievers.

---

[3] This is not a new command. See Deuteronomy 13:6–11 and Exodus 32:25–29. Talking separately about making Jesus our "Saviour" and our "Lord" is therefore ridiculous. If he isn't our Lord, nor is he our Saviour.

[4] The Greek word *nēphizō* in 14:28 means *to calculate using pebbles* and it probably refers to bankers using an abacus to calculate complex sums. "Count the cost" is therefore not just a metaphor. Jesus means it literally.

In 14:33, Jesus states the cost very clearly. He tells the crowd literally that *"Every one of you who does not wave goodbye to all his possessions cannot be my disciple."* It's all or nothing. It's terribly difficult and yet at the same time it is so much easier than what passes for discipleship in so many of our churches. Because we fool ourselves that Christianity consists of a series of sacrifices, we never experience the power that comes to those who fully surrender their lives to the Lord straightaway. Instead we struggle to cut our own way through the impenetrable jungle of manmade obedience each day. C. S. Lewis explains in his essay "Is Christianity Hard or Easy?" that there is no contradiction between Jesus' command for his followers to carry crosses by dying daily and his promise in Matthew 11:28–30 that following him is an easy yoke and a light burden:

> *The Christian way is different: harder, and easier. Christ says, "Give me All. I don't want so much of your time and so much of your money and so much of your work: I want You. I have not come to torment your natural self, but to kill it. No half-measures are any good. I don't want to cut off a branch here and a branch there, I want to have the whole tree down... Hand over the whole natural self, all the desires which you think innocent as well as the ones you think wicked – the whole outfit..." ...The terrible thing, the almost impossible thing, is to hand over your whole self – all your wishes and precautions – to Christ. But it is far easier than what we are trying to do instead... Cutting the grass may keep it short: but I shall still produce grass and no wheat. If I want to produce wheat, the change must go deeper than the surface. I must be ploughed up and re-sown... It is hard; but the sort of compromise we are all hankering after is harder – in fact, it is impossible. It may be hard for an egg to turn*

into a bird: it would be a jolly sight harder for it to learn
to fly while remaining an egg.[5]

In 14:34–35, Jesus encourages us that it is always worth the cost of partnering with the Holy Spirit. We have already come too far with him to go back to our old lives now. We have seen too much of what it means for us to become the salt of the world, his change agents who repel the corrupting work of the Devil. Having witnessed this call to partner with God, we can never now be satisfied with anything less. Only a fool would choose to become unsalty salt.[6] We have to hit full throttle and give him everything.

If we say yes to this, we will graduate from his school of ministry with distinction. We will become fully qualified to partner with the Holy Spirit through love, prayer, Bible reading, courage, generosity, clear eyesight, clarity and humility. Though it will cost us all that this world has to offer us, it will also grant us entry into all of the blessings of the age that is to come. Jesus promises us that the Father will delight to give us the badge and gun of his Kingdom (12:31–32), that he will give us access to heavenly blessings that we could never have earned (14:17) and that he will declare to us, *"Everything I have is yours"* (15:31).

What an offer. Jesus indicates that school is out by ending this chapter with one of his favourite stock phrases,[7] so let's respond to what C. S. Lewis says on our graduation day:

This is the whole of Christianity. There is nothing else...
The Church exists for nothing else but to draw men into
Christ, to make them little Christs. If they are not doing

---

[5] Broadcast on BBC radio in 1944, this essay is included as a chapter in his book *Mere Christianity* (1952).

[6] The Greek word *mōrainō* in 14:34 primarily means *to become foolish*. It only secondarily means *to become unsalty*. Jesus is therefore using a play on words here and in Matthew 5:13.

[7] Jesus uses this phrase three times in Matthew, twice in Mark, twice in Luke and eight times in Revelation. He is warning us to respond today if God has enabled us to understand his words. He may not do so tomorrow.

that, all the cathedrals, clergy, missions, sermons, even the Bible itself, are simply a waste of time. God became Man for no other purpose.

It is not a sort of special exercise for the top class. It is the whole of Christianity. Christianity offers nothing else at all.

Reckless Love (15:1–32)

The tax collectors and sinners were all gathering round to hear Jesus. But the Pharisees and the teachers of the law muttered, "This man welcomes sinners, and eats with them."

(Luke 15:1–2)

In September 1957, nine black students enrolled at the all-white Central High School in Little Rock, Arkansas. The white majority made it very clear that the new students were not welcome. They were spat on and verbally abused. Their clothes were set on fire. One of them even had acid thrown in her face. Eventually President Eisenhower had to call in the 101st Airborne Division to protect the fact that the school was now open to anyone.

Jesus is experiencing his own Little Rock Crisis at the beginning of chapter 15. Although the three parables in this chapter are much loved in their own right, if we truly want to appreciate them, we mustn't overlook what prompted him to tell them. The Pharisees and rabbis were unimpressed when Jesus sent out the Twelve and the Seventy-Two, but when they see how inclusive Jesus is with his next batch of students they can bear it no longer. They look at the lowlifes that are signing up to follow Jesus and they complain, *"This man welcomes sinners, and eats with them."* Jesus therefore tells these three parables to protect his students and his under-fire school admissions policy.

In 15:3–7, Jesus tells the Parable of the Lost Sheep.[1] If you

---

[1] Jesus tells a similar parable on another occasion in Matthew 18:12–14. "Sinners" and "righteous people" are meant to be in inverted commas in this chapter. We are all sinners. What matters is whether we admit it.

know these verses well, watch out that your familiarity with the story does not make you miss its meaning. This is not a story about a good shepherd, but about a reckless one. No shepherd in their right mind would ever leave ninety-nine sheep unguarded for the sake of retrieving one that had been lost. A shepherd's business plan always included a contingency for losing one or two animals to a wolf along the way. What the shepherd in the parable does is ludicrous. It is the equivalent of you or me going to the bank to pay in a thousand pounds in ten-pound notes, counting them in the queue, discovering that a ten-pound note is missing, and leaving ninety-nine banknotes on the counter while we retrace our steps back down the road. Maybe it's safer where you live than it is in my part of London. If I did that, the notes would not be on the counter when I returned!

Jesus is therefore telling us that God loves people with a reckless love. He doesn't count their sins like a Pharisee or create an inventory of their shortcomings like a teacher of the law. He loves them so much that, when they turn to him in humility, he is always happy. He does not put them on a probation period. He dances for joy in front of all the angels in heaven. The doorway to salvation may be narrow, but it is open to anyone.

In 15:8–10, Jesus tells the Parable of the Lost Coin. It is very similar. When the woman invites her friends and neighbours to a party because she has found a coin, they don't admire her thriftiness. They think she must be out of her mind. *Just tell us that again: you had ten coins, you lost one, you did the housework, you found it down the back of the sofa – seriously, this is the worst excuse for throwing a party we have ever heard!* Jesus wants us to grasp that God is not like a battlefield general, happy to lose a few of his men just as long as the rest of them carry the day. God is radically and lavishly in love with every person he has made. Jesus repeats to us that God does a dance in front of all the angels.

In 15:11–24, Jesus tells the Parable of the Lost Son. Once

more the story is the same. Although the younger son is usually referred to as prodigal – wastefully extravagant or reckless – the real prodigal in this story is the father. In a shame culture such as first-century Israel, the younger son brings disgrace on his family by wishing his father dead and by squandering family money on sinful living in a pagan land. The father ought to say no to his request for money, or at the very least disown him when he uses it to get far away from home. The Pharisees and teachers of the law imagine that God reacts that way towards sinners. Sadly, so do many churches.

But God isn't like us. Although he loathes sin, he also loves humility.[2] When the younger son hits rock bottom, he comes to his senses, like any person whose sin convicts them that they need God's salvation.[3] He does not expect to be accepted back as a son and as a partner in the family business, but he rehearses a speech in which he asks at least to be readmitted as a slave. He never gets to deliver it. The father has such a generous love towards him that he has been looking out down the road for him ever since he went away. When the father sees him, he ignores the Jewish custom that grown men should never run. He sprints towards his sinful son, throws his arms around him, kisses him and interrupts him.[4] He doesn't make his son squirm and offer to pay penance for his wrongs by asking to become a household slave. Instead, he dresses him in the clothing of a master and gives him a signet ring that expresses his renewed authority and power. He throws a party that makes it clear to everyone that the boy is now back in the family. *"This son of mine was dead and is alive again; he was lost and is found."*

---

[2] *Pigs* in 15:15–16 does more than stress it is a foreign land. For a kosher Jew, this was absolute rock bottom.

[3] Note the clear parallels here with the Gospel. In Greek the son says literally *"I am perishing"* or *"I am lost"* (15:17), and to forgive him costs the father a blood sacrifice (15:23).

[4] The key word in 15:20 is *compassion*, since it highlights the great difference between God's heart and those of the Jewish leaders. *Kataphileō* means literally that *he showered him with kisses*.

If you are conscious of your own sin, Jesus told these three parables for you. God isn't interested in making you feel bad. He will not put you through a probation period.[5] Pride is toxic because it puts us in the place of God (that's why claiming that we haven't sinned is one of the worst sins of all), but there's a flipside to this. Humility brings delight to God's heart because it confesses freely that we need a Saviour. Humility is the opposite of sin. It restores God to his proper place in our hearts, confessing that we are creatures and that he is the all-powerful Creator. Jesus encourages you that in order to be saved all you have to do is the same thing as this sinful son. If you admit your sin and believe that God will forgive you, and commit to follow him whatever the cost may be, then you will be forgiven. *Admit, Believe* and *Commit*. It is as easy as A-B-C.

In 15:25–32, Jesus returns to the main point of these three parables. The elder son in the story represents the Pharisees and teachers of the law. When he hears that his kid brother has been accepted back into the family, he is furious and chooses to shut himself out of the salvation party. The father goes out to him because he loves him. He has no favourites. He gives him the same Gospel invitation – *"Everything I have is yours"* – but the elder son is too proud to accept the father's lavish offer. He fails to see his own sin (*"I've never disobeyed your orders"*) and exaggerates the sins of others (*"he squandered your property with prostitutes"*).[6] He fails to grasp the joy of partnership (*"I've been slaving for you"*) or how much grace has been given him (*"you never gave me even a young goat"*). He shows his lack of love by disowning his brother as *"this son of yours"*. The father corrects him firmly. No, he is *"this brother of yours"*.

---

[5] The father kisses the son while he is still in his pigsty clothes. We do not have to clean ourselves up to be accepted. The *ring* and the *sandals* in 15:22 speak of God wishing to partner with us straightaway.

[6] Jesus does not actually tell us that the younger son wasted his money on prostitutes. The Pharisees are offended that Jesus eats with other people (15:2) but think nothing of the fact that he eats with them (14:1).

In the second *Lord of the Rings* book, in the midst of a brutal attack by an army of orcs, King Théoden asks Aragorn, *"How shall any tower withstand such numbers and such reckless hate?"* Jesus turns to us as he ends these three parables and he turns that question on its head. What can the Devil do against such utterly reckless love?

The chapter ends with the elder brother still standing outside. There is a choice that has to be made. Will we complain about God's inclusivity or will we grasp it with both hands? Will we accept his school admissions policy and partner with him in the world?[7]

---

[7] Romans 15:7 commands us to *"Accept one another, just as Christ accepted you, in order to bring praise to God."*

The Joy Luck Club
(16:1–31)

Remember that in your lifetime you received your good things, while Lazarus received bad things, but now he is comforted here and you are in agony.

(Luke 16:25)

In Amy Tan's novel, a group of Chinese women discover greater happiness in the midst of trouble than they would have known in better times. As they are forced to flee the Japanese invasion, they meet to turn their attention away from the pains of the present and towards a better future. *"We could hope to be lucky. That hope was our only joy. And that's how we came to call our little parties the Joy Luck Club."*[1]

Jesus has not finished defending his schools admission policy. Remember, the chapter divisions in our Bibles are medieval additions to the text. We are told in 16:14 that the Pharisees are still sneering.[2] Jesus explains to his disciples why it is that degenerates and down-and-outs flock to follow him, while the refined and respectable run the other way. If you have ever asked the question "Why do good things happen to bad people and bad things happen to good people?" then listen carefully. Jesus has his own Joy Luck Club.

In 16:1–9, Jesus tells what surely must be the most confusing parable in the gospels. Is he actually commending

---

[1] Amy Tan in her bestselling novel *The Joy Luck Club* (1989).

[2] The continuity is even clearer in the Greek text, since 16:1 reads literally, *"Jesus **also** said to the disciples"*, and since 15:13 and 16:1 are the only places in the entire Bible where *diaskorpizō* is used to mean *wasting* money.

this dishonest manager for his financial impropriety? Obviously, the answer is no. Jesus is simply pointing out that the manager gave no thought to eternity while times were good. He lived the high life on his master's money, completely unaware that his possessions had begun to possess him. When he heard the news that he was about to be fired for his mismanagement, that all changed. He had nothing: no money, no talents, no friends and no Saviour to turn to in his hour of need.

Like Amy Tan's Chinese women sitting at the mah-jong table as Japanese bombs rain down on them, the manager learns that some of the bad things that happen to us are God's kindness in disguise. In a moment, he is set free from his slavery to money. Instead of using people to gain wealth, he starts using wealth to gain friends. Instead of living for his bank balance, he starts preparing for the day of real reckoning. When he is finally called in to be fired, his employer cannot hide his admiration for the dishonest manager. He has a clear perspective on what really matters. By granting buyers generous discounts on their invoices, he has lost money but he has won many friends. He has become a member of the Joy Luck Club. What looked like disaster taught him how to invest what is temporary in what will last for eternity.[3]

In 16:10–13, Jesus brings some application to the parable. God gives us money for the same reason a parent entrusts a child with pocket money. He lets us handle the temporary riches of this world in order to train us to handle the riches of his Kingdom.[4] The word that Jesus uses for money in 16:13 is *Mammon*, the Aramaic word for *Confidence* personified as

---

[3] Jesus speaks literally in 16:8 about *"the sons of this age"* and *"the sons of the light"*. How we use money reveals whose children we really are. Jesus also speaks literally in 16:9 about *"eternal tabernacles"*.

[4] These verses warn would-be leaders that God will only entrust them with leadership if they serve faithfully on someone else's team. They also tell leaders to promote on the basis of track record, not of charm.

a god.[5] He uses wealth to reveal whether or not we can be trusted to use money as a tool, through generous giving to our church, to Christian projects and to the poor, or whether we will turn a good tool into a deadly god. Jesus warns us not to fool ourselves: transactions speak louder than words. *"No one can serve two masters. Either you will hate the one and love the other, or you will be devoted to the one and despise the other. You cannot serve both God and Mammon."*

In 16:14–18, Jesus brings specific application to the Pharisees, since they love money. He points out that their wealth has robbed them of true riches. It has bought them such great honour in the world's eyes that they have become blinded to the fact that *"What people value highly is detestable in God's sight."* Because their lives have been so fortunate, they sneer at his invitation to become part of his Joy Luck Club. They despise the students that are enrolling into Jesus' school of ministry instead of queuing up behind them.

God sees through their designer clothes and straight into their hearts. Although they claim to love the Jewish Law, they twist and doctor it to suit their own desires. They threaten him by saying that Herod wants to kill him, yet they hear no threat themselves because they sold out to the world long ago. They would never challenge Herod, like John the Baptist, that divorcing his own wife to marry the wife of his brother was contrary to God's Law. They know that God's Word is final, yet they circumvent the verses that treat remarriage after divorce as adultery.[6] They are so wedded to the ways of this evil world

---

[5] The word *Mammon* is only used in 16:9, 11 and 13, and in Matthew 6:24. However, Hebrews 13:5–6 also tells us that the love of money is an insidious attempt to find security without needing to trust in God.

[6] Although these verses clearly echo Matthew 5:17–20 and 19:1–12, don't miss the fact that they are also meant to echo 3:19–20 and 13:31. The Bible only permits divorce and remarriage for the victims of adultery (Matthew 19:9), abandonment (1 Corinthians 7:12–16) or serious abuse (Exodus 21:10–11).

that they have actually come to regard the Good News as bad news.[7]

In 16:19–31, Jesus therefore tells one of his hardest-hitting parables in order to warn the Pharisees that their wealth is buying them a first-class ticket to hell. We will look in detail in the next chapter at what Jesus teaches about hell, but for now let's simply note what the parable means. Everyone assumes that the rich man in the story is the lucky one. He dresses in clothes that trumpet his wealth, status and luxurious lifestyle.[8] The beggar Lazarus, on the other hand, is patently unlucky. He has no fine clothes or food. He doesn't even have his health. Jesus nauseates us with the detail that *"The dogs came and licked his sores."*

But here's the thing. When the two men died, it became instantly clear that luck in this world can spell disaster for eternity. Unlucky Lazarus had no money in which to place his confidence, so he lived a life of undistracted gazing towards God. As his world fell apart, he learned to place his faith in the world to come. He became a member of the Joy Luck Club.

The rich man never joined it. He was too distracted by the things of this world to pay attention to the world that was to come. He is therefore told in hell that *"In your lifetime you received your good things, while Lazarus received bad things, but now he is comforted here and you are in agony."*

These are sobering words. Affluent Westerners reject the Gospel far more readily than people in the developing world. If you have been lucky in this life, don't make the same mistake as the rich man, and if you are fortunate enough to be less lucky don't complain. Give thanks that God has done what it takes to make you a member of his Joy Luck Club.

---

[7] Jesus is deliberately ambiguous in 16:16 and in the parallel Matthew 11:12. Does he mean that humble people forcefully enter God's Kingdom or that proud people forcefully push it away? Probably both.

[8] Since *purple* was the proud garb of Roman senators, Luke is indirectly challenging Theophilus here.

Hellfire (16:19–31)

Father Abraham, have pity on me and send Lazarus
to dip the tip of his finger in water and cool my
tongue, because I am in agony in this fire.

(Luke 16:24)

Luke's gospel is full of beautiful parables. You don't have to be a Christian to enjoy them. We talk in everyday English about prodigals returning, houses being divided, hiding our light under a bushel, phoning the Samaritans, building on sand, needing new wineskins and the dangers of the blind leading the blind. One story that never makes it into that list, however, is the Parable of the Rich Man and Lazarus. It's far too unpleasant. It is a story in which Jesus talks clearly about hellfire.

Many Christians rush to explain away the offence of this story. They point out that it's a parable. When Jesus says the rich man is *"in torment"* and that he screams, *"I am in agony in this fire,"* we are meant to see it as a metaphor. Granted, but it must be a metaphor for something horrible. The eighteenth-century theologian Jonathan Edwards reminds us that *"When metaphors are used in Scripture about spiritual things... they fall short of the literal truth."*[1] Other metaphors used by Jesus to describe hell in Luke's gospel include people weeping and gnashing their teeth (13:28)[2] in a place like the incinerator in a valley outside Jerusalem where rubbish was burned night and

---

[1] From his sermon "The Torments of Hell Are Exceedingly Great" in *Sermons and Discourses 1723–29*.

[2] Jesus also uses this as a metaphor in Matthew 8:12, 13:42, 50, 22:13, 24:51 and 25:30.

day (12:5).[3] Whatever reality such vivid metaphors describe, it ought to send shivers running down our spines.

Other readers have more sophisticated ways of explaining these verses away. They claim that hell will not go on forever: there still remains a chance for repentance. However, Jesus specifically denies that this is true. He talks of people being cut in two (12:46) in order to emphasize that the Final Judgment is called final for a reason: its verdict is irreversible. Abraham confirms that here in 16:26: *"Between us and you a great chasm has been set in place, so that those who want to go from here to you cannot, nor can anyone cross over from there to us."*[4] Luke will not even allow us to console ourselves that hell will eventually run its course and be snuffed out along with the souls of the damned. He tells us that hell is an eternal place of *"unquenchable fire"* (3:17).[5]

Jesus knows that this will offend many people, but he doesn't soft-pedal. He talks about the horrors of hell more in the four gospels than Milton and Dante do in all their poems put together. He is more interested in saving our souls than he is in sparing our feelings, and in this parable we find at least four reasons for his honesty with us.

Jesus speaks clearly about hell because *the Day of Judgment will soon be upon us.* We must not let our familiarity with this parable blind us to the fact that Jesus intends the crunching gear change in verse 22 to shock his listeners to the core. Nothing in verses 19–21 prepares us for the fact that the rich man and Lazarus are about to die suddenly, but that's what death is like. Jesus wants the thought of eternity to make us live each day as if

---

[3] Jesus also uses this Greek word *Gehenna* (literally *the Valley of Hinnom*) in Matthew 5:22, 29–30, 10:28, 18:9, 23:15 and 33, and in Mark 9:43, 45 and 47.
[4] See also 13:25. This parable also denies the idea of any temporary halfway house named Purgatory.
[5] The Greek word *asbestos* means *inextinguishable* and therefore, by implication, *eternal*.

it were our last. One day it will be, because death takes everyone by surprise.

Jesus also talks clearly about hell because *all of us have sinned*. It is easy to see sin on the faces of the Pharisees, but this parable is intended as a mirror to show us the sin on our own faces too.[6] The rich man does not rape or murder anyone. He does not lie or take drugs or blaspheme. He does not do anything that we might call a sinful action. James 4:17 warns us that we become guilty, not just through the evil things we do, but also through the good things that we fail to do. The only sin committed by the rich man in the parable is his self-centred neglect of others. Affluent Westerners tend to ask how a loving God could ever judge them, but this parable warns us that the real question is how a loving God could ever not.[7] He talks about hell because we are guilty of sin and he wants to save us from it.[8]

Jesus talks clearly about hell because *the time for repentance is quickly running out*. Many of us think like the German poet Heinrich Heine, who joked flippantly on his deathbed, *"Of course God will forgive me: that's his job."*[9] But Jesus warned us in 13:25–27 that there is no second chance for a person to repent after the final curtain falls. Now he warns us that those who reject God's kindness towards them in this life will continue to reject him even in hell. The rich man cries out in his torment to Abraham for water but not to the Lord for forgiveness. Far from repenting of the sinful way in which he treated Lazarus, he

ACT TWO: HE CAN USE YOU

174

---

[6] It is easy to see that Jesus is targeting the Pharisees when he talks about the *Law and Prophets* in 16:31, and when he says that heaven will be full of down-and-outs and hell full of money-lovers like themselves.

[7] One of the biggest themes of Luke is *salvation*. There is a terrifying reality from which we need to be saved.

[8] Luke uses the pagan word *Hades* to refer to hell in 16:23 because he has Theophilus in his sights too. The issue isn't money (Abraham was very rich yet he appears in heaven) but how we handle our money.

[9] Sigmund Freud recounts Heine's final words in *The Joke and Its Relation to the Unconscious* (1905).

still demands that he serve as his water boy in hell. Instead of praising God, he tries to pin the blame on him for his condition. Abraham has to point out that his real problem has never been too little proof about the Day of Judgment in the Scriptures, but far too much stubbornness towards it in his heart.

Jesus speaks clearly about hell because *he wants to save us from it.* That's the great crescendo upon which this parable ends.[10] The rich man begs for Lazarus to be raised from the dead so that his brothers will believe. A few weeks after Jesus told this parable, a different man named Lazarus actually would be raised in John 11. For now, Jesus prophesies about his own impending death and resurrection.[11] He will endure hell for us on the cross to save us from hell, and he will come back from the dead as definitive proof that what he says about salvation is entirely true. Jesus does not talk about hell lightly. He does so as one who knows that he is going to experience it very soon. The only reason Lazarus can enjoy heaven is that Jesus has endured hell for him.

So don't try to sweep what Jesus says about hell under the carpet. Don't get offended or embarrassed by his words. What Jesus says here is actually amazingly good news. A day is quickly coming on which God will judge every foul deed that has ever been perpetrated throughout history. One day our cries for justice will receive their definitive answer. Even better news is that Jesus has already drunk the Day of Judgment down to its last bitter dregs for us. No one need go to hell unless they reject his sacrifice for them and decide stubbornly that they want to go it alone.

---

[10] Lazarus represents the down-and-outs despised by the Pharisees. The rich man would not even let him through the gate into his courtyard, but Abraham allows him literally to *lean back on his chest* in 16:23!

[11] Jesus never normally names people in his parables. Perhaps he does so here to stir us to cry out for salvation, since the name *Lazarus* (the Greek form of the Hebrew name *Eleazar*) means *God Is My Helper*.

Swoosh (17:1–19)

The apostles said to the Lord, "Increase our faith!"

(Luke 17:5)

You don't have to be a fan of the *Star Wars* movies to pretend to use the force to open automatic doors. If you have never tried it, you are missing out on one of life's little pleasures. I guarantee that if you try it once, you'll find yourself doing it again and again.

I taught my youngest son Ethan to do it when he was four years old. I don't know which of the two of us laughed more, because he didn't really grasp what he was doing. He had no idea that a pressure sensor under his feet was activating an electrical mechanism. He just shouted, *"Look at me, Daddy!"* He began to believe that the swoosh of his hand was actually opening the door.

The twelve apostles are a bit like my son Ethan in these verses. As graduates from Jesus' school of ministry and with two successful field trips under their belts, they are starting to prepare themselves for the next one. They think they are getting the hang of swooshing at demons and illnesses with their hands. They therefore ask Jesus for help to open bigger doors. They ask him to *"Increase our faith!"*

Jesus has to explain gently that, for all of their successes so far, they still understand about as much about ministry as my four-year-old son does about opening automatic doors. Don't judge them harshly, because we are often the same. We assume that healing people is about saying the right words at the right volume (the louder the better) and with enough belief in our hearts to bring down a miracle from heaven. The Twelve aren't the only ones to think that all they need is a bit more faith. The correction that Jesus gives them in 17:6 is therefore recorded here for us all.

Jesus tells them that their focus is wrong. They don't need more faith. They simply need to use the faith that they already have. He assures them that *"If you have faith as small as a mustard seed, you can say to this mulberry tree, 'Be uprooted and planted in the sea,' and it will obey you."* Our power to heal people doesn't depend on the size of our faith or on our formulae any more than Ethan's power to open automatic doors depends on the way he swooshes his hand. We mustn't be as foolish as a four-year-old. We are in partnership with the third Person of the Trinity. Our power to heal people is entirely his.

Jesus demonstrates this for us in 17:11–19 when he meets ten lepers at the northernmost stop-off on his tour of Perea, on the border between Samaria and Galilee. The apostles know exactly what Jesus must do to heal them because they remember what he did to the leper in chapter 5. He must touch them in order to allow the Holy Spirit to flow out of him and into their leprous bodies. Then he must command them to *"Be clean!"* But they are in for a surprise. Jesus neither touches them nor commands them to be healed. He simply tells them to go in faith and ask the priests to perform a skin inspection. As the ten lepers set out in faith, they are all miraculously healed.

Think about it. It matters very little how much faith a policeman places in his badge and gun. What matters is whether or not the badge is real and whether or not the gun is loaded with live ammunition. So long as he possesses faith the size of a mustard seed to use them, it is all about the quality of the badge and gun that he carries. In the same way, just as long as we have a mustard seed of faith to partner with the Holy Spirit, it does not matter what formula we use. Our power lies in his size and quality, not in ours. Jesus demonstrates this by constantly shifting his methods, but never his partner. Sometimes he heals by driving out a demon (8:29; 11:14). The next moment he heals by rebuking a physical malady (4:39). Next time he heals by commanding the ill person to be healed (5:13). Another time he heals by touching people so that his body can become a conductor of God's power supply to them (4:40; 14:4).[1] On other occasions he commands people to do what he knows their illness prevents them from doing (5:24; 6:10; 7:14; 8:54). He even heals unconsciously when a person creeps up behind him and touches his cloak (8:44). We will search in vain for a method here, because there isn't one. It is not about the swoosh of the hand. It is all about the Spirit.

Jesus therefore teaches the twelve apostles three important principles in these verses that are make or break when it comes to our partnership with the Holy Spirit. In 17:1–2, he warns us not to lead anybody astray from the Scriptures. Since the Spirit inspired those words, tampering with the Bible damages our partnership with him. We would be better off at the bottom of the ocean than on a platform preaching a message of our own.

In 17:3–4, Jesus reminds us what he taught us in 11:4. If we want to be forgiven and to enjoy unbroken fellowship with God's Spirit, we need to forgive others just as generously as he forgives us and to guard the purity of our relationship with them.[2] If we harbour bitterness and unforgiveness towards others in our hearts, we will very quickly drive the Holy Spirit away from what is meant to be his home.

In 17:7–10, Jesus warns us not to fool ourselves that partnering with the Holy Spirit earns us brownie points in heaven. Although he promises to reward us for our willingness

---

[1] In Luke's gospel Jesus is like a human battery, who gets charged with God's power in prayer (5:16–17) and then touches people to let God's power flow out from him (6:19 and 8:46). We are to be the same (24:49).

[2] People are not to be put out of the church because they sin, but only if they refuse to repent of their sin. Church discipline exists to humble the proud, not to punish the penitent. See Matthew 6:12–15; 18:21–35.

to die to self and to live for his Kingdom, he points out that we are not doing him a favour by partnering with him.[3] The privilege is all ours. Just like the twenty-four elders in Revelation 4, we need to cast our victory crowns down at the feet of Jesus and to declare that every soul we bring to Christ, every demon we drive out, every illness we heal and every church we plant makes us even more indebted to his mercy. Not only did he stoop to save us, but now he stoops again to use us. Instead of basking in pride, we must humbly confess that *"We are unworthy servants; we have only done our duty."*

In 17:11–19, Jesus therefore ends by showing us what faith the size of a mustard seed is able to achieve. The ten lepers are clueless. One of them is even a heretic Samaritan.[4] But they believe enough in the power and authority of Jesus to obey what he tells them to do. As they set off to see the priests for a skin inspection, they are all healed.[5] Jesus explains to the leper who comes back to thank him that *"Your faith has made you well."* Not the method that he followed, not the swooshing of his hand, not the size of his faith, but the object of his faith. If we honour God's Word, forgive other people and keep humble, we will also see similar miracles. It's not the size of our faith as we partner with God that matters. It is the size of the Spirit with whom we partner.

---

[3] Luke 12:44; 19:17–19. These rewards appear to be opportunities to serve Jesus even more.

[4] The healing of the 10 lepers is only mentioned in Luke's gospel. Not only is it an object lesson in gratitude towards God, but it is also a reminder to Theophilus that the Gospel is for Gentiles as well as Jews.

[5] Faith is not measured by how much we feel a sense of belief in our hearts, but by how much we obey.

Now and Not Yet
(17:20–18:8)

*Once, on being asked by the Pharisees when the
kingdom of God would come, Jesus replied...*

(Luke 17:20)

My wife and I can never agree when it comes to choosing
movies. She loves period dramas, simple and predictable. I like
quirky films with a non-linear narrative. You know the kind I
mean. Think *Memento* or *Eternal Sunshine of the Spotless Mind*,
where the story lurches back and forth in time and you have to
piece together the complete picture.

But however much I'm used to that kind of movie, even
I find it hard to follow the plot when Jesus talks about the
Kingdom of God in Luke's gospel. In the same chapter he tells
us that *"the kingdom has come"* and that we still need to pray
"your kingdom come". Well, has it come or hasn't it? On another
occasion, in two consecutive verses, he assures us that *"Your
Father has been pleased to give you the kingdom"* and yet warns
that we still need to *"seek his kingdom"*. How can that make
sense? Has the gift somehow got lost in the mail? To top it all,
having just corrected a group of people for thinking *"that the
kingdom of God was going to appear at once"*, he assures a dying
man who asks to be remembered *"when you come into your
kingdom"* that his prayer will be answered that very same day![1]
Even Christopher Nolan, the master of non-linear-narrative

---

[1] Luke 11:2, 20; 12:31–32; 19:11; 23:42–43.

movies, would struggle to follow the plotline of God's Kingdom throughout Luke's gospel.

We therefore ought to be grateful that the Pharisees ask Jesus to clarify the plotline of his Kingdom here in 17:20–21. Although they no doubt ask the question sarcastically, the answer Jesus gives them is sincere and it matters hugely.[2] Since he commands us to *"seek his kingdom"*, to *"enter the kingdom"* and to *"preach the good news of the kingdom"*, we can only obey him if we find out what his Kingdom really means.[3] His reply to the Pharisees provides us with four helpful headings in the storyline. The Kingdom is both about Jesus and about God's work in us. It is both about now and about the future.

First, these verses show us that God's Kingdom is about *Jesus right now*. Jesus is deliberately ambiguous in 17:21 when he tells the Pharisees in Greek that *hē basileia tou theou entos humōn estin*. One way of translating this is that *"the kingdom of God is in your midst"* – in other words, the Kingdom has come through his own arrival in the world. Jesus said something similar in 9:27, when he assured his disciples that to see him in his transfigured glory was to *"see the kingdom of God"*, and in 11:20 when he declared that his miracles proved that *"the kingdom of God has come"*. Because Jesus is heaven's King, he can claim to be God's Kingdom personified.

At the same time, these verses also show us that God's Kingdom is about *you and me right now*. The ambiguous Greek phrase can also be translated that *"the kingdom of God is within you"* – in other words, it comes whenever a person is filled with the Holy Spirit and learns to partner with God's rule in the world. That's why Jesus points out to the Pharisees in 17:20 that its coming is unobservable. The world has no idea that a

---

[2] The Pharisees ask because they expect God's Kingdom to mean the violent overthrow of the Romans. They are trying to taunt Jesus that he is a failure as Messiah.

[3] Luke 4:43; 6:20; 8:1, 10; 9:2, 11, 60; 12:31; 16:16; 18:16–17, 24–25; 23:51.

Revolution has begun.[4] Christians look so normal and yet, when they partner with God's Spirit to extend God's rule in the world, they become powerful agents of God's Kingdom.[5]

When we read further, we discover that God's Kingdom is also about *Jesus sometime in the future*.[6] Jesus tells the Pharisees that, before it can come fully, he must be rejected by the Jewish nation and crucified (17:22–25). He must be raised again and ascend to heaven for such a long period that people will start to doubt if his Kingdom was ever among them in person at all (17:26–29). Centuries will pass during which people will be given time to choose whether to live for this world or for the age that will dawn when the King returns (17:30–36).[7] When this grace period is over, God's Kingdom will definitively come *"on the day the Son of Man is revealed"* (17:30).[8] Four times Jesus refers to himself by this name that was given to the great King of kings in Daniel's vision. He warns the Pharisees to make no mistake: though he lets them sneer at his Kingdom now, everybody will bow the knee to him on the Day it dawns in all its fullness.

Finally, Jesus tells us that God's Kingdom is about *you and me sometime in the future*. Although the revolution that has taken place in our hearts is unobservable, there will be nothing invisible about what happens to us on that Day. Just as everybody

---

[4] Jesus tells the Pharisees that God's Kingdom is not about the overthrow of Caesar, but of Satan. It is not about a revolution in the Senate, but in the Spirit. It is not about an army of warriors, but of worshippers.

[5] See 10:8–11. Jesus often appears to equate the Kingdom coming with our being filled with the Holy Spirit to continue his ministry. See, for example, Luke 22:29; John 20:21–22.

[6] That's why the Kingdom can be said both to *have come* (11:20) and to be *nearly here* (21:31). We will never understand the plotline of the Kingdom of God unless we grasp that it is now and not yet.

[7] This is so important that Jesus repeated this teaching a few weeks later in Matthew 24:23–28 and 37–41.

[8] Noah's Flood and the destruction of Sodom (both in Genesis) are often used in the New Testament as pictures of the suddenness of Jesus' second coming (see 2 Peter 2:5–8; 3:3–7; Jude 7). The death of Lot's wife in the destruction of Sodom ought to remind us to take these words of Jesus very seriously.

knows that a dead carcass must be hidden from view when they see vultures circling, so will everybody know that the days of this present age are truly numbered when Jesus suddenly returns. He will light up the sky from one end to the other, and those who have followed him will be revealed in glory to the world (13:28–30). Those who laugh at us now, just as they laughed at him back then, will suddenly stop laughing on the great Day when he invites us to *"eat and drink at my table in my kingdom and sit on thrones, judging the twelve tribes of Israel"* (22:30).

So have you got that? The Kingdom came to earth in Jesus and it has still come to earth in us through his Holy Spirit. It hasn't yet come in all its fullness, though, which is why the Parable of the Persistent Widow in 18:1–8 belongs with this block of teaching. It ends with another reference to the second coming of the Son of Man because we are often tempted to stop praying for God's Kingdom to come on earth as it is in heaven. Jesus warns us not to retreat into Christian defeatism, battening down the hatches until he returns. We must remember that God's Kingdom is within us and that he wants us to bring the power of that Day to bear on the earth right here and right now. If even an unjust judge will dispense justice for the sake of a quiet life when besieged strongly, we must not doubt that God will answer our persistent prayers for his Kingdom to come.[9]

God's Kingdom came to earth in Jesus. It is still on the earth inside us through the Holy Spirit today. It is coming down to earth in all its fullness someday soon, so let's pray with confidence for God to demonstrate the glory of his coming Kingdom through our lives today. Let's pray, pray, pray and then let's pray some more: *Our Father in heaven, please let your Kingdom come!*[10]

---

[9] The unjust judge uses the word *hupopiazō* in 18:5 to complain that the widow keeps *pummelling him in the face like a boxer*. God really wants us to lay into him in prayer. Don't stop until you see his Kingdom come.

[10] Jesus teaches on prayer and then asks in 18:8, *"When the Son of Man comes, will he find faith on the earth?"* Faith is therefore seen, not by how much we say, but by how much we pray. Prayer is faith made visible.

Mr. Topsy-Turvy (18:9–34)

All those who exalt themselves will be humbled, and
those who humble themselves will be exalted.

(Luke 18:14)

My children have always loved the Mr. Men book series. One of their favourites is *Mr. Topsy-Turvy*. He wears his bowler hat upside down, he holds his walking stick at the wrong end, he walks the wrong way up and down escalators and he gets thrown out of the library for turning all the books upside down. To my children, all of this is hilarious.

But there is something deadly serious about the topsy-turvy Kingdom that Jesus personifies. He describes it to us in these verses, and it isn't child's play. He is just about to cross the River Jordan and ride in triumph into Jerusalem on a donkey to be crowned King on a cross and to win a stunning victory by losing everything. These verses continue to unpack what he means by God's Kingdom. He wants to teach us all of its topsy-turvy principles.

In 18:9–14, Jesus talks about *forgiveness*. Everybody knew that the Pharisees were obsessive–compulsive about religion. Everybody also knew that any Jew who worked as a tax collector for the Roman Empire had committed an act of treachery towards God. Jesus therefore tells the Parable of the Pharisee and the Tax Collector to reveal the topsy-turvy nature of forgiveness in God's Kingdom.[1]

The Pharisee is so well behaved that he misses out on

---

[1] This parable is unique to Luke's gospel, but it shouldn't come as a surprise. It repeats the message of 1:52 and 14:11, as well as Old Testament verses such as Psalm 18:27 and 138:6, and Isaiah 57:15 and 66:2.

God's mercy. He doesn't even think to ask for it because he is too busy reeling off all the good things he has done: *"God, I thank you that I am not like other people – robbers, evildoers, adulterers – or even like this tax collector. I fast twice a week and give a tenth of all I get."* Note how his devout religion has engendered self-worship. He imagines that he has become his own saviour.[2]

The tax collector is so sinful that he grabs God's mercy with both hands. He is under no illusion that he has earned himself any credit with God, much less that he has become his own saviour. He is so aware of his long list of sins that he stands at a distance and does not even dare look up to heaven. His prayer is very simple: *"God, have mercy on me, a sinner."* Now for the punchline. Jesus says that it's the tax collector and not the Pharisee that goes home from the Temple forgiven. In God's topsy-turvy Kingdom, religion is as fatal as irreligion if it makes us too proud to squeeze through the narrow doorway of salvation. God always exalts the humble and he always banishes the proud.[3]

In 18:15–17, Jesus talks about *power*. When Luke says that the religious leaders *looked down* on other people in 18:9, he uses a Greek verb that means literally *to set at nothing*. Unless people looked good on this world's terms, they regarded them as nobodies.[4] Jesus therefore catches his disciples displaying the same attitude (this time towards children, but at other times towards women, Samaritans, Gentiles and members of the crowd) and he points out that it is always a case of the weaker the better in God's Kingdom.[5] Children know they are not the

---

[2] The Greek text of 18:11 tells us literally that the Pharisee *"prayed to himself"*!

[3] This is just as much a danger for us when we compare ourselves with others. We must not respond by praying, *"Thank you I am not like the Pharisee"*! The tax collector prays literally, *"Have mercy on me, **the** sinner."*

[4] The verb *exoutheneō* comes from the noun *oudeis*, which means *nobody* or *nothing*.

[5] Recognizing that Jesus imparted power through the laying on of hands, these parents wanted him to touch their children and to pray a powerful blessing over them. Note the echo here of 9:46–48.

most important individuals in their family and they know to cry out for help when it is needed. They model what makes us powerful in God's Kingdom. Proud people don't just miss out on the power of the Spirit. They never become part of God's family at all.

In 18:18–27, Jesus talks about poverty. He meets a very wealthy man who has used his money to buy power. Unlike the Pharisee in the parable, he appears to be rich towards God, asking Jesus eagerly, *"Good teacher, what must I do to inherit eternal life?"*

Jesus sees right through his hypocrisy. He refuses to be reduced to being this man's spiritual life coach, as nothing more than a good teacher. He points out that the only one who is truly good is God – he is therefore either a bad teacher for claiming falsely to be God or he is Yahweh in human flesh and blood. The rich young ruler must decide. Jesus quotes five of the Ten Commandments to convict him of his sin and, when he proves as blind to his shortcomings as the Pharisee in the parable, he adds a sixth commandment of his own: *"Sell everything you have and give to the poor."*

Jesus turns our thinking on its head through this encounter.[6] We tend to think of wealth as a mark of God's blessing, but Jesus says that it is often a heavy curse that prevents people from entering the narrow doorway of salvation. Very few rich people cry out to God for help because they have such great resources of their own, although Jesus points out that the Holy Spirit still has power to melt rich hearts too: *"What is impossible with man is possible with God."*[7] Sadly, the rich young ruler

---

[6] We can tell we are proclaiming the Kingdom clearly if it provokes confused and horrified questions like the one in 18:26: *"Who then can be saved?"* If you never get asked this, perhaps your message isn't topsy-turvy.

[7] Jesus exclaims literally in 18:24, *"How difficult it is for **those having property** to enter the Kingdom of God!"*, yet a rich man is saved only a few verses later, in 19:1–10. Jesus is not saying that all Christians need to give away their possessions, but revealing how little the rich man truly loves his neighbour.

ignores this offer of salvation. Like the rich man in the parable in chapter 16, he is too engrossed with this world's riches to become a member of the Joy Luck Club and to place his hope in eternity.

In 18:28–30, Jesus talks about *sacrifice*. Peter has left his boats, his house, his wife and his children behind to follow Jesus. He expects affirmation for having said yes to the invitation that the rich young ruler has just turned down. Jesus reassures him that, although the world currently despises him, he will not just receive a reward in eternity. He will also be honoured in this age. Little did Peter know that his name would one day be attached to thousands of churches and to the name of the second-largest Russian city.

In 18:31–33, Jesus talks about *death and resurrection*. He isn't just a teacher of God's topsy-turvy Kingdom. He also personifies it. He is Mr. Topsy-Turvy. He announces that the time has finally come for him to cross the River Jordan and start his journey towards crucifixion in Jerusalem. He is the King of kings, but his path to power will be surprising. He will defeat Satan by appearing to lose to him. He will receive all power by becoming a corpse. He will secure all authority by surrendering to Rome.[8]

In 18:34, Luke says that the disciples had no idea what Jesus is saying. They could not understand how God's Kingdom works, but by God's grace we can. We are able to fall to our knees, like a tax collector or a little child, and to tell Jesus that we have had enough of playing by this world's rules. We are able to tell him that from now on our world has been turned upside down by the principles of his topsy-turvy Kingdom.

---

8 Whereas Matthew writes for Jews and emphasizes that the Jews murdered Jesus, Luke pins the blame on the Gentiles. He does not want Theophilus to pray like the Pharisee in 18:11.

God at Work (18:35–19:10)

Jesus entered Jericho and was passing through.

(Luke 19:1)

When Joshua crossed the River Jordan to conquer the Promised Land, the first place he came to was the city of Jericho. He felt intimidated. Although the Lord had promised to give him every place where he set his foot, the walls of Jericho looked exceptionally strong. How could he capture such an impregnable city? Suddenly an angel appears. *"Are you for us or for our enemies?"* Joshua stammers. *"Neither. But as commander of the army of the Lord I have now come."*[1] Joshua suddenly sees that gaining ground in God's Kingdom is never about devising strategies of our own and asking God to bless them. It is about spotting where God is at work and joining in with whatever he is doing.

Jesus demonstrates this same principle as he passes through Jericho on the first leg of his journey to Jerusalem. In the past few chapters he has mainly taught about his Kingdom, but now he demonstrates it in action. If you are a Christian, I'm sure you want to see people saved, bodies healed and lives transformed all around you, so let's watch Jesus as he models for us how to go about doing so. Act 2 of Luke repeatedly assures us that God can use us, and these verses show us how.[2]

In 18:35–39, Jesus looks out for what his Father is doing.

---

[1] Joshua 5:13–14. *Joshua* and *Jesus* are the same name in Hebrew and Greek. Jesus is the true and better Joshua.

[2] The parallel passages in Matthew 20:17–34 and Mark 10:32–52 record an argument among the disciples over who was greatest. Luke ignores this in order to focus on his main purpose: training us for ministry.

Note that for once Jesus is not the major player in these verses. He is doing what Joshua had to learn to do in order to conquer Jericho. He is looking to see where his Father God is already at work in the city. Jesus explains this ministry method in John 5:19–20: *"I tell you, the Son can do nothing by himself; he can do only what he sees his Father doing, because whatever the Father does the Son also does. For the Father loves the Son and shows him all he does. Yes, and he will show him even greater works than these, so that you will be amazed."*

In 18:40, Jesus suddenly stops. He has just spotted his Father God at work in the crowd. A blind beggar is shouting out to him, *"Jesus, Son of David, have mercy on me!"*[3] Those at the front of the procession try to stop him because they assume that Jesus has many busy plans to see to. Perhaps he is meeting the mayor of Jericho or is down to preach at the synagogues in the old and new cities.[4] The beggar couldn't care less about his diary clashes. He is desperate to see. He cries out even more loudly and, far from avoiding him like the priest and Levite in the Parable of the Good Samaritan, Jesus is delighted to help. The only item he has in his diary is to fit in with his Father's plans, and the man's faith-filled prayer has just revealed to him what those plans are. Nobody would pray like this unless God were at work. This is also how Paul operated in Acts 14:9, when he looked around a pagan city, spotted a lame man and *"saw that he had faith to be healed"*.

In 18:41–43, Jesus dispenses the power of the Kingdom to meet the beggar's needs. It might seem a bit odd to you that he asks the man, *"What do you want me to do for you?"* After all, it's pretty obvious that he wants to see! However, Jesus has a holistic

---

[3] *"Son of David"* was an Old Testament name for the Messiah (1 Chronicles 17:11–14; Isaiah 16:5). Note that the beggar also hails Jesus in 18:41 as *kurios*, or *Lord*. He has more faith than a synagogue full of rabbis.

[4] Don't be confused that Matthew 20:29 and Mark 10:46 say this happened as Jesus *left* Jericho while Luke says it was as he *drew near* to Jericho. The healing took place on the road between the old and new cities.

view of God's Kingdom. The beggar's blindness is only one of the ways in which he needs God. If he asks for forgiveness, for provision, for freedom from fear, for the Holy Spirit or for insight into the Scriptures, Jesus can give him all of those things too. Having dispensed healing as a small sliver of what the Gospel means, Jesus encourages him to open his eyes to the whole of God's Kingdom by following him along the road.[5]

In 19:1–4, Jesus keeps on looking around to spot his Father God at work in Jericho. Again, he is not the major player in these verses. They are about a wealthy tax collector who climbs a tree to get a better view of Jesus because he is too short to see over the crowd.[6] Jesus spots him in 19:5 and stops again. He can see his Father's fingerprints all over what is happening. He knows that Psalm 14:1–3 and 53:1–3 clearly state that *"There is no one who understands; there is no one who seeks God"*, and yet here is someone so convicted of his sin that he has climbed a tree to seek an audience with God![7] Knowing that this can only be the work of the Holy Spirit, Jesus calls up to Zacchaeus that his diary is entirely free. He has nothing to do and nowhere to stay other than with him.

In 19:6–10, we see what happens when we clear our diaries of man-made plans and start looking for God at work around us instead. In our partnership with the Holy Spirit, he is always the senior partner. He initiates and we follow, never the other way around. In John 15:26–27, Jesus explains our intended ministry method: *"When the Advocate comes, whom I will send to you from the Father – the Spirit of truth who goes out from the Father – he will testify about me. And you also must testify."* Note the order

---

[5] It's good to be realistic that miraculous healings do not always lead to salvation (17:17–18), but don't forget that they often do! In Romans 15:17–19, Paul tells us that they were essential to his own Gospel ministry.

[6] This event is unique to Luke's gospel. Note that Zacchaeus wasn't merely a tax collector, but a *chief* one.

[7] This is how Paul quotes from those psalms to state this as a Gospel principle: Romans 3:10–18. Looking for God at work simply means keeping your eyes open to spot what things are happening that only God can do.

here: first it's the Father at work, then it's the Son at work, then the Spirit at work and only then is it us at work in fourth place too. This is immensely liberating. God has not promised to help you in your efforts. He has promised to reveal what he is doing so that you can join in with him!

Joshua demolished the walls of Jericho by faith when he looked to see what God was doing and simply shouted when he was told. Luke 18:24–27 tells us that what happens to Zacchaeus is equally impossible. When Jesus joins in with what his Father is doing, he demolishes the wall of self-sufficiency that years of worshipping money have built up around the tax collector's heart. He announces joyfully to the crowd that *"Today salvation has come to this house, because this man, too, is a son of Abraham."*

The crowds are not happy. They aren't used to this kind of Spirit-led ministry and, besides, Zacchaeus is the last person they would have slotted into the diary for Jesus. Nevertheless, they cannot deny how fruitful we become when we look for God at work instead of concentrating on our own plans. With very little prompting, the tax collector gives half of his possessions to the poor and spends the other half obeying God's Law.[8]

So what's it to be? Will you ask God to bless your own plans or will you surrender your agenda to his Spirit? Will you choose frenzied activity to extend God's Kingdom through your own power, or look out for God at work and join in with him?

---

[8] Jesus treats his actions, and not just his earnest profession of faith, as proof that he is saved – especially his care for the poor and his costly obedience to the Law (Exodus 22:1; 2 Samuel 12:6).

Whole Again (19:10)

For the Son of Man came to seek and to save what was lost.

(Luke 19:10)

Little misunderstandings with words can make a massive difference. Just ask the four journalists suspended by the state-owned *China News Service* in December 2015. Reporting on a trade summit in Johannesburg, they intended to report that President Xi Jinping had delivered a dramatic speech (*zhi ci*), but unintentionally reported his dramatic resignation (*ci zhi*). Chinese premiers are not famous for suffering fools gladly, and so it proved. Little misunderstandings with words can cost us dearly.

You don't have to be a linguist to understand the message of Luke's gospel, but it definitely helps if you can understand a few of his key words. He wrote in Greek, the language of the great classical historians and the international language of his day. One of his favourite words is *sōzō*, which looks quite little but don't be fooled. It conveys a wealth of understanding about the true nature of the Gospel and the Kingdom of God.

The simple English translation of the word *sōzō* is *to save*. Luke uses it in that general sense in verses such as *"your faith has saved you"* (7:50), *"believe and be saved"* (8:12), *"are only a few people going to be saved?"* (13:23) and *"who then can be saved?"* (18:26). Luke speaks of salvation in this general sense – being rescued from Satan's clutches through our sins being forgiven – but he also speaks of far more through this word *sōzō*. It isn't just about forgiveness and deliverance from hell. That is only part of what Luke says we can expect from God's great act of salvation.

The key verse in which Luke unpacks the meaning of the word *sōzō* is here, in 19:10. Jesus is so excited by what has happened to Zacchaeus that he announces to the crowd that scenes like this are the very reason he came into the world. He returns to the great mission statement that he read out in the synagogue in 4:16–21, but now he summarizes it even more succinctly as *"The Son of Man came to seek and to save what was lost."* He says that *sōzō* means more than rescuing lost people, amazing though that is. It also means retrieving *"what was lost"* by Adam in the Garden of Eden.[1] It means a complete reversal of all the dire effects of the Fall. If Adam lost it, Jesus came to earth to restore it. If Satan does it then Jesus came into the world to undo it.[2]

This is extremely important when we consider the healing miracles of Jesus. It's not uncommon to hear Christians debating whether such miracles are still on offer to us today, but Luke would not understand that kind of question at all. He uses the word *sōzō* in a far broader manner than our own narrow view of salvation as something purely spiritual. He makes it correspond to the Hebrew word *shalōm*, which means far more than *peace*, describing a complete restoration of the world back to how things were always meant to be. If Adam made a mess of it in the Garden of Eden, then *shalōm* fixes it. If it will no longer exist in the age to come, *shalōm* gets rid of it now. *Shalōm* makes everything whole again.

Luke therefore uses the word *sōzō* repeatedly throughout his gospel to describe the healing miracles of Jesus. It is the word he uses for the healing of a shrivelled hand (6:9), for the cure of a menstrual problem (8:48), for the resurrection of a

---

[1] Not every English Bible translation spots the significance of this, so some Bibles refer to Jesus coming *"to save the lost"*. However, this Greek neuter singular has to mean that Jesus came to save *"what was lost"*.

[2] See Romans 5:12–21; 6:23; 1 Corinthians 15:21–22, 45; 1 John 3:8.

dead girl (8:50), for the cleansing of a leper (17:19) and for gifting sight to a man who is blind (18:42). Luke also uses an intensified form of the word (*diasōzō* means *to save utterly*) to describe the healing of a dying slave (7:3). Since sickness and death entered the world as a result of Adam's sin, its reversal is an integral aspect of God's salvation package.[3] Galatians 3:13 says that when Jesus died on the cross he bore the curse of Adam away. When he shouted out that *"It is finished!"* as he died in John 19:30, he meant not just in part but as a whole. No wonder Luke is so excited. Our salvation is far bigger than we thought.

Luke also uses the word *sōzō* to describe Jesus casting out demons – for example, when delivering a man in a graveyard from a legion of demons (8:36). Luke says that salvation also freed him from his catalogue of mental health issues: *"They found the man... sitting at Jesus' feet, dressed and in his right mind"* (8:35).[4] The other gospel writers share Luke's holistic view of how entirely salvation has robbed the Devil of his arsenal of weapons. Matthew 8:16–17 tells us categorically that the death and resurrection of Jesus has secured our healing and deliverance from demons every bit as much as it has secured our forgiveness and deliverance from hell.

The death and resurrection of Jesus has also won for us freedom from fear and from poverty. Salvation made Zacchaeus poorer, not richer, so I am not trying to argue that God has promised to inflate our bank accounts and make our lives problem free. When salvation came to the house of Zacchaeus, it reduced his wealth and increased his godliness, whereas prosperity teaching tends to do the reverse. Nevertheless, we mustn't miss the vast scope of the salvation package that Luke describes through this Greek word *sōzō*. It brings deliverance

---

[3] Romans 5:12; Deuteronomy 28:21–22, 58–62.

[4] Luke also uses verbs of physical healing, such as *therapeuō* and *iaomai*, to describe deliverance from demons (6:18; 7:21; 8:2; 9:42). Even as a doctor, he sees these things as one indivisible salvation package.

from fear, from discontent, from guilt, from shame, from doubt and from meaninglessness. God's salvation transforms everything.

Understanding this therefore should change the way we live as churches. Jesus explains the true meaning of salvation to the crowds in Jericho because they are surprised he lodges with sinners. He explains that the whole purpose of his coming to earth was to drive out the kingdom of darkness by transforming lost lives like this one. In saying this, he passes judgment on any church that is more focused on its meetings, its rituals and its internal friendships than it is on its call to go out and reverse the effects of Adam's curse in the name of Jesus. Since we are told in 1 John 3:8 that the reason Jesus came into the world was to destroy the Devil's work, the mission statement of any church must include enforcing its utter destruction.

Understanding this should also change the way we live as individual believers. Satan has been utterly defeated, so his last remaining hope is to fool us that we haven't the authority to resist him in large areas of our lives. If you bought a house and found dirty dishes in the kitchen, people asleep in all the bedrooms, the previous owner watching TV in the living room, the garage still full of his junk and his car parked in the driveway, you would not content yourself that he had vacated the hallway. You would send him packing and demand the whole house from him. Do the same with the Devil.

It is not enough to know that we have been saved from hell tomorrow, when our calling is to bring heaven down to earth today. Use the little Greek word *sōzō* to resist the Devil. Tell him that all that Adam lost is now yours.

The Long Wait (19:11–27)

He went on to tell them a parable, because he was near Jerusalem and the people thought that the kingdom of God was going to appear at once.

(Luke 19:11)

None of us is very good at waiting. We are the generation that complains when the queue at a drive-through restaurant is two cars long or when our internet browser forces us to wait a few seconds to connect with a friend on the other side of the world.

Previous generations have not found waiting any easier. The Roman poet Ovid had to remind himself to *"Have patience and endure; this unhappiness will one day be beneficial."*[1] The first-century Jews needed reminding too. They were so desperate for the day when their Messiah would finally overthrow the Romans that, now that Jesus is less than twenty miles away from Jerusalem, they want him to commit to a deadline. Luke says in 19:11 that Jesus told the Parable of the Ten Minas because the crowds outside the house of Zacchaeus were pushing for God's Kingdom to come *"at once"*.

In 19:12–13, Jesus informs them that they are going to have to wait a whole lot longer. The man of noble birth in the parable represents the Messiah, so he explains that the Messiah will have two arrivals, not just the one. The first time, he will come in peace to call the world to receive him as their King. The second time, he will return to enforce his rule. Before the man goes off to *"a distant country"*, he entrusts his servants with money to invest during their long period of waiting for a

---

[1] Ovid wrote this in 16 BC in his *Amores* (3.11.7).

long-term investment. Jesus warns the crowd that the plotline of God's Kingdom isn't nearly over. It has only just begun.

In 19:14, Jesus explains that the long wait is *for the sake of the Jewish nation*. The Greek word *politai* means *citizens*, so in the context of the question this can only refer to the Jews.[2] Jesus points out that their nation is not ready for its Messiah. If he took his rightful place on the throne of Israel straightaway, they would actually side with Caesar and say, *"We don't want this man to be our king."* Jesus wants the Jews to receive him gladly, so he will give them time to do so.[3] He will not be like the present emperor Nero, who ruled through the murder of his stepbrother, his mother and a whole host of senators and noblemen. The symbol of God's Kingdom would not be the sword, but the cross; not the iron fist, but the nail-pierced hand which gently beckons people to follow.

In 19:15–19, Jesus explains that the long wait is also *for the sake of the Church*. The consummation of the Kingdom of God will end the story of this world, but it will also start the story of the age that is to come. Jesus therefore wants time to train up his people to hold positions of authority during that eternal age. These are normally referred to as "heavenly rewards", but note two things. First, the rewards consist of being entrusted with serving Jesus even more. There is no contradiction here with 17:7–10, because these rewards are nothing like the self-indulgent paradise of Islam. Second, these rewards are very earthy. They are not out in the ether. They are cities in an age in which the heavens and the earth have been remade and fused together into a single place where God dwells with his people

---

[2] Jesus is talking to a Jewish crowd that is complaining that he has saved Zacchaeus instead of honouring the more respectable Jews of Jericho (19:7, 11). This parable is therefore part of his reply.

[3] Although 19:27 speaks of judgment on the Jews that reject him, Romans 9–11 promises that the long wait will succeed in converting a large number of Jews to Christ before his second coming.

forever.[4] God is using the long wait to develop character within us so that we are prepared to rule with him throughout eternity.

One of the servants has taken his mina and used it to earn ten more. Another has taken his mina and earned five more. Jesus is thrilled with both of them. He praises them as good servants, pointing out that the three months' wages he gave them was just *"a very small matter"*, spiritual pocket money to train them in how to handle greater things. Because both were trustworthy in little, he can now entrust them with major responsibility at the consummation of his Kingdom. Jesus does not reveal what eternal reality is represented by these cities, but he says enough to convey to us that it is very real and very good.

In 19:20–23, Jesus explains that the long wait is *for the sake of the Church on Judgment Day*. Christians will not have to give an account for their sins – praise God, Jesus has seen to that – but they will give an account for how well they have stewarded their salvation.[5] Unlike the similar parable that Jesus tells on a different occasion in Matthew 25:14–30, the servant who does nothing with his mina is not cast out of heaven. This is not a parable about redemption, but about reward. The lazy servant is admitted to Paradise, but with very little to show for how he lived during the long wait for his Master. Whereas the Jewish crowd made the mistake of thinking that God's Kingdom had come too fully, the wicked servant represents the Christian who thinks that it has come too little.[6] His view of Jesus is, *"I was afraid of you, because you are a hard man. You take out what you did not put in and reap what you did not sow."* He represents

---

[4] Isaiah 65:17; 66:22; Matthew 19:28; Acts 3:21; Romans 8:19–23; 2 Peter 3:13; Revelation 21–22.

[5] Romans 14:10–12; 1 Corinthians 3:8–15; 2 Corinthians 5:10; Revelation 22:11–12.

[6] The parable in Matthew 20:1–16 addresses the competitive Christian. This parable addresses the lazy one.

Christians who treat Jesus as a hard taskmaster, instead of as the one who sends his Spirit to be our partner.[7]

In 19:24–27, Jesus explains that the long wait is *for the sake of the Jewish nation on Judgment Day*. The crowd in the parable are upset that the wicked servant has lost his mina and that it is going to the one who already has ten, but that is how it will be when Jesus returns. *"I tell you that to everyone who has, more will be given, but as for the one who has nothing, even what they have will be taken away."* Jesus says that even though the Jewish nation has the Scriptures, the Covenant, the Temple and the Law, all those things will be taken away from them on Judgment Day unless they say yes to their Messiah. In case they are in any doubt about it, he declares that those who were *citizens* in verse 14 are now *enemies* in verse 27. The parable ends with their slaughter. Unless the Jewish nation repents during the long wait, Jesus warns that it is heading for disaster.

These words close Act 2 of Luke's gospel. Jesus has stated plainly that God can use anyone and has explained how to go about partnering with the Holy Spirit. Now he commands us to choose how we will live between his ascension to heaven and his return. Will he say to you on that Day, *"Well done, my good servant!"* or *"I will judge you by your own words, you wicked servant!"*?[8]

Don't move on from Act 2 of Luke until you have made a firm decision. How will you respond to Jesus' promise that he can use you? All of this happened for you.

---

[7] How we view God affects how we live for him. That's why we have to take to heart verses such as 12:32, 14:17 and 15:31. We are meant to see this long wait as our happy harvest time!

[8] Jesus issues a stern warning in 19:22 even to those who know little of the Gospel. When people ignore the Scriptures, he still says to them, *"I will judge you by your own words."*

Act Three:

He Made a Way for You

Make Way (19:28–48)

As he went along, people spread their cloaks on the road.

(Luke 19:36)

It is April 30 AD. Jesus has climbed the steep and winding road from Jericho to Jerusalem and he is finally able to look down on the city from the Mount of Olives. He is about to ride as King into his capital. It is the moment we have all been waiting for.[1]

Jesus knows how he is expected to do it. Almost 200 years earlier, Judas Maccabeus rode into the city in triumph after liberating Israel from Seleucid rule. His soldiers cried out, *"Make way!"* and the people of Jerusalem lined the streets to welcome him as their saviour. We are told in 2 Maccabees 10:7 that *"The people, carrying green palm branches and sticks decorated with ivy, paraded around, singing grateful praises to him."*[2] As the curtain rises on the third and final Act in Luke's gospel drama, we are therefore meant to think we know what is about to happen. It is going to be just like Judas Maccabeus.

But Jesus has already read that script and thrown it away. Act 3 of Luke's gospel is going to be by far the most surprising. He will make a way all right, but the way will lead to something

---

[1] In John's gospel, Jesus constantly shuttles back and forth between Galilee and Jerusalem, but Luke does not record those visits in order to build suspense for now. This is Jesus' first visit to Jerusalem since Luke 2:51. Luke also omits the anointing of Jesus' feet in Bethany, which appears in all the other gospels, to keep us focused on this moment of high drama. Jericho is the lowest-lying city in the world, over 250 metres below sea level, so Jesus has had to climb over 1,200 metres in order to get to here.

[2] 2 Maccabees is the book in the Old Testament Apocrypha which records his great victory and triumph.

far better than a temporary victory over Israel's military oppressors. In Acts 1 and 2 Jesus told us that God wants to use people like you and me, but he never fully explained how it is possible for a holy God to partner with sinners. Now he rides into Jerusalem to make a way for that to happen. It isn't what anyone is expecting.

His way involves a very different approach to *power*. Maccabeus comes from the Aramaic word *maqqaba*, meaning *sledgehammer*. It became his nickname because of the ruthless way in which he shattered the Seleucid armies at the Battles of Beth-Horon and Emmaus. In deliberate contrast, Jesus chooses to ride into Jerusalem, not on a mighty warhorse, but on a donkey so young that it has never been ridden before.[3] He bears no weapon in his hands. The Messiah hasn't come to slaughter his foes, but to be slaughtered by them.

His way also involves a very different approach to *money*. Luke knows that Theophilus will automatically compare this scene to one of the great Roman triumphs in which victorious generals returned to the capital in a fanfare of pomp and glory. When Julius Caesar entered Rome in 46 BC after conquering the Gauls, he distributed 2,000 tons of silver and gold to the cheering crowds.[4] In contrast, Jesus bears no treasures. He has even had to borrow the donkey and the makeshift saddle on which he rides. The only gift he offers Jerusalem is his own flesh and blood. The Messiah is riding in to die.[5]

His way involves a very different approach to *significance*. The Pharisees try to downplay his arrival in Jerusalem. They get angry when the crowds throw their cloaks in the road to

---

[3] Luke refers to it as a *pōlos*, which can just as easily refer to a horse's *foal* as to a donkey's *colt*. Matthew 21 tells us it was a donkey. Jewish kings had ridden on donkeys before (1 Kings 1:33), but never on a baby one.

[4] See Appian of Alexandria's *History of the Civil Wars* (2.15.101–102).

[5] Jesus entered Jerusalem four days before the Passover Feast – that is, on the tenth day of the month. This was the day on which lambs were brought into the city ready to be slaughtered (Exodus 12:3; 1 Corinthians 5:7).

form the equivalent of a modern-day red carpet, just as they did when Jehu was crowned in 2 Kings 9:13. They get even angrier when the crowds start shouting out the words of the Messianic prophecy in Psalm 118:26: *"Blessed is the king who comes in the name of the Lord!"*[6] We are told in John 11:48 that the Pharisees were frightened that the Romans might view such words as rebellion, and they weren't prepared to risk a showdown with their rulers over a non-event like this. Jesus corrects them: *"If they keep quiet, the stones will cry out."* The Pharisees might fool themselves that what is happening here is insignificant, but the Messiah has entered Jerusalem to change the face of the world.

His way involves a very different approach to *religion*. Judas Maccabeus had ridden into the capital to purge the Temple of the idols put there by the pagans. Jesus weeps as he rides down the short road from the Mount of Olives into the city because he recognizes that the idols in our hearts are far harder to clear. He prophesies the destruction of Jerusalem by the Romans in 70 AD, because he knows that the Jews are about to fail to recognize that his arrival means God's Kingdom has come. He doesn't drive out pagans from the Temple courtyards in verses 45–46, but merchant Jews. He accuses them of turning God's great worship centre into *"a den of robbers"*, and he promises to end their profiteering from religion. God will demolish their defunct Temple at the hands of the Romans in order to make way for a far better Temple instead: *"My house will be a house of prayer."*[7] The Messiah makes it clear that he has entered Jerusalem to

---

[6] John 12:13 says that they also waved branches to fulfil Psalm 118:27: *"With boughs in hand, join in the festal procession."* Luke omits this detail because it was likely to be lost on Theophilus. In the same way, instead of quoting from Zechariah 9:9 like Matthew and John, he inserts the extra word *"king"* to his quotation from Psalm 118:26 in order to explain to Theophilus what the crowd's words meant to Jewish ears.

[7] These are quotations from Isaiah 56:7 and Jeremiah 7:11. By quoting from what is known as Jeremiah's "Great Temple Sermon", Jesus warns that Herod's Temple will be destroyed like Solomon's was in 586 BC.

replace corrupt religion with Christian partnership with God's Spirit through obedience and prayer.[8]

Make no mistake about it: Jesus has ridden into Jerusalem to prepare a way for us to be saved into partnership with God, but it isn't the way that any of us would have expected. It takes a very different approach to power, to money, to significance and to religion. But here's the thing: Jesus is more in control of events at this moment than Judas Maccabeus and Julius Caesar put together. He renounces the resources of this world in order to operate on the resources of heaven. This enables him to prophesy where his disciples can find the right donkey.[9] It enables him to overcome the objections of its owners with just a handful of words.[10] He demonstrates his mastery over all of creation through his miraculous ability to ride on a donkey that has not yet been broken in.[11] Let's not mistake the Messiah's meekness for weakness.

Act 3 of Luke's gospel therefore begins with high drama. Jesus has arrived in Jerusalem to make a way for the holy God to partner with sinful people, a way that is going to cost him everything. As the Messiah makes his way down the death-and-resurrection road, he turns and beckons an army of believers to fall in behind him.

---

[8] Luke emphasizes through Jesus' tears and through the fact that he does not complete the quotation from Isaiah that God still loves the Jews. It actually says, *"a house of prayer **for all nations**."* His statement in 19:42 that *"it is hidden from your eyes"* goes alongside Matthew 23:37: *"you were not willing."* See also Luke 7:30.

[9] Jesus also displays similar miraculous prophetic insight in 22:7–13.

[10] The word for *owners* in 19:33 is actually *kurioi*, or *lords*. When the disciples say, *"The Lord needs it"*, the owners are forced to recognize that Jesus is the *kurios kuriōn* – the Lord of lords (Revelation 17:14).

[11] Unless you live on a farm, you might not appreciate how big a miracle this is. It is every bit as big a miracle as the one in 8:24.

The Way of the Jews
(20:1–47)

The teachers of the law and the chief priests looked
for a way to arrest him immediately, because they
knew he had spoken this parable against them.

(Luke 20:19)

Theophilus and his Roman friends knew Christianity as *the Way*. The early believers did not fight it when people mockingly called them "Christians" but that is not how Luke describes them in the book of Acts. He calls them followers of *the Way* because they believed that God had opened up a pathway along which people could be saved.[1]

Theophilus had a big question, however, and it was crucial that Luke answer it if he wanted to see the apostle Paul set free. Theophilus wanted to know whether *the Way* was a continuation of Judaism (and therefore protected as a religion by Roman law) or whether it was something new (and therefore outlawed as a danger to the cohesion of the Roman Empire).

Luke works very hard in chapter 20 to demonstrate that the Way of Jesus is in fact the true way of the Jews. He seeks to drive a wedge in the minds of his readers between the Jewish leaders and the common Jews. That isn't his only aim in these verses (Matthew and Mark include these clashes in the Temple courtyards in their gospel accounts too), but look at the way he introduces them at the end of chapter 19: *"Every day he was teaching at the temple. But the chief priests, the teachers of the law and the leaders among*

---

[1] Acts 9:2; 19:9, 23; 24:14, 22. *Christian* is used as an insult in Acts 11:26 and 26:28, and 1 Peter 4:16.

the people were trying to kill him. Yet they could not find any way to do it, because all the people hung on his words."

In 20:1–8, Luke points out that the Jewish crowd sides with Jesus, not with their leaders, when it comes to John the Baptist. The fact that Jesus is teaching in the Temple courtyards is already a clear sign that the Jewish crowd accept him as one of their own. When he is interrupted by members of the Sanhedrin (the ruling council of seventy-one priests, rabbis and elders) and asked to name the source of his authority, it becomes clear that their chief problem is not one of doctrine but of his not being one of them![2] Jesus responds with a question of his own. He will only name his source if they will do the same regarding John the Baptist.[3] It is a trap. If they say that John was a genuine Jewish prophet, they are guilty of ignoring what he said. If they say he was a false prophet, they will find themselves on the wrong side of the Jewish crowd. Either way, it is one–nil to Jesus. He is clearly the real rabbi who teaches the historic way of the Jews.

In 20:9–19, Jesus tells the Parable of the Tenants, which predicts that the Jewish leaders will reject him as Messiah. The nation of Israel is often pictured as a vine in the Old Testament, so he tells the Sanhedrin that they are merely stewards of God's people.[4] The Lord is the real owner, and the Jewish leaders have a terrible track record of killing his prophets who point them back to the true road. Even now, they know deep down that he is the Son of God, the true heir of the Kingdom, yet they would rather murder him than follow him back to their historic faith.[5] To prove it, Jesus quotes from Psalm 118:22 – the very

---

[2] The *Sanhedrin* was led by the high priest and governed internal Jewish affairs. For his Roman readers, Luke explains in 20:1 that it comprised *"the chief priests and the teachers of the law, together with the elders"*.

[3] We looked at Jesus' use of questions in his teaching in the earlier chapters on 2:41–50 and 9:18–26.

[4] Psalm 80:8–16; Isaiah 5:1–7; Jeremiah 2:21; Ezekiel 17:5–8; Hosea 10:1.

[5] The tenants mistreat the servants and throw them out, but they throw out the son before they kill him. Jesus is predicting that he will be crucified outside the city walls of Jerusalem (Hebrews 13:11–14).

psalm from which the crowd quoted two days earlier when he rode into Jerusalem.[6] Even their own people recognize him as the true Messiah!

Luke does two things here to reach out to Theophilus and his Roman friends. First, he points out in verse 16 that the fact that many Jews have rejected Jesus should not stop them from following him: it is the reason the Gospel has gone out to them.[7] Second, he emphasizes in verse 19 that this parable is not so much condemning the Jews as condemning their leaders. The Jewish nation rejected Jesus because its leaders went bad.

In 20:20–26, Jesus proves that the Jewish leaders are not as devout as they appear. First, Luke tells Theophilus that the Jewish leaders *"sent spies, who pretended to be sincere... so that they might hand him over to the power and authority of the governor"*. He wants the judge to see that the apostle Paul's accusers are not devout Jews either. They are cunning liars who want to make their Roman rulers puppets in their own plans. Second, Luke reveals that the Jewish leaders are nowhere near as committed to their religion as they pretend. Their own interpretation of the Jewish Law insisted that it was blasphemy to bring the image of a foreign god into the Temple courtyards. However, they quickly produce a coin bearing the face of the divine Tiberius when it suits them. They have strayed so far from the way of the Jews that even a satnav couldn't bring them back to it.

In 20:27–40, Jesus proves that the Jewish leaders have turned their backs on the founder of their religion. The Sadducees accepted only the first five books of the Old Testament

---

[6] Don't miss how clever Jesus is being here. He quotes from Psalm 118:22 in 20:17 to point back to the crowd's quotation from Psalm 118:26 in 19:38. He also uses a play on words for his Jewish hearers, since the Aramaic words for *son* and *stone* are *ben* and *eben*. To reject the Son is to reject the Stone of Psalm 118.

[7] The Jewish leaders are disgusted by the thought of God saving Gentiles in 20:16, but not disgusted enough to repent of their sin and turn back to the way of the Jews.

as inspired Scripture: the five books of Moses that are known as the Pentateuch or the Torah.[8] They did not believe in heaven, hell, angels, demons, miracles or much else supernatural. Since they know that Jesus sides with historic Judaism on all these things, the Sadducees believe that they have found his weak spot. They toss out one of the convoluted hypothetical scenarios that were so loved by the debating Jewish rabbis, but Jesus is far too quick for their poor exegesis of Deuteronomy 25:5–10. He tells them that their muddled thinking about the resurrection stems from muddled thinking about angels, even though Moses mentions angels over thirty times in the Torah! Jesus quotes God's words to Moses at the burning bush in Exodus 3:6 to prove that even the Torah preaches resurrection by talking about dead patriarchs as if they were alive. It is so clear to everybody that it's the Sadducees, not him, who have left the true way of the Jews that the other rabbis applaud him for defending historic Judaism far better than they can!

In 20:41–47, Jesus goes on the offensive. He takes Psalm 110, one of the most famous Messianic prophecies in the Old Testament, and asks the Jewish leaders how this Scripture fits inside their world view. When they cannot reply because it clearly doesn't, he attacks their pretence and self-promotion, all to the delight of the Jewish crowd.[9]

Luke uses these clashes between Jesus and the Jewish leaders to make it abundantly clear to his readers that it is the priests and rabbis, not the Christians, who have abandoned the way of the Jews. The Christian faith is therefore recognized and protected by Roman law. Judge Theophilus must set the apostle Paul free.

---

[8] *Sadducee* comes from the name of Solomon's high priest *Zadok*. They controlled the Temple in the same way that the Pharisees tended to control the synagogues, which is why we only meet them now in Jerusalem.

[9] We have a much longer account of this warning in Matthew 23:1–39. Three verses are enough for Theophilus, especially given that Luke has already recorded similar teaching in 11:37–54.

The Way of Rome
(20:20–26)

They hoped to catch Jesus in something he said,
so that they might hand him over to the power and
authority of the governor.

(Luke 20:20)

It was easy to die quickly in the Roman Empire. All you had to do was question the authority of the emperor. Pontius Pilate, the Roman governor of Judea, quickly caved in and crucified an innocent man when threatened in John 19:12, *"If you let this man go, you are no friend of Caesar. Anyone who claims to be a king opposes Caesar."* Every Roman official knew that certain sacrifices had to be made to stay on the right side of the emperor.

Theophilus knew it too. Emperor Nero had murdered his own mother, his stepbrother and a whole host of noblemen, so he was hardly likely to think twice about killing a two-a-penny judge like him. The court case to decide the fate of the apostle Paul would set an important precedent, effectively passing an official imperial verdict over Christianity as a whole. Theophilus was therefore in the spotlight, and Luke does not leave us guessing as to the low-down tactics employed by the prosecution. In 23:2, he gives us an example of what they were saying about Jesus: *"We have found this man subverting our nation. He opposes payment of taxes to Caesar and claims to be Messiah, a king."*

Luke therefore needs to use the clash between Jesus and the spies sent by the Jewish leaders in 20:20–26 to show Theophilus that the Way of Jesus poses no threat to Emperor

Nero. Luke needs to use it to expose the dirty tricks that are being played by Paul's accusers. He points out that these spies only *"pretended to be sincere"* and that they were actually hoping to manipulate a Roman governor.[1] Theophilus must not be fooled.

Luke assures Theophilus that the Christians are good citizens of Emperor Nero. After all, Jesus healed the slave of a Roman centurion in 7:1–10. That's a double whammy. Not only did he accept the presence of Roman soldiers in the Holy Land, but he kept quiet about the injustice of slavery too. Furthermore, he told would-be insurrectionists that he was not the rebel leader they were looking for.[2] If he was ever going to have a Rosa Parks moment and come out against the emperor, it is surely now, because the spies are asking whether Jews ought to pay taxes to Rome. For Judge Theophilus and for Paul in the dock, his answer is absolutely critical.

Jesus asks the spies to show him a denarius coin and to read out the inscription on it. *Tiberius Caesar Divi Augusti Pontifex Maximus* was Latin for *Tiberius Caesar, son of the divine Augustus, the Great High Priest.* There's just so much that Jesus can say in reply. There is the obvious: Tiberius is not really the son of Augustus. They are not blood relatives and never even really liked each other. As for the claim that Augustus is a god and Tiberius the great mediator between the gods and men, it is so blasphemous that the Jewish spies ought to be ashamed to have carried such a coin into the Temple courtyards. Instead of saying all this, Jesus simply asks whose face is on the coin. When they confirm that it is Caesar's, it is the cue for any rebel leader to shout the great war cry of the Maccabeans: *"Pay back to the Gentiles what they deserve!"*[3] Instead, Jesus delivers his own

---

[1] The Greek word *hypokrinomai* in 20:20 is the origin of our word *hypocrite*.

[2] One of the Twelve was named Simon *the Zealot*, part of a group that planned violent revolution against Rome (6:15). It must have been a shock for him to discover that Jesus wasn't the Messiah he expected.

[3] The echo of 1 Maccabees 2:68 in Jesus' reply is entirely intentional.

twist on that old war cry: *"Pay back to Caesar what is Caesar's, and to God what is God's."*

Even the spies can see that there is nothing seditious in his answer. They are so taken aback by the skilful way in which he sidesteps their trap that they have nothing else to say.[4] Luke will stress this further when he tells us that Pilate stated three times at Jesus' trial that *"I find no basis for a charge against this man."*[5] He will keep repeating throughout the book of Acts that the followers of Jesus pose no threat to Emperor Nero, and that it is their accusers who are the real troublemakers.[6] Luke therefore tells Theophilus that he can put his mind at ease. There is nothing revolutionary about Jesus.

Except, of course, for the fact that there is. Luke's gospel is a brilliant example of how to communicate the Good News of God's Kingdom to a hostile world. Jesus speaks no threat against the emperor, but he entirely rejects the way of Rome. He is its greatest critic because he is its Saviour. *"Give back to Caesar what is Caesar's"* is only half of his new war cry. The other half proclaims his Kingdom Revolution: *"And give to God what is God's."*

Jesus calls us to revolt against *the currency of Rome*. He asks to borrow a Roman denarius, not because he lacks money, but because he spots a chance to expose the hypocrisy of the spies. He treats Caesar's coinage with great disdain when he tells the spies to send it back to Caesar, where its blasphemous inscription belongs, because God's Kingdom cannot be founded on Rome's currency. By all means give *that* back to Caesar. He is welcome to it all. Just be sure to give God all the things that

---

[4] He has actually trapped them. They question the Messiah's authority in 20:2 yet kowtow to Caesar's authority every day. Their silence in 20:26 is a picture of what will happen to every rebel on Judgment Day.

[5] Luke 23:4, 14–16, 22 (see also 23:41, 47). Jesus' accusers manipulated Pilate's cowardice to ensure that an insurrectionist and murderer was released instead of him (23:25).

[6] Acts 13:50; 14:2; 16:19–40; 17:5, 13; 18:12–17; 19:35–41; 21:27–39; 23:12–35; 24:10–21; 25:7–27.

really matter: love, honour, obedience, holiness and devotion. That is, all the things that money just can't buy.

Jesus also calls us to revolt against *the power play of Rome*. The fact that he allows the spies to taunt him when he has power to command the angels and the elements to smite them displays that he has come to be a very different type of King. While senators and politicians scheme to climb their way up the greasy pole in Rome, he opens up a new pathway of humility.[7] Not the Roman way, but the death-and-resurrection road. His coronation day will not involve a marble throne but a wooden cross, not a crown of gold but a crown of thorns, not bejewelled fingers but nail-pierced hands and feet.

As a result of this new pathway, Jesus is able to call us to revolt against *the enemy of Rome*. Rome's true foe was not the barbarians of the north, any more than Israel's true foe was Caesar. It was Satan and all that he stood for. Jesus did not come into the world to kill the Romans, but to save them. He came to make them part of a far better Kingdom than the puny empire of which they were so proud. He came to make them more than conquerors by restoring to them all that Satan stole from their first father. That's why the angels used imperial language when they appeared to the shepherds. The Gospel was good news for the Romans. Since we have the same enemy, it's still good news for us too.

Jesus is safe. He poses no threat to the Roman emperor. He is telling the truth to Governor Pilate when he reassures him in John 18:36 that *"My kingdom is not of this world… My kingdom is from another place."* Yet at the same time Jesus is massively dangerous. He means to overturn this world's way entirely. Caesar can keep his failed currency of earthly wealth and human power. We have a better way. We have *the Way*. We are children of the true God and he has made us partners in his Kingdom Revolution.

---

[7] Even Jesus' enemies are forced to admit in 20:21 that he never plays any of their power games.

Get Out of the Way (21:1–4)

"Truly I tell you," he said, "this poor widow has put in more than all the others."

(Luke 21:3)

It wasn't easy for Hudson Taylor to sacrifice his hopes and dreams to sail as a missionary to China. His journal is full of his intense loneliness and pain. Yet far greater than the pain of his own sacrifice was watching other people making sacrifices with him.

As his ship sailed out of the dock gates in Liverpool, he saw a look on his mother's face that haunted him throughout the long voyage to China.

> *I shall never forget the cry of anguish wrung from that mother's heart. It went through me like a knife. I never knew so fully, until then, what "God so loved the world" meant. And I am quite sure that my precious mother learned more of the love of God to the perishing in that hour than in all her life before.[1]*

All of this was simply preparation for a greater pain to come. Deciding to throw away his own life for the sake of the million dying each month in China was one thing. Asking people to throw their lives away with him was almost too much for him to bear. As he walked along the beach in Brighton on the morning of Sunday 25th June 1865, he found himself quite unable to ask anybody else to make the great sacrifice of joining his team.

> *I feared that in the midst of the dangers, difficulties and trials which would necessarily be connected with such*

---

[1] Hudson Taylor recalls this in his autobiography *A Retrospect* (1894).

a work, some who were comparatively inexperienced
Christians might break down, and bitterly reproach me
for having encouraged them to undertake an enterprise
for which they are not equal... I feared I should lose my
reason... They will break down. They will reproach you.
Can you stand that?... Why did we come? Oh, why did
that man deceive us?[2]

If you are a Christian leader, you can identify with Hudson
Taylor's inner torment. At least, you should be able to. Christian
leadership is largely about asking people to die. I have lost count
of the number of people that I have had to call to make costly
sacrifices – people who gave up well-paid jobs to become full-
time church workers, people who gave up their friends to move
and plant a new church in another part of the world, people
who decided to forfeit their summer holiday or a new car or a
bigger house in order to help the poor. That's one of the reasons
Luke records for us how Jesus taught his disciples to pastor a
vulnerable widow. He told them to get out of her way.

Jesus is still in the Temple courtyards, having seen off all the
attempts of the Jewish leaders to entrap him. He looks across the
courtyard and sees many rich people throwing large amounts of
money into the Temple offering box, but his eyes are glued to one
particular donor. The widow has nothing. Not only does she lack
a husband and any kind of welfare state to support her, but she
only has to her name two tiny copper coins known as a *lepton*.
There are 128 lepta to a denarius, so both coins put together are
worth less than 2 per cent of the denarius that Jesus told the
spies to send back to Rome. She is in desperate straits. Mark tells
us literally that she is *needy*. Yet Jesus tells the disciples to take
note when she drops both coins into the offering box: *"Truly I
tell you, this poor widow has put in more than all the others. All*

---

[2] John Pollock in his biography *Hudson Taylor and Maria* (1962).

these people gave their gifts out of their wealth; but she out of her poverty put in all she had to live on."[3]

Now for confession time. If I am honest, I would have tried to stop her. I would have pointed out that her gift was unwise. It was unnecessary, since Jesus only mentions giving 10 per cent in 11:42. It was irresponsible, since it would worsen her poverty. I would have told her to give less, or give later, or maybe not give at all. Honestly, I would have tried to redirect her off the death-and-resurrection pathway. I would have told her to go home and die another day.[4]

Jesus reacts very differently, however. He doesn't shout *"Nooo!!"* like my wife did the time she saw me about to put petrol in our diesel car. He doesn't run across the courtyard and rugby tackle the widow before she can land her copper coins across the try line. He commends her to his disciples and, since his words made it into the Bible, he implicitly commands us, whenever we see similar sacrifices, to get out of people's way.

Back on the beach, Hudson Taylor was learning to do this:

*There the Lord conquered my unbelief... I told Him that all the responsibility as to issues and consequences must rest with Him; that as His servant, it was mine to obey and to follow Him—His to direct, to care for, and to guide me and those who might labour with me. Need I say that peace at once flowed into my burdened heart? There and then I asked Him for twenty-four fellow-workers... If we are obeying the Lord, the responsibility rests **with him**, not with us! **Thou**, Lord! **Thou** shalt have the burden. All the responsibility lies on Thee, Lord Jesus! I surrender. The consequences rest with Thee.*[5]

---

[3] What matters is not how much we give, but how much we have left over. This is repeated in Mark 12:41–44.

[4] Luke 16:13 and Hebrews 13:5–6 actually suggest that generous giving is extremely responsible financial planning. It weans us off trusting in this world's riches and on to trusting in the resources of heaven.

[5] Taken from *A Retrospect* and from Pollock's *Hudson Taylor and Maria*.

Jesus wants us to learn this lesson too. It isn't kindness to suffocate a person's eager desire to give God more money than they can afford. Spreadsheets can put out fire as fast as fire blankets. Nor is it kindness to dissuade a friend from breaking up with her non–believing boyfriend, a man in an unhappy marriage from staying and making it happier, a gay friend from submitting his sexuality to Christ or a happy-go-lucky student from throwing it all away to go as a missionary to Nepal. If Jesus is stirring somebody to obey him and you discourage them, you are not partnering with the Holy Spirit. Matthew 16:23 insists that you have become the mouthpiece of Satan.

Instead, get ready to call people to walk the death-and-resurrection pathway with you. Of course, that means you must walk it first, but we have already seen in 14:25–35 that that's simply what Christianity means. There isn't a diluted version. Get used to giving away more money than you can afford. Throw the meticulous measuring stick of the Pharisees away. Get used to spending more time serving at church and sharing the Gospel with unbelievers than you think you can spare. Get used to living life in the deep end of discipleship, saying yes to going to places you don't wish to visit, to tasks you don't wish to do and to a destiny you would never have chosen in a month of Sundays.

Hudson Taylor assures us that it will always be worth it:

> *Fruit-bearing involves cross-bearing... We know how the Lord Jesus became fruitful – not by bearing His Cross merely, but by dying on it. Do we know much of fellowship with Him in this?... If I had a thousand pounds China should have it – if I had a thousand lives, China should have them. No! Not China, but Christ. Can we do too much for Him? Can we do enough for such a precious Saviour?*[6]

---

[6] The first half of this quotation comes from *Hudson Taylor and the China Inland Mission* by Howard Taylor (1918). The second half comes from a letter home to his sister on 14th February 1860.

The Big Wait (21:5–38)

*At that time they will see the Son of Man coming in a
cloud with power and great glory.*

(Luke 21:27)

Jesus is leaving the Temple courtyards. He will never return to
the Temple again. As if that's not enough to make him emotional
already, his disciples start admiring all its beautiful stones. They
are not exaggerating. The Jewish historian Josephus tells us that
some of them were eleven metres long, five metres deep and
three metres high.[1] But they are nowhere near as big as the
wait that Jesus describes for his return from heaven.

On one level, these verses are all about what is about to
happen to the Temple in Jerusalem. Jesus prophesies that it is
about to be razed to the ground. Huge though its stones are,
there won't be one left on another. Jumping down to 21:20–24,
we see that Jesus prophesies that Jerusalem will be surrounded
by Roman armies. Those who fail to get out in time will either
be slaughtered or sold in the slave markets of the empire. Jesus
says this is *"the time of punishment"* that the Old Testament
prophets predicted would come upon the nation of Israel if it
rejected its Messiah.

Forty years after Jesus spoke these words, and less than
ten years after Luke wrote them down, they came horribly true.
When the Jewish high priest was deposed by the Romans for
having illegally executed James, the main leader of the church
in Jerusalem, a backlash swept the Zealots into power and
provoked a full-scale Jewish revolt against Roman rule. The

[1] Josephus in his *Antiquities of the Jews* (15.11.3).

Jews enjoyed some early successes but were eventually pushed back inside Jerusalem by the well-armed and tightly disciplined Roman legions. Josephus was present when the city fell in August 70 AD, and he estimates that over a million Jews were slaughtered: *"They killed those they overtook without mercy and set fire to the houses into which the Jews fled, burning every soul in them... They ran through everyone they met and obstructed the very lanes with their dead bodies, making the whole city run with such blood that the fire of many of the houses was quenched."*[2] The Roman general refused a victory wreath because he saw *"no merit in vanquishing people forsaken by their own God"*.[3]

These verses became very important to the Christians in Jerusalem at that time. The majority of them escaped the destruction as a result of their obedience to the prophecy in 21:21: *"Let those who are in Judea flee to the mountains, let those in the city get out, and let those in the country not enter the city."*[4] That's a salutary reminder to take these verses seriously. They once saved the lives of many Christians, and they may yet save yours.

I say that because it is obvious that these verses were not just written for the generation that lived through the destruction of Jerusalem. Some of the things that Jesus says here must describe the whole of AD history, from the ascension of Jesus to his return. The disciples ask about the destruction of Jerusalem, but his answer encompasses the final destruction of the world and its renewal in God's completed Kingdom.[5]

Jesus warns that there will be many false messiahs (21:8),[6]

---

[2] Josephus in his *Wars of the Jews* (6.8.5–6.9.3). He adds that *"nothing was left there to make visitors believe it had ever been inhabited"* (7.1.1). Jesus wept over Jerusalem for a reason.

[3] Philostratus II in his *Life of Apollonius of Tyana* (6.29).

[4] Their escape is recorded by Eusebius in *Church History* (3.5.3) and by Epiphanius in *Panarion* (29.7.7–8).

[5] In the parallel Matthew 24:3, the disciples ask, *"What will be the sign of your coming and of the end of the age?"*

[6] Another word for false messiah in Greek is *antichrist*. See 1 John 2:18, 22; 4:3; 2 John 7.

many wars and revolutions (21:9–10), and many natural disasters such as earthquakes and famines and epidemics and *"fearful events and great signs from heaven"* (21:11). There will be many waves of persecution against his followers at the hands of the Jews and the Romans and the barbarians (21:12).[7] His earlier warning in 12:49–53 will be fulfilled with such force that many believers will die (21:12–19). I don't think I have ever seen the verse *"Everyone will hate you because of me"* inside a Christian greeting card, but these verses are full of promises of deliverance. Jesus reassures us that his Spirit will come to the rescue and will reveal to us what we need to say to convert our persecutors to Christ (21:13–15). He pledges to give us life, even if receiving it means that many of us are going to die.[8]

Some of the verses that speak most clearly about the destruction of Jerusalem in 70 AD also convey a longer-term meaning. The whole of AD history will spell judgment for the Jewish nation for having rejected its Messiah, but there will finally come a moment when *"the times of the Gentiles are fulfilled"* (21:22–24). Paul prophesies about this in Romans 11, explaining that *"Israel has experienced a hardening in part until the full number of the Gentiles has come in"* and that *"Salvation has come to the Gentiles to make Israel envious... In this way all Israel will be saved."*[9] That's why there has been such a big wait for Jesus to come back. He has worked out a way to make the Jewish nation regret having rejected him, provoking a wave of mass Jewish conversions to him before his glorious return.

Jesus describes this second coming in 21:25–28. We are not to be alarmed when the planet that we are living on seems

---

[7] *Synagogues* refers to Jews, *governors* refers to Romans and *kings* refers to the tribute rulers of the barbarians.

[8] Verses 18–19 do not mean that we will not be harmed. Verse 16 warns bluntly that some of us will die! Rather, it means that our souls will be delivered safely to eternal life, even as they are ripped from our bodies.

[9] *All* Israel does not mean that 100% of Jews will turn to Jesus. It is a stock phrase in the Old Testament, which means *a vast number representing every single tribe and clan within Israel.*

to be endangered, or when terrors and terrorists rule. We are to stand strong, even as the unbelievers around us drop their heads in despair. All of this is the necessary prelude to the moment when the big wait will finally be over: *"At that time they will see the Son of Man coming in a cloud with power and great glory."*[10]

Jesus does not hide any of this from us. He expands on these verses even further in the final book of the Bible. If you are interested, you can read *Straight to the Heart of Revelation*, but for now let's end with the list of things that Jesus says we are to do.

We are to *be discerning*. He has given us this prophecy of what will happen throughout AD history so that we can watch and see the plotline of his Kingdom unfurling before our eyes (21:29–31). We are to *be jubilant*. These events are not disasters. They mean that the Kingdom of God is about to be consummated. The "now and not yet" is about to become simply now (21:31). We are to *be confident*. Neither the Jewish race nor the Word of God will be destroyed during this big wait. God has it all under control (21:32–33).[11]

We are to *be watchful*, not allowing ourselves to get caught up in the things of this brief passing age that will soon disappear and be replaced by the new heavens and the new earth (21:34–35). We are to *be prayerful* that God will protect us and help us to stand before Jesus as faithful servants and to receive our reward (21:36).

If we do this, the big wait will all be worth it when Jesus finally returns. The Messiah came once to be rejected, but he is coming back again to rule.

---

[10] In 21:27, Jesus claims to be God, paraphrasing Daniel 7:13 to present himself as the starter and finisher of history. In 21:33, he equates his own words with the words of God, and in 21:36 says he is the divine Judge.

[11] The Greek word *genea* must refer to the Jewish *race* in 21:32 rather than to the disciples' *generation*. The survival of the Jewish race against all odds is a powerful testimony that all these promises will come true.

Snakes and Ladders
(22:1–38)

Who is greater, the one who is at the table or the one who serves?... But I am among you as one who serves.

(Luke 22:27)

My children love the game Snakes and Ladders. I'm sure you have played it too. They love the way somebody can roll a six and look as though they are on track to win the game, only to discover with horror that a six lands them on a snake and sends them plummeting right back down to the bottom of the board. Meanwhile, someone else rolls a one and looks as though they are getting left behind by the other players. Suddenly they realize that a one brings them to the bottom of a ladder and permits them to climb past all the other players to take the lead. Snakes and Ladders is full of surprises – a bit like chapter 22 of Luke's gospel.

In 22:1–6, Judas Iscariot rolls what looks like a winning number. He has found a way to get rich fast. The Jewish leaders are desperate to kill Jesus, but they are afraid of the crowd of pilgrims that has packed the city for the Passover Festival.[1] At night, when the crowds are asleep, they have no idea where to find him, for he is too smart to sleep in any of the houses in their city.[2] As one of the twelve apostles, Judas knows where he sleeps each night on the Mount of Olives, looking out across the

---

[1] Luke 19:47–48 is echoed by Matthew 26:3–5 and Mark 14:1–2.

[2] Jesus slept in a secret location on a hillside (21:37) because his enemies would otherwise have surrounded and stormed his city lodgings while the crowds were asleep (1 Samuel 19:11–12; 23:7).

Kidron Valley towards Jerusalem. None of the other disciples has thought to turn this knowledge into money, so Judas moves fast. He agrees to lead the Jewish leaders to Jesus' hideout in return for cash.[3]

Judas has rolled a six, but it lands him on a snake. We are meant to be horrified by the words, *"Satan entered Judas, called Iscariot, one of the Twelve."* Judas was one of the Twelve sent out by Jesus to see many people saved, healed and delivered throughout Galilee. He helped train the Seventy-Two sent out by Jesus on a second mission trip throughout Judea, who rejoiced in 10:17 that *"Lord, even the demons submit to us in your name."* Now he rejects partnership with God's Spirit and enters into partnership with Satan.[4] By choosing the path of money instead of the death-and-resurrection pathway, he trades in happiness for misery, significance for infamy, obedience for rebellion and heaven for hell.[5]

In 22:7–13, Jesus looks as though he has rolled a one. The population of Jerusalem trebled at Passover time, so there is barely a spare bed in the city. Anyone who wants to hire a room that can seat thirteen for dinner needed to have booked it days ago. But Jesus isn't worried. Today is *"the day of Unleavened Bread on which the Passover lamb had to be sacrificed"*, so he knows that his Father will provide all that he needs to fulfil the Passover Festival through his own body.[6] Dependence on God

---

[3] Luke does not tell us how much money Judas received. Matthew 26:15 says that it was 30 silver coins, the equivalent of 6 weeks' wages for a labourer or the usual price tag for a slave (Exodus 21:32).

[4] Luke 22:3 and John 13:27 use language normally reserved for people being filled with the Holy Spirit. If we refuse to partner with God's Spirit then we open ourselves up to unwitting partnership with evil spirits.

[5] Despite having once wielded the badge and gun of God's Kingdom, Judas went to hell because he played around with sin (John 12:1–6; 17:12). That's a pretty sobering thought.

[6] Different rabbis counted dates differently, so Jesus was able to celebrate the Passover in the evening with his disciples according to one calendar yet fulfil it the following afternoon according to another.

as our Father may look weak and foolish, but it always lands us on a ladder. The Holy Spirit reveals to Jesus where he can find a fully furnished function room, just as he revealed where to find a donkey in 19:30.[7] When the disciples do as Jesus commands, they discover that their Master's simple faith is the perfect dice roll.

In 22:14–23, Jesus tries to teach the disciples that it always is. Puffing ourselves up always pulls us downwards, whereas bowing down in humility always leads us upwards. Jesus explains to the disciples that the bread and wine that lie at the heart of the Passover meal speak of something that is about to be fulfilled in the coming of the Kingdom of God.[8] As he breaks the bread, he tells them that his body is about to be torn apart so that, through his death, they will be able to live.[9] As he passes round the wine, he explains that his blood is about to be shed to inaugurate a new and better Covenant than the one that the original Passover generation received from the Lord at Mount Sinai.[10] Whenever it looks as though the game has turned against them, they are to remember that his crucifixion forms the centrepiece of God's plan. *"The Son of Man will go as it has been decreed."* The glorious promises of Scripture are about to be fulfilled.

In 22:24–30, the disciples demonstrate how little they understand this. They start to argue over which one of them has

---

[7] It was very unusual to see a first-century Jew carrying water through the streets, since fetching water from a well was considered a menial chore for women and for children.

[8] Although writing in Greek, Luke records Jesus' very Hebrew way of expressing himself in 22:15: *"I have eagerly desired with eager desiring."* He wants to emphasize the Jewishness of this festival moment.

[9] Jesus tells the disciples to eat bread *"in remembrance"* of his sacrifice, so *"this is my body"* cannot possibly mean that bread becomes his body as we eat it. Rather, it is a symbol that helps us to remember.

[10] God's covenants throughout the Bible are always made through the shedding of sacrificial blood (Exodus 24:8; Hebrews 9:15–28). The blood of an innocent lamb also lies at the heart of the Jewish Passover meal.

rolled the biggest number on the dice.[11] They are so like Judas Iscariot in their thinking that, in verse 23, they cannot even tell which one of them is the fake believer.[12] All of them still hope to use Jesus to further their own ambitions. They want to become top dog in a Church that exists to flatter their own egos. Jesus has to correct them fast. They will one day sit on thrones and rule the universe with him, but first they need to follow in his footsteps down the death-and-resurrection road.[13] They need to assume the position of the youngest child in the family or the most junior servant in the household. In this Snakes and Ladders world, the only way to go up is down.[14]

In 22:31–38, Jesus turns to Simon Peter, the emerging leader among the Twelve. He has been rolling sixes throughout Luke's gospel. Jesus preached from his boat and healed at his house. Jesus invited him and only two other disciples to witness his glory on the Mount of Transfiguration and at the raising of a dead girl to life. Jesus had even renamed him Peter to declare that he was precisely the kind of rock with which he loves to build. But here he calls him Simon. He warns that he will deny his Master three times before the night is through.[15]

---

[11] Luke records this here because he failed to mention a similar debate on the road to Jerusalem in Matthew 20:25–28 and Mark 10:41–45. This question was evidently the source of frequent fighting among the disciples. It is still the true source of many of the disputes within our churches today.

[12] John 13:29 tells us that Judas looked like such an authentic disciple that the others assumed he must have left dinner to run an errand for Jesus or to take a gift to the poor.

[13] Since Jesus uses a Greek present participle in 22:30, he isn't merely promising them a one-off role on Judgment Day. He is saying that they will rule with him forever. This should end all our rivalry. Those who have been promised a Ferrari tend not to argue over who owns the clapped-out banger in the driveway.

[14] This promise is for us too. The Greek verb *to confer* in 22:29 is the root of the Greek noun *covenant* in 22:20.

[15] *"That's enough!"* in 22:38 probably means *"That's enough talking!"* Jesus isn't so much telling his disciples to arm themselves as pointing out that the night will be even more violent than it is cold (John 18:10–11, 18).

Nevertheless, these verses end in hope. In 22:37, Jesus quotes from Isaiah 53 to assure his disciples that all that the Snake wants to do to them is about to be reversed through a single winning dice roll. It will look as if the Messiah has failed. Whenever God's Kingdom is forcefully advancing, it usually does. Like in a game of Snakes and Ladders, Jesus is about to win a mighty victory by appearing to have thrown it all away.

Parallel Lives (22:39–53)

Yet not my will, but yours be done.

(Luke 22:42)

A long time ago there was a man named Adam. He lived in a garden that was entirely free from sorrow and from pain. He enjoyed face-to-face chats with God every evening and he only had to do one thing to maintain his garden paradise forever. He had to say no to eating from the one tree in the garden the fruit of which he was forbidden to taste. To make their friendship genuine, the Lord invited him to make an active daily choice. He was to look at the tree and pray obediently, *"Lord, not my will but yours be done."*[1]

I'm sure you know the story. Adam made the wrong choice. He was with his wife Eve when Satan appeared as a snake to tempt her, yet he failed to lift a finger to defend her.[2] Having failed to do right by his wife, he then did wrong by the Lord. He joined her in eating the forbidden fruit. Instead of choosing friendship with God in an eternal paradise, he chose to speak defiant words to his Creator: *"Lord, not your will but mine!"*

Genesis 3 describes the curse which fell on the world as a result of Adam's sin. When the human race yielded its authority on the earth to Satan, it lost its immunity to his hatred towards them. The ground started to produce thorns and destructive weeds that choked the crops they needed for their food, turning their sweet gardening into sweaty and exhausting

---

[1] Genesis 3:3 says that God placed the tree in the middle of the garden so that Adam made a choice each day.

[2] Genesis 3:6 tells us that Adam *"was with her"* when she was tempted.

toil. Marriage had been created to be one of their greatest joys, but it morphed into power play: men abusing their wives and women manipulating their husbands. Family had been created to be another great joy, but it soon became shrouded in pain. From the pangs of childbirth to fierce fighting among siblings, everything the Devil touched began to smell of hellish death instead of heavenly life. Death lay at the heart of the curse on humankind.

It is a pretty bleak start to the Bible, but if you read Genesis 3 carefully you will also notice that it's a story filled with hope. Even as he pronounces a curse over the world, God prophesies that a man will be born who will succeed where Adam failed. He warns the Devil, *"I will put enmity between you and the woman, and between your offspring and hers; he will crush your head, and you will strike his heel."*

When we read about what happened to Jesus in the Garden of Gethsemane, we are meant to spot that these are parallel lives.[3] This is no paradise. We are told that Jesus is in such anguish that he sweats drops of blood. Since these words do not appear in all Greek manuscripts, many scholars used to laugh at 22:43–44 until the trenches of World War One produced several similar cases of what doctors now call haematidrosis. Several soldiers were observed to sweat drops of blood in the last few minutes before they died of shock during a battle. Jesus feels the same anguish as he faces up to Adam's curse here, except he doesn't die. He is the Offspring of Eve, the one who succeeds where Adam failed and who looks death in the face and stares it down. He is the one that Paul describes in 1 Corinthians 15:45 as *"the last Adam"*.

These are parallel lives, so note how different Jesus is from

---

[3] Luke merely tells us that Jesus prayed somewhere on the Mount of Olives. John 18:1 and 26 say that it was in a *garden* on the hillside. Matthew 26:36 names it as the Garden of Gethsemane, or the *Garden of the Oil Press*. Jesus evidently had permission from the owner of an olive orchard to sleep on his land.

Adam. Adam failed to protect Eve from temptation in the Garden of Eden, but Jesus warns his disciples to *"Pray that you will not fall into temptation."*[4] Adam blamed Eve for her failure, but Jesus overlooks the failure of his disciples by waking them up and urging them a second time to *"Get up and pray so that you will not fall into temptation."*[5] Adam fooled himself that he was strong enough to resist temptation, but Jesus is very honest with his Father that he wants to say no to the death-and-resurrection road.[6] The biggest difference of all is what the two men say at the end of their struggle with temptation in the garden. Adam said, *"Not your will but mine,"* but Jesus ends his prayer with *"Yet not my will, but yours be done."*

Jesus has succeeded in the garden where Adam failed. As a result, the curse on the human race goes into sudden reverse. Can there be any worse example of this fallen world's hypocrisy and sinfulness than the moment when Judas Iscariot betrays Jesus with a kiss, feigning friendship to identify him in the darkness to the men who want to kill him? Yet Jesus responds to him with love and truth, full of concern for the fate of Judas rather than his own: *"Judas, are you betraying the Son of Man with a kiss?"* Adam blamed Eve and pushed her away, but Jesus forgives Judas and reaches out to him.

Can there be any clearer example of the violence of this fallen world than an army of five to six hundred men, armed with swords and clubs, who are dispatched to arrest one preacher

---

[4] Matthew and Mark emphasize that Jesus said this to Peter, James and John. Luke adds that he also said it to the other disciples. He did not ask the Eleven to pray for him as much as for themselves.

[5] Luke only mentions that the disciples fell asleep once. This is generous. Matthew and Mark tell us that they actually fell asleep three times in succession.

[6] Jesus prayed to be spared the crucifixion if there were any other way in which people could be saved. The fact the Father refused his request is very powerful proof that no salvation exists outside Jesus (Acts 4:12).

of peace while he prays alone?[7] Yet Jesus intervenes to stop his outnumbered disciples from attempting to defend him, and he heals one of the violent gang that suffers a severed ear.[8] Luke is the only gospel writer to record this healing – the last miracle that Jesus performed before he died – to show us that, even at this late stage, Jesus was fully in control.[9] Adam took matters into his own hands in the Garden of Eden and lost control to Satan, but Jesus submits to his Father's will in the Garden of Gethsemane and remains Lord of all that happens to him here.[10]

Think of the scene in the famous Christmas movie *It's a Wonderful Life*, where George Bailey sees his home town of Bedford Falls as it would have been had he never lived. Renamed Pottersville, it is a hotbed of crime and oppression and abject misery. Jesus performs the reverse of that famous scene here. By succeeding in the garden where Adam failed, he paves the way for Adamsville to be restored as Paradise. All that Adam lost in the Garden of Eden, Jesus wins back in the Garden of Gethsemane.

So take a moment to reflect on these two parallel lives in worship. Luke proclaims that the curse over humanity has been lifted through the obedience of Jesus. The reign of sin and death is over. The new Adam has overcome.

---

[7] John 18:12 says that they were led by a *chiliarch*, the commander of several centuries of soldiers.

[8] John 18:10 tells us that the servant was named Malchus and that Peter was the disciple who chopped off his ear. Lashing out at our enemies seldom results in our gaining a healthy hearing for our message.

[9] Matthew 26:53, Mark 14:49 and John 18:5–8 make the same point in different ways. If he had wanted to, Jesus could have escaped their clutches as easily as he did in Luke 4:29–30.

[10] He declares literally in 22:53 that he is submitting to their arrest only because this is the brief hour that God has decreed for *the authority of darkness* to reign.

Innocent (22:54–23:25)

Pilate announced to the chief priests and the crowd,
"I find no basis for a charge against this man."

(Luke 23:4)

Following Jesus in a world that was ruled by Emperor Nero was a dangerous affair. When Paul invoked his right as a Roman citizen to have his case heard by Caesar's court in Rome, he was under no illusion about how much justice he could expect to find there. The Roman historian Suetonius tells us that Nero *"showed neither discrimination nor moderation in putting to death whoever he pleased on any pretext whatsoever"*.[1] As Paul waited to be heard by Judge Theophilus, the Christian faith therefore stood in grave peril.

Theophilus must have been deeply suspicious of Paul and his Christian friends. After all, a Roman governor had executed Jesus as a criminal. As for Paul, he knew full well that Nero brooked no rivals, yet he preached that Jesus had risen from the dead and been declared by God to be the true King of kings. That's why Luke works so hard in these verses to convince Theophilus that Jesus was the innocent victim of a terrible miscarriage of Roman justice. Luke knows that Paul's trial will quickly become a test case for Christianity as a whole, so the stakes are very high. He therefore records five of Jesus' trials that proved beyond all doubt that he was innocent of any crime.

---

[1] He wrote this in c. 120 AD in his *Life of Nero* (37). Paul's appeal in Acts 25:11–12 was a dangerous gamble.

Luke tells us about the first trial in 22:54–65.[2] Jesus is taken to the house of the Jewish high priest Caiaphas, where the members of the Sanhedrin cannot contain their delight to finally have him in their power. Luke gives much less detail about this trial than Matthew and Mark, choosing instead to focus only on the areas where the trial contravened both Jewish and Roman law. He tells us that it took place at the dead of night, which was forbidden in order to prevent shady kangaroo courts such as this one.[3] The Sanhedrin are not interested in seeking justice, but in settling old scores, so they break the law a second time by beating their prisoner before they have passed judgment on him.[4] Luke wants Theophilus to know beyond all doubt that Paul's Jewish accusers care nothing for law and for justice. They are attempting to manipulate Rome.

When Jesus goes on trial for a second time, in 22:66–71, it is a tacit admission that his first trial was illegal.[5] The Sanhedrin reconvenes at daybreak to pass sentence because it knows that its secret night-time session was against the law. The process does not take long because the leading Jewish judges are not seeking justice as much as a legal fig leaf that will cover up their naked crime. The only fault they can find in Jesus is that he claims to be the Son of Man and the Son of God.[6] When they use this to convict him of blasphemy, the irony is not

---

[2] Jesus was actually put on trial 6 times in 12 hours. Luke misses out the very first of the 6 trials, which took place before the deposed former high priest Annas. You can read about it in John 18:12–24.

[3] This is explicitly forbidden in Sanhedrin 4:1, which is part of the Mishnah in the Jewish Talmud.

[4] See Acts 23:3. The Greek word *derō* means *to thrash* or *to flay*, suggesting a severe beating that drew blood. The Jewish leaders can't wait to inflict on Jesus' body the hatred that sinful humanity feels towards God.

[5] In 22:66, Luke uses the Greek words *sunedrion* (Sanhedrin) and *presbuterion* (council of elders) in order to ensure that Theophilus understands the function of the Sanhedrin in Jewish Law.

[6] Although *Son of Man* and *Son of God* describe Jesus as fully human and fully divine, they are meant primarily as titles of the long-awaited Messiah (see Daniel 7:13; 1 Chronicles 17:13–14).

lost on Theophilus. The Greek word that Luke used in 22:65 to describe the Sanhedrin insulting Jesus is *blasphēmeō*. Luke makes it very clear that it's the enemies of Jesus who are the real blasphemers.[7]

Things get even more uncomfortable for Theophilus when Jesus goes on trial for a third time, in 23:1–7. Pontius Pilate is the Roman governor of Judea and is therefore the highest representative of Roman justice in the land. He knows that the Jewish leaders are spinning lies in order to manipulate him.[8] Jesus had explicitly commanded the crowds to pay their taxes to Caesar and resisted all of their attempts to cast him as the leader of an armed rebellion against Rome. What's more, the Sanhedrin has subtly shifted its charge from one of blasphemy (which was of little concern to Pilate) to one of subverting Caesar's rule (which Pilate could not afford to be seen to ignore). Pilate tells them frankly that *"I find no basis for a charge against this man,"* yet astonishingly he lacks the moral backbone to follow through on his own verdict and to set Jesus free.[9] Instead, he takes the coward's way out. He latches on to the fact that Jesus is from Galilee, Herod the tetrarch's jurisdiction, and sends him on for yet another trial instead of releasing him. Luke wants Theophilus to stop thinking of Jesus as a convicted criminal and to consider him a victim of the well-recounted injustices of Rome.

---

[7] The plural *archiereis* in 22:66 cannot refer to the two *high priests*. It must refer to the *chief priests* who led the 24 priestly clans (1 Chronicles 24:6–18) and who held seats on the 71-man Sanhedrin. All of the priestly clans therefore gathered as one team in order to sacrifice the innocent Lamb of God together.

[8] The Sanhedrin lacked authority to execute anyone for blasphemy so they had to go through Pilate. In doing so, they merely fulfilled Jesus' prediction in 9:22–23 and Matthew 20:18–19 that he would be crucified in the Roman fashion rather than stoned in the Jewish fashion.

[9] Pilate knew that the Jewish leaders were simply jealous of Jesus (Matthew 27:18; Mark 15:10), but he feared that they might ruin his career by complaining about him to the Emperor Tiberius (John 19:12). Ironically, Josephus tells us in *Antiquities of the Jews* that he lost his governorship over a separate incident shortly afterwards and was recalled to Rome in disgrace, never to recover (18.4.1–2).

When Jesus goes on trial for a fourth time, in 23:8–12, it makes Roman justice look even worse.[10] Herod Antipas is Caesar's man in Galilee, yet, instead of seeing through the accusations of the Jewish leaders, he turns his courtroom into an amusement arcade, demanding that Jesus perform a miracle to entertain the courtiers who have travelled with him to Jerusalem for the Passover Feast. When Jesus refuses to perform like a circus pony, Herod treats him as shamefully as the Jewish leaders. He then cosies up to Pilate, having found common ground in their mutual disregard for Roman justice.

This leads into the fifth and final trial, in 23:13–25. Although Jesus is standing in the dock, Luke makes it clear that sentence is being passed on Roman justice in this scene. Pilate declares for a second time that Jesus is innocent – *"I have examined him in your presence and have found no basis for your charges against him. Neither has Herod... He has done nothing to deserve death"* – then he astonishes us by ignoring his own verdict: *"Therefore, I will punish him and then release him."* Pilate demonstrates that Roman justice matters far less than peace in the provinces. It is something which can be bought and sold.

The Jewish leaders know how to work the crowd, so Pilate's verdict provokes uproar.[11] The crowd have no new evidence to bring against Jesus, yet they demand that he must be crucified all the same. Pilate repeats a third time that *"I have found in him no grounds for the death penalty. Therefore I will have him punished and then release him."*[12] Yet it is clear now that mob rule will prevail. Pilate releases a convicted murderer and insurrectionist against Roman rule before crucifying an

234

[10] The trial before Herod is unique to Luke's gospel. It represents Roman rule at its very worst.

[11] Luke is warning Theophilus not to listen to the public prejudice against Christians in Rome. Crowds are fickle, hailing Jesus as their Messiah one moment and demanding his execution the next.

[12] Luke follows up these statements in his gospel that Jesus is innocent with similar statements in Acts that Paul could have gone free had he not appealed to Caesar (Acts 25:10–12, 25; 26:31–32; 28:18–19).

innocent man. As Theophilus prepares to hear Paul's defence in his courtroom, Luke therefore wants these five trials to make him hang his head in shame over the Roman injustices that have brought him there.

On the other hand, Luke wants us to lift our faces in triumph. He wants us to grasp that, if even the sworn enemies of Jesus could not prove him guilty, he truly is the only innocent person who has ever lived. He truly is the only spotless, sinless sacrifice that can atone for our own sin. He truly is the one that John the Baptist says he is in John 1:29, when he exclaims, *"Look, the Lamb of God, who takes away the sin of the world!"*

Three Men in a Boat
(22:54–23:25)

He released the man who had been thrown into prison for insurrection and murder, the one they asked for, and surrendered Jesus to their will.

(Luke 23:25)

I like the metaphors that Alistair Maclean uses in his novels. Here's one of my favourites: *"We were in the same boat and it was sinking fast."*[1] In these verses, Luke talks about three men whose boats were sinking fast with that of Jesus. He wants to use their differing reactions to what happened to Jesus to call us to make our own response to him. He reminds us once again: *All of this happened for you.*

The first man whose boat is sinking fast is a newcomer to the story. We are meant to see Barabbas as a satanic parody of all that is good about Jesus. Although his Aramaic name means *Son of the Father* and he has been arrested as a would-be messiah, he is a far cry from the real Son of God.[2] Jesus respected authority, even that of Caesar, whereas Barabbas has led an armed insurrection against Roman rule. Jesus established his Kingdom through the power of the Holy Spirit, whereas Barabbas has put his faith in force of arms. Even at this very moment, Jesus is laying down his life for others, whereas Barabbas has murdered

---

[1] This line comes from *Fear Is The Key* (1961). His most famous novels are *Where Eagles Dare* and *The Guns of Navarone*.

[2] Although Luke gives his short name in 23:17–25, some Greek manuscripts of Matthew 27:16–17 give his full name as *Jesus Barabbas*. He is an antichrist, a false messiah, a satanic imposter.

those who got in his way. Even as a prisoner, Jesus is in control of what is happening to him, whereas Barabbas is languishing on death row, powerless to prevent his crucifixion later that day. Jesus is godly even in the face of death, while Barabbas is at the very bottom of the pile.

But a glimmer of light shines into his prison cell. Jesus is willing to step into his sinking boat for him. Luke tells us in 23:17 that *"Pilate was obliged to release one prisoner to them during the feast."*[3] That's Roman justice for you: the law can be set aside at the blink of an eye, but unjust traditions are inviolable. Pilate hopes to use the tradition to release Jesus without having to cross the Sanhedrin. After all, Jesus can remind the crowd that it was he who healed them, he who fed them, he who taught them and he who loved them – not the members of the Sanhedrin, who ooze charm to win their votes now but who fiercely despised them only yesterday. Pilate therefore offers Jesus his freedom on a plate, but Jesus refuses to court votes like a contestant on *The X Factor*. He lets the crowd cry out for Barabbas to be freed, because he is dying to save sinners just like him.[4]

In 23:25, Barabbas finds himself blinking in the sunlight and soaking up the sweet smell of freedom. Jesus has stepped into his sinking boat so that he can place his feet back on firm ground. The true Messiah dies so that the pretender can live.

The second man whose boat is sinking fast is Judas Iscariot. He has done the unthinkable. He has betrayed the Messiah into the hands of his enemies. Luke emphasizes his aloneness by saying nothing about what he did after the arrest of Jesus. He only tells us later, in Acts 1:15–20, that *"Judas, who served as guide for those who arrested Jesus... fell headlong, his body burst open and*

---

[3] Many of the most accurate Greek manuscripts do not contain 23:17. It may have been added later by someone who felt Luke's gospel required the same explanation as Matthew 27:15–26 and Mark 15:6–15.

[4] Luke emphasizes in 23:9 that Jesus remained largely silent throughout his trials. He could have talked himself out of crucifixion, but his silent willingness to die fulfilled the prophecy in Isaiah 53:7.

all his intestines spilled out." Matthew 27:1–10 tells us that he only hanged himself after he saw *"that Jesus was condemned"*, so the news about Jesus trading places with Barabbas must have spread quickly across Jerusalem. This offered hope to Judas. If Jesus had been willing to step into the sinking boat of a false messiah, maybe he was willing to step into the sinking boat of a failed disciple too. Judas refused to believe it. The Gospel sounded too good to be true. He regretted his actions, but he did not repent. He died stubborn and alone.

If you have been reading Luke's gospel closely so far, you must have sensed your own sin. Which of us has consistently said what Mary says in 1:38: *"I am the Lord's servant"*? Which of us has resisted the Devil's temptations as firmly as Jesus in 4:1–13 or partnered consistently with the Holy Spirit? We are all sinners, every single one of us, so Luke warns us not to mistake sorrow for faith or remorse for repentance, like Judas. He calls us to come to Jesus and ask him to switch places with us. He tells us to pray that what he did for Barabbas he will do for us too.

The third man whose boat is sinking fast is Simon Peter. He too has done the unthinkable. He has watched Jesus heal the sick and drive out demons and raise corpses back to life. He has seen him transfigured into his heavenly glory. He has listened to three years of teaching and emerged as the leading apostle among the Twelve. Since Jesus says that we are guilty in proportion to the revelation we have received, Peter's denials make him even guiltier than Judas and Barabbas. Having boasted in 22:33 that *"Lord, I am ready to go with you to prison and to death,"* he has saved his own skin by denying three times that he even knows him. He has deserted his Master at the very moment when he needed him most. Luke says that as the cock crowed, fulfilling Jesus' prediction that Peter would deny him, Jesus was being led across the courtyard and *"turned and looked straight at Peter"*. The former fisherman was overwhelmed by the scale of his sin. *"He went outside and wept bitterly."*

Unlike Judas, however, Peter repents. He remembers what Jesus promised him in 22:31–32: *"Simon, Satan has asked to sift all of you as wheat. But I have prayed for you, Simon, that your faith may not fail. And when you have turned back, strengthen your brothers."*[5] He accepts that Jesus knows the very worst about him but still wishes to forgive him and continue to partner with him. He accepts that however much his sin has surprised him, it didn't surprise God. Peter steps out of his sinking boat by believing that Jesus has made a way for sinners, just like him.

So before you move on to the next few verses and read about the crucifixion of Jesus, make sure that you have laid your own sin down at the foot of his cross. Make sure that you have grasped the full scandal of the Gospel. God knows the very worst about you but he still loves you. The same grace that saved Barabbas from death row is also extended to you. If you step out of the sinking boat of your sin, you will be saved.

---

[5] Note Satan's limited authority. He even has to ask for permission to test us! The Greek text says that Satan asked to tempt all the apostles (*you plural*) but that Jesus prayed for Peter to bring them back (*you singular*). Even as he prophesied Peter's failure, Jesus reassured him that he had still chosen him to lead.

Read Between the Lines
(23:26–46)

There was a written notice above him, which read:
THIS IS THE KING OF THE JEWS.

(Luke 23:38)

A boss was forced to write a job reference for a lazy and incompetent former employee. His words are glowing, but read between the lines what he really thinks about him.

> *I cannot say enough good things about him or recommend him too highly. He never cared how many hours were needed to complete a task, and when he left our firm all of us were very satisfied. Many times I felt that there was nothing I could teach him and that his true ability was deceiving. You will be very lucky if you can get him to work at your company and I urge you to waste no time in interviewing him, because nobody would be better for this job than him. I therefore commend him to you as a job candidate with no qualifications whatsoever, certain that he will move on from your firm just as he has arrived at it: fired with much enthusiasm.*

Luke wants us to read between the lines when we study his account of the crucifixion of Jesus. On the surface, he appears to be describing defeat and disaster, but he gives us several hints that this is actually the account of an astonishing victory over the Devil.

In 23:26, Luke hints that Jesus is marking out the death-

and-resurrection pathway for each one of us to follow. Like a jungle explorer with a machete, he goes on ahead of us to carve out what he has kept on telling us is the way to victory. In 9:23–24, he warned his followers that *"Whoever wants to be my disciple must deny themselves and take up their cross daily and follow me. For whoever wants to save their life will lose it, but whoever loses their life for me will save it."* In 14:27, he repeated, *"Whoever does not carry their cross and follow me cannot be my disciple."* When Jesus proves too weak from his flogging to carry his own cross to Calvary, the Roman soldiers therefore become unwitting Gospel preachers.[1] They press-gang Simon of Cyrene into carrying the cross behind him, illustrating what it truly means for us to follow Jesus.[2] Discipleship means dying to our own desires in order to experience God's resurrection power. The Calvary road is our pathway too.[3]

In 23:27–31, Luke hints that Jesus is the sinless sacrifice who suffers in our place. Anyone can conceal dark aspects of their character when everything is going well, but times of adversity reveal our hearts for what they really are. A lemon can masquerade as an orange in a fruit bowl, but not in a juicer. Jesus therefore demonstrates the true depth of his character by caring deeply for the fate of Jerusalem, even as Jerusalem rejects him. He quotes from a prophecy of judgment against Jerusalem in Hosea 10:8 because, even as they kill him, he still invites them to be saved through him. Instead of cursing them for their dead-wood religion, he points out that he is being nailed to a cross for them.[4]

---

[1] Luke does not describe much of Jesus' pre-crucifixion torture, but see Matthew 27:27–31 and John 19:1–3.

[2] *Cyrene* was a city in modern-day Libya, so Simon was presumably a Passover pilgrim. Luke is the only gospel writer to emphasize that he carried the cross *behind* Jesus, deliberately tying in with 9:23 and 14:27.

[3] *Calvaria* means *the Place of the Skull* in Latin (23:33). It is *Golgotha* in Aramaic.

[4] The prophecy warns Israel that, if they reject God's King (Hosea 10:3), their children will pay (Hosea 9:11–17). The proverb about dead wood and green wood shows he is more horrified by their fate than his own.

In 23:34, Luke hints that Jesus is the one who intercedes for us in heaven. Recording three of his seven sayings from the cross, Luke is the only gospel writer to tell us that Jesus interceded for his murderers as he died: *"Father, forgive them, for they do not know what they are doing."*[5] The New Testament letters inform us that Jesus is offering prayers of intercession to God the Father in heaven on our behalf right now, but they give us little detail about what he says in those prayers.[6] Luke fills in the blanks for us here. Even as Jesus dies, he starts praying to the Father that our many sins will be forgiven.[7]

In 23:38, Luke hints that the sufferings of Jesus are how he has defeated the Devil. Pontius Pilate was easily manipulated by the Jewish leaders, but he finds enough courage to express his resentment towards them by ordering a notice to be nailed above the head of Jesus which declares that *"This is the King of the Jews."*[8] Matthew 8:16–17 explains that the cross lies at the heart of the coming of God's Kingdom. By stretching out his arms to embrace the toxic effects of our sin in his own body, Jesus completely rid Satan of the authority and power which he wielded against us. Colossians 2:15 repeats this, saying that Satan is now a disarmed enemy who is on the run from God's Kingdom. At first glance, these verses appear to describe the defeat of the Messiah and the victory of the Devil, but read between the lines. In fact, it is the other way round.

In 23:39–43, Luke hints that Jesus is rejoicing in his victory

---

[5] The other four sayings from the cross can be found in Matthew 27:46 and in John 19:27, 19:28 and 19:30.

[6] See Romans 8:34; 1 Timothy 2:5; Hebrews 7:25; 1 John 2:1.

[7] A very small percentage of Greek manuscripts do not contain 23:34. We can be confident that this verse belongs to the text and that Jesus therefore practised what he preached in 6:27–38. Although he quotes in 23:46 from Psalm 31:5, note the marked difference between his attitude and that of David in Psalm 31:17!

[8] John 19:20 tells us that the sign was written in Latin, Greek and Aramaic. Jesus is the King of the Jews but he invites people from every nation and language to enter into his Kingdom.

even through the pain. When one of the criminals crucified with Jesus declares that *"This man has done nothing wrong"* – clearly another pointed challenge to Theophilus – Jesus responds to his faith with an astonishing promise. Today his Kingdom has finally come. Crucifixion may be the most painful way that anyone can die, but Jesus tells the forgiven criminal that they will both be enjoying the delights of Paradise together by nightfall and forevermore.

In 23:44–46, Luke hints that Jesus is in control of every detail of his own crucifixion. The sun goes dark for the final three hours of his life because creation weeps over the murder of its Creator. The wind that Jesus stilled on Lake Galilee proclaims once more that he is Master by ripping apart the Temple curtain as a great sign to the Jewish nation that the Old Covenant has been superseded by the New. Even the way in which Jesus dies declares his sovereignty. His life is not taken from him. When he sees that his act of sacrifice has been completed, he permits his spirit to leave his broken body, praying loudly, *"Father, into your hands I commit my spirit."*[9]

Throughout these verses, Luke therefore presents the death of Jesus as the fulfilment of God's great plan. The fact that the Romans meet Simon of Cyrene at the city gate hints that Jesus fulfilled the ancient prophecy that the Messiah would die outside the city.[10] The fact that he is executed alongside criminals, afflicted by thirst, while soldiers divide his clothing as plunder fulfils the ancient prophecies in Isaiah 53:12, Psalm 69:21 and Psalm 22:18.[11] The fact that he dies at three in the afternoon, the very moment when the Passover lambs are being sacrificed a few hundred metres away in the Temple courtyards,

---

[9] The Greek word *ekpneō* is only used elsewhere in the New Testament in Mark 15:37 and 39. Jesus voluntarily *gave up his spirit* (John 10:18). He didn't just endure death for our sake; he embraced it willingly.

[10] Leviticus 4:21 and Numbers 19:3, as explained in Hebrews 13:11–13.

[11] See Luke 22:37; John 19:28, 24.

proclaims that he is the true Passover Lamb.[12] Scripture has been fulfilled.

So don't be fooled into thinking that these verses describe a defeat. Read between the lines. Although Jesus is dead by the end of the chapter, he is not down and out. He is halfway down the death-and-resurrection pathway that spells victory for God's people.

---

[12] *Twilight* in Exodus 12:6 describes the period between 3 p.m. and nightfall. See 1 Corinthians 5:7.

The Way Back (23:26–56)

They seized Simon from Cyrene, who was on his way in from the country.

(Luke 23:26)

Five years after the British fashion designer Alexander McQueen committed suicide, the Victoria and Albert Museum in London held an exhibition to mark his legacy. Quotes on the walls charted his troubled pathway to suicide. First, the self-glorification of human sin: *"I want to be the purveyor of a certain silhouette or a way of cutting, so that when I'm dead and gone people will know that the twenty-first century was started by Alexander McQueen."* Next, the toxic effects of that way of living: *"I oscillate between life and death, happiness and sadness, good and evil."* Then a final quote on the wall that serves as a lament for his condition: *"There is no way back for me now."*[1]

Alexander McQueen grappled with the question that most people ask themselves when they become aware of God. If the holy God we've read about is real, where does that leave us? What about the things we've done? Can there be any way back for us? As Jesus dies on the cross, Luke answers that question for us once and for all.

Luke begins by telling us that Simon of Cyrene *"was on his way in from the country"*. In other words, he represents the many Jews scattered across the Roman Empire who returned to Jerusalem for the Passover Festival each year. He thinks he is making his way back to the mother city, but God has better plans for him. Although the Roman soldiers seize him at the

---

[1] The *Savage Beauty* exhibition took place at the V&A Museum in 2015.

gateway to the city and force him to follow Jesus, we can tell that he and his two sons, Alexander and Rufus, soon became willing followers of Jesus from the fact that they are clearly well known to the Christians in Rome in Mark 15:21. He accepts that Jesus is clearing a pathway back to God for repentant Jews like him.

Luke wants to make it clear that none of us need despair like Alexander McQueen. Jesus even prays in 23:34 for those who are crucifying him, *"Father, forgive them, for they do not know what they are doing."* There is therefore a way back to God for even the worst of us. That's the irony when the Jewish leaders sneer at Jesus in 23:35, *"He saved others; let him save himself,"* because he is only able to save others because he refused to save himself.[2] He is only able to make guilty people righteous because he, the Righteous One, was willing to be punished as if guilty. This great exchange lies at the very heart of the Gospel and it is why there is a way back for anybody who believes. His perfect sacrifice eclipses all our imperfections.

Luke illustrates this immediately through one of the criminals who was crucified with Jesus.[3] The other gospel writers say he was a burglar or a bandit. He had lived a terrible life of sin and he was about to die. He had no chance left to redeem himself. His only hope lay in tearing his eyes away from himself and on to Jesus. While his companion insults Jesus and sneers, *"Save yourself and us!"*, he believes that Jesus is making a way back to God even for the likes of him. *"We are punished justly, for we are getting what our deeds deserve. But this man has done nothing wrong... Jesus, remember me when you come into your kingdom."* Jesus does not respond with a list of theological

---

[2] Note how closely the words of the Jewish leaders echo the words of Satan in 4:1–13. Satan's most dangerous temptations are those that sound most logical, just like this one which claims that if God loves us then our lives will be trouble-free. Jesus sees through their frail human logic and so must we. See Acts 14:22.

[3] Matthew and Mark say that both robbers heaped insults on Jesus. Luke is the only gospel writer who says that one of them had a change of heart before he died, emphasizing that there is a way back for all of us.

questions. He does not demand that he do penance.[4] He tells him that his faith is enough to bring him back to God. *"Truly I tell you, today you will be with me in paradise."*[5]

So much for the Jews, but what about Gentiles like Theophilus? In 23:47, Luke tells us that even the Roman centurion who oversaw the crucifixion of Jesus came to saving faith in him. When he saw the way that Jesus refused to retaliate, looking at him and his soldiers – men with blood on their clothes from hammering nails through his hands and his feet – and praying, *"Father, forgive them, for they do not know what they are doing",* he exclaims, *"Surely this was a righteous man!"*[6] Even a pagan with blood on his hands can find his way back to God if he believes that Jesus is the spotless sacrifice for his sin.

That's not all. In 23:50, Luke says that even a member of the Sanhedrin was saved. Joseph of Arimathea chose this very moment to come out as a follower of Jesus and to break ranks with his colleagues by laying the corpse of Jesus in his own tomb, helped by the women who followed Jesus faithfully to the end.[7] We therefore have a member of the Sanhedrin that demanded the death of Jesus, the leader of the soldiers who carried out their demand and an out-and-out criminal – all of them far from

---

[4] This is a powerful rebuttal of the idea that our salvation is dependent on our own good works. The forgiven criminal wasn't even able to do so much as be baptized as a new Christian.

[5] *Paradise* means literally a *pleasure garden*, but in 2 Corinthians 12:4 and Revelation 2:7 it refers to *heaven*.

[6] A plural participle in Matthew 27:54 suggests that the entire squad of soldiers was saved along with their centurion. Luke focuses on the one individual in order to call us to make an individual response and in order to challenge Theophilus that yet another high-ranking Roman has recognized that Jesus was innocent.

[7] Luke says that Joseph did not condone the Sanhedrin's verdict the night before, but nor did he speak up against it. John 19:38 says that he was a secret believer until this moment.

God, yet all granted a way back to him. This is what people mean when they marvel at God's amazing grace.[8]

Luke therefore gives us one final picture to illustrate that all of us now have a way back to God. The Jews had built their Temple in a way that emphasized exclusion from the holy presence of the Lord. Anyone who was not a Jew was barred on pain of death from the inner courtyard of the Temple. Anyone who was not a priest was excluded from entering the Temple building, and even the priests were confronted with a four-inch-thick curtain that barred them from the inner room where God's presence dwelt.[9] Only the high priest was permitted to enter that inner sanctuary, and even he was barred except on one particular day of the year. Everything about the Temple shouted out, *No Entry*, yet at the very moment Jesus died the mighty curtain was torn in two as a sign from heaven to earth that God had made a way back into his holy presence for us all.

So read these verses and rejoice. No matter who you are and no matter where you've been, you have a way back to God. It's just as we are told in Hebrews 10:19–22: *"Since we have confidence to enter the Most Holy Place by the blood of Jesus, by a new and living way opened for us through the curtain, that is, his body... let us draw near to God with a sincere heart and with the full assurance that faith brings, having our hearts sprinkled to cleanse us from a guilty conscience."*

Luke is deliberately ambiguous in 23:48. Do the Jews beat their chests in celebration or in repentance? It's as if he is telling us that the way back to God is open for us all, but now it can go either way. It is time for each of us to decide.

---

[8] Note that Luke describes those who had faith in the coming Messiah as those *"waiting for the kingdom of God"*. To be a Christian and not to proclaim the Good News of God's Kingdom is a contradiction in terms.

[9] The Jewish Mishnah tells us that the curtain was a handbreadth thick (Shekalim 8:4–5).

Trust Me, I'm a Doctor
(24:1–12)

They did not believe the women, because their words
seemed to them like nonsense.

(Luke 24:11)

Luke has never been the most popular historian in the faculty library, but he has always ended up top of the class. Whenever people cast doubt on his writings because they don't like what he says, the historical evidence rallies to Luke's support every time.

Scholars used to rubbish Luke for stating in Acts 17:6 that the rulers of Thessalonica were known as *politarchs*. That is, until archaeologists unearthed five separate inscriptions which revealed that Luke was right and the scholars were wrong. They used to insist that Luke was mistaken in referring to Gallio as *proconsul* of Achaia in Acts 18:12, until archaeologists discovered the Delphi Inscription, dating back to 52 AD, in which the Emperor Claudius refers to *"Lucius Junius Gallio, my friend and proconsul"*. Scholars used to argue that Luke was wrong to say *Lysanias* was tetrarch of Abilene in Luke 3:1, since the only ruler known by that name had been executed by Mark Antony in 33 BC. Then they discovered an inscription from the reign of Tiberius which recorded that *"The tetrarch Lysanias created this street."*[1] Luke's repeated vindication by archaeology brings new

---

[1] This is all old news today, but it was completely revolutionary when William Ramsay presented the case in support of Luke in *The Bearing of Recent Discovery on the Trustworthiness of the New Testament* (1913).

meaning to his words in Luke 19:40: *"I tell you... the stones will cry out!"*

So we need to take Luke seriously as a historian when he describes the events that surrounded the resurrection of Jesus. It isn't enough for us to say with the apostles in 24:11, *I don't believe him because his words sound like nonsense.* Luke knows that dead people don't come back to life again – he is a medical doctor – yet he records the simple facts about what happened so that we might believe. However much we might wish to doubt his words, the weight of history and archaeology supports his claim in the opening verses of his gospel that *"I myself have carefully investigated everything from the beginning... so that you may know the certainty of the things you have been taught."*

There can be no doubt that Jesus was truly dead and that he was buried in Joseph of Arimathea's tomb. Luke states these basic facts so confidently because he is certain that Paul's accusers will not attempt to deny them before Judge Theophilus. Once the Roman executioners were certain that Jesus was dead, they released his body to Joseph. He wrapped it in linen grave clothes and laid it in a tomb cut into a rock face, with no back door and with its front door sealed shut by a very heavy stone.[2] No corpse had ever been laid in the tomb before, so there could be no mix-up, and everything that Joseph did was watched carefully by a group of women. These hard facts help us understand why none of Jesus' enemies ever tried to explain away the resurrection at the time by saying anything like *he wasn't really dead* or *the women went to the wrong tomb.* It takes 2,000 years of distance from these facts to make such an entirely unhistorical claim.

Nor can there be any doubt that the corpse of Jesus

---

[2] The large stones which sealed ancient tombs could weigh over two tons and were usually rolled down a slope to seal a tomb. Only a large team of people could therefore open a tomb by rolling the stone back up. Matthew 27:62–68 adds that the sides of the stone were sealed to prevent tampering, probably with clay.

disappeared from the tomb. He was buried just as a special Jewish Sabbath was beginning and the women came back to the tomb at the crack of dawn once the Sabbath rest was over.[3] They found that the heavy gravestone had been rolled away from the entrance and that, while the grave clothes were still in the tomb, the corpse of Jesus had entirely disappeared.[4] They were terrified by the sudden appearance of two angels, who reminded them what Jesus had prophesied: *"Why do you look for the living among the dead? He is not here; he has risen! Remember how he told you, while he was still with you in Galilee: 'The Son of Man must be delivered over to the hands of sinners, be crucified and on the third day be raised again.'"*[5]

It is hugely significant that none of the enemies of Christianity tried to deny these facts at the time. Nobody claimed that the women had gone to the wrong tomb because the crowds would have asked them to prove it by taking them to the right tomb! Nobody claimed that the Jews or Romans had removed the body, because the crowds knew full well that they would have produced the corpse to quash the rumours of resurrection if only they could. Nobody claimed that grave-robbers had stolen the body, because grave-robbers were interested in stealing linen grave clothes and funeral spices – the very things that were left behind. Instead, the enemies of

---

[3] John 20:1 says they set off while it was still dark. The other gospel writers say they arrived at sunrise.

[4] The other gospel writers tell us that the stone was rolled back by an earthquake. The tomb was not opened to let Jesus out, since he could now walk through walls, but to let witnesses into it (24:31; John 20:19).

[5] *The third day* either refers to the days of burial, Sabbath and resurrection, or else it refers to the fact that the first day of the Feast of Unleavened Bread was always an extra Sabbath day, even if it fell the day before a Sabbath (Leviticus 23:6–7; John 19:31). This particular Sabbath might therefore have lasted two days.

Christianity conceded that the corpse of Jesus had disappeared, accusing the disciples of having stolen the body.[6]

This was the only counter-argument left to me when, as a history student at Cambridge University, I began to investigate these facts in earnest. I had recently experienced Jesus through reading the Bible and praying, but I wanted some hard facts to confirm whether or not my experiences were real. As I trawled the bookshelves of the Cambridge History Library, I found Luke's account of events very difficult to deny. The empty tomb had been discovered, not by the disciples, but by a group of women. Far from having staged these events, it seemed clear that the disciples *did not believe the women, because their words seemed to them like nonsense*". Even as he names the female witnesses, Luke is fully aware that a woman's testimony counts far less in a Roman courtroom than that of a man. If he were making up the story, all these witnesses would have been male, but he is committed to recounting events as they happened – even the inconvenient details.[7]

Besides, as I started studying the primary sources, it quickly became clear that the enemies of Christianity very quickly dropped the claim that the disciples stole the body. There was simply too much evidence against it. Roman guards who lost a corpse were executed, but these guards had been paid off and set free.[8] Men who had stolen a body would not have been willing to die for what they knew was a lie. I was forced to agree with the conclusion of the eighteenth-century historian Gilbert West that Christianity conquered the Roman Empire because it

---

[6] See Matthew 28:11–15. Luke omits to mention that the tomb was guarded by Roman soldiers who failed in their duty. He does not want to make it any harder for Theophilus to accept that these basic facts are true.

[7] Perhaps Jesus chose these women because, unlike the men, they had not deserted him in his hour of need.

[8] Contrast Matthew 28:11–15 with Acts 12:18–19.

was based on *"an argument whose conclusiveness was visible to the dullest capacity"*.[9]

So don't miss this. Luke's message may not be what many people want to hear, but it is definitely true. Jesus really died. Jesus was really buried. Jesus really rose again. The Christian Gospel is therefore really true. *"His unique identity as Son of God was shown by the Spirit when Jesus was raised from the dead, setting him apart as the Messiah, our Master."*[10]

---

[9] *Observations on the History and Evidence of the Resurrection of Jesus Christ* (1747). See Acts 17:31 and 26:26.

[10] The apostle Paul says this in Romans 1:4, paraphrased here in *The Message*.

The Main Event (24:13–35)

It is true! The Lord has risen and has appeared.

(Luke 24:34)

Luke has established that the body of Jesus disappeared from his tomb. So far, so good. The Oxford history professor Géza Vermes accepts that this is undeniable:

> *When every argument has been considered and weighed, the only conclusion acceptable to the historian must be that the opinions of the orthodox, the liberal sympathizer and the critical agnostic alike – and even perhaps of the disciples themselves – are simply interpretations of the one disconcerting fact: namely that the women who set out to pay their last respects to Jesus found to their consternation, not a body, but an empty tomb.*[1]

But finding that a dead man's tomb is empty is not the same thing as finding out that he is alive. If we are to believe in the resurrection of Jesus, we need to hear about the witnesses who saw him alive again after the discovery of his empty tomb. We need Luke to substantiate his claim to Theophilus in Acts 1:3 that *"After his suffering, he presented himself to them and gave many convincing proofs that he was alive. He appeared to them over a period of forty days and spoke about the kingdom of God."* That's what Luke does for us here.

He does not mention the appearances of Jesus to Mary

---

[1] Géza Vermes in his book *Jesus the Jew: A Historian's Reading of the Gospels* (1973).

Magdalene and to the other women in the garden on their way back from the tomb.[2] Instead, he brings in a new witness to convince Theophilus. Not another woman and not one of the disciples. Someone slightly more removed. Luke is the only gospel writer to tell us about Cleopas.[3]

There is a strange statement in John 19:25 that Mary the mother of Jesus had a sister named *"Mary the wife of Clopas"*. It seems odd that a single set of parents should decide to give their two daughters the same name, which is why we need the second-century historian Hegesippus to explain to us that *"Clopas was a brother of Joseph."*[4] The two Marys were sisters-in-law, one married to Joseph of Nazareth and the other to his brother. Although Luke spells the name slightly differently, it appears that the witness Luke now calls into the courtroom is this brother. When Theophilus asks questions about Cleopas, he will have to conclude that an uncle knows how to identify his nephew.

Cleopas and his companion live in Emmaus, which is the Greek form of the Hebrew name *Hamat*, meaning *Hot Springs*. They have stayed late in Jerusalem because the city is abuzz with news that this morning the tomb of Jesus was discovered empty, but despite the late hour they decide to walk the seven miles home. They are met on the way by a traveller who appears to know nothing about the main event that is happening in the city. They explain to him that this is the third day since the crucifixion of Jesus of Nazareth. Surely he has heard about the famous prophet and miracle worker? Jesus prophesied that three days after his crucifixion he would be raised to life, and

---

[2] Cleopas has clearly not yet heard about them (24:24), but we read about them in Matthew, Mark and John.

[3] Mark 16:12–13 mentions this event in passing but does not describe it in any detail.

[4] Eusebius of Caesarea records these words of Hegesippus in his *Church History* (3.11). Since the companion of Cleopas is not named yet lived with him, it was most likely his wife Mary.

now a group of women have found his tomb empty. This has been verified by his disciples. How can the stranger not have heard about the main event dominating the news?[5]

The stranger does not pull his punches. *"How foolish you are, and how slow to believe all that the prophets have spoken! Did not the Messiah have to suffer these things and then enter his glory?"* He then launches into an overview of the entire Old Testament, explaining that the main event in Scripture has always been the death and resurrection of the Messiah. Why are their faces so *skuthrōpoi* (the Greek word in 24:17 means *gloomy* or *miserable*) when what has happened represents the fulfilment of all God's promises in Scripture?

I find this encounter hugely challenging. If I'm honest, I tend to think that what I really need to grow in my walk with Jesus is to see a glorious vision of him in his risen glory, but Luke says that Jesus hid his identity from Cleopas and his companion because what they really needed at this moment was a Bible study![6] They were miserable because all they had done was chat about what they had seen. They needed somebody to explain the Scriptures properly to them.[7] Good preaching is what turns gloomy sinners into glad saints. It is what turns miserable churches, which are about as joyful as a funeral, into exuberant communities that excitedly proclaim the resurrection.[8]

---

[5] The temporary disappointment that Cleopas describes was foretold in Lamentations 4:20.

[6] A literal translation of 24:16 is that Jesus *held their eyes under his power* to prevent them recognizing him.

[7] If we truly want to impart joy to people then we need to give them more than a *homily* (*homileō*, 24:14). We need to *expound* (*diermēneuō*, 24:27), *open up* (*dianoigō*, 24:32) and *give an exegesis* of Scripture (*exēgeomai*, 24:35).

[8] Wonderful though charismatic experiences are, they quickly fade. A firm grip on the truths of Scripture, however, lasts a lifetime. Luke is probably also stressing here that Jesus is the true fulfilment of the Jewish Scriptures, emphasizing that Christianity is a *religio licita* that is protected under Roman law.

Jesus is right. When he imparts to them a proper understanding of the Bible, it changes their attitude completely. When they reach their house, they invite him in. The roads are not safe after sundown and, besides, their hearts that were weighed down with sorrow before they heard his Bible study are now burning with joy. Jesus agrees to stay with them so that they can celebrate together, but as soon as he sits down to dinner with them he decides that they are ready to see him in his risen glory.[9] As he breaks bread for the first time since he broke it with his disciples at the Last Supper as a symbol of his broken body, he finally permits them to recognize him. Once they have seen him in his risen glory, he miraculously disappears.[10] They have seen enough. Despite the dangers of night-time travel, they hurry back the seven miles to tell their friends in Jerusalem.

When they arrive back in the city, they discover that Jesus has been busy. He has also appeared to Simon Peter. The empty tomb had been compelling proof on its own, but it is even more significant now that people are claiming to have witnessed the risen Jesus alive and well. Luke indicates that Cleopas and his companion have understood the importance of grounding our experiences in Scripture, using the Greek word *exēgeomai* to tell us that they *gave an exegesis* to the Eleven. They do not merely talk about seeing the risen Jesus at their dinner table. They describe *"what happened on the way"*. They repeat the Old Testament Scriptures that Jesus taught them are pointers to the death and resurrection of the Messiah. How could they have missed it? The labour pains of their weekend had actually given birth to the main event in human history.

We are coming to the end of this commentary on Luke's gospel. I am so grateful that you have permitted me to give you

---

[9] Having hidden his identity from them in 24:16, Jesus now makes out in 24:28 that he is planning to walk further. He never forces his way into our lives, but awaits our invitation (Mark 6:48; Revelation 3:20).

[10] The Greek phrase *aphantos egeneto ap'autōn* in 24:31 means literally that Jesus *became invisible to them.*

an exegesis of the Scriptures. Now it's time for you to decide. Do you believe that Jesus is truly risen? If so, are you willing to make it the main event of your own life too? Don't put down this book before responding to the challenge that the apostles preached across the Roman Empire. Paul warns in Acts 17:31 that *"God has set a day when he will judge the world with justice by the man he has appointed. He has given proof of this to everyone by raising him from the dead."*

No Fear (24:36–49)

They were startled and frightened, thinking they saw a ghost.

(Luke 24:37)

The disciples were scared. They had run away on the night that Jesus was arrested. Despite all the events of that first Easter Sunday, their fear still remained. They locked the doors and huddled together for safety that evening, convinced that the Jewish leaders were about to come and kill them.[1] They struggled to accept the news that Jesus was alive. Even when Cleopas and his companion told them how they had met with Jesus on the road to Emmaus, we are told in Mark 16:13 that *"they did not believe them."*

That's why the first words that Jesus speaks to the disciples when he suddenly appears in their locked room are *"Peace be with you."* This is more than the traditional Hebrew greeting, *shalōm*. Jesus is recognizing that their hearts are full of fear and making them a promise that he has come to turn their panic into peace and their fear into faith.

At first, the disciples respond badly. Instead of drawing courage from seeing Jesus, Luke says that they were *"startled and frightened, thinking they saw a ghost"*.[2] Jesus has to ask them why their hearts are so troubled and their minds so doubtful.

---

[1] John 20:19–23 gives us this extra detail when it recounts the same event described in Luke 24:36–49.

[2] The Greek word that Luke uses for *ghost* in 24:37 and 39 is *pneuma*, meaning literally a *spirit*. The disciples were happy to believe that Jesus' spirit lived on after death, like those of the Old Testament believers, but they struggled to believe that he had been raised to life physically as the first-fruits of their

He has to invite them to put their fingers in the nail-holes in his hands and feet in order to believe. Ghosts do not have flesh and blood. He is therefore truly alive. They need have no fear.

This is not enough for the disciples. Luke tells us that *"they still did not believe it because of joy and amazement."* Jesus therefore asks them to give him something to eat so that he can prove to them that he is no mere spectre. He eats some broiled fish to show them that they are looking at his resurrected body. Yes, it is different. It can disappear in front of Cleopas and appear to his disciples behind locked doors, but it is real in every way, just like the bodies that believers will receive on the Day of Judgment at the resurrection of the dead. Jesus looks around at the worried faces of his disciples and can tell that he is still not getting through. There is only one way to dispel their fear once and for all.[3]

Luke says that the disciples were only delivered from their fear when Jesus took them through a Bible study, like the one he had given to Cleopas and his companion.[4] They needed more than an exciting experience. They needed a complete change of world view. Jesus therefore takes them on a whirlwind tour of the Old Testament, starting with the first five books that were written by Moses, progressing through the book of Psalms and concluding with the seventeen books of prophecy that bring our Old Testament to an end. Luke tells us in 24:45 that the remedy to their fear was for Jesus to open their minds so that they could understand what the Scriptures truly mean. We ought to find that challenging. If we want to know Jesus so deeply that he drives out all our fear, we don't need to get on a plane to chase

---

own resurrection from the dead. See Job 19:26; John 5:28–29; Acts 24:15; 1 Corinthians 15:12–58; Philippians 3:21.

[3] John 20:24–29 tells us that Thomas was not with the other ten surviving apostles when Jesus appeared to them on Easter Sunday evening. He had to wait for another appearance on the following Sunday instead.

[4] One of the reasons Luke emphasizes the importance of Bible study at the end of his gospel is that he wants to help Theophilus and his other readers to find a route to a faith of their own. See Romans 10:17.

revival or celebrity preachers. We simply need to open up the Bible and ask Jesus to explain to us whatever we read.[5]

To help us, Jesus summarizes the entire Old Testament for us in just thirty-seven English words. We need to read these verses slowly, because they show us whether we have truly understood the message of the Bible. *"This is what is written: the Messiah will suffer and rise from the dead on the third day, and repentance for the forgiveness of sins will be preached in his name to all nations, beginning at Jerusalem."* Note Luke's three clear themes.[6]

First, Luke checks that you have understood that the Bible is all about the death and resurrection of Jesus the Messiah. Have you seen his sacrifice foreshadowed in Genesis 3:21, when God forgives Adam and Eve by slaughtering an innocent animal to atone for their sin? Have you spotted it in Genesis 4, when Abel finds forgiveness through killing an innocent lamb, while his brother Cain fails to find it through the work of his own hands? Have you grasped that this is why Abraham comes down from the mountain on which a ram has died to save his son Isaac and prophesies in Genesis 22:14 that its sacrifice points to something greater in the future: *The Lord **Will** Provide*?[7] Have you grasped that the only reason the sacrifices that were offered in the Tabernacle and in the Temple were ever able to grant forgiveness for people's sin was that they pointed to Jesus, the true Lamb of God? Jesus insists that we have not understood the Bible until we grasp that his bloodstains are on every page.

---

[5] John 20:19–23 suggests that Jesus opened the eyes of the disciples by breathing on them and commanding them to receive the Holy Spirit. Paul backs this up in Ephesians 1:17 by talking about *"the Spirit of wisdom and revelation"*. If you want to have insight into the Scriptures, like the apostles, be filled with the same Spirit.

[6] It is no coincidence that the Devil has done all he can throughout Church history to distract people from these three things: from *the cross of Jesus*, from *world evangelization* and from the call to *be filled with the Holy Spirit*.

[7] Mount Moriah was later the site of the Temple and one of the mountain's outcrops was Calvary.

Second, Luke checks that you have understood that the Bible is all about God's plan to forgive sinful people from every nation. The Old Testament focuses mainly on the people of Israel, because the message of salvation goes out from Jerusalem, but it constantly reminds us that the God of Israel is the Saviour of the whole world. Whether it is through penitent foreigners, such as Rahab or Ruth, or through King David's invitation for all nations to come and worship at his new Tabernacle, or through the words of the prophets – over and over again it describes the Lord's passion to save people from all nations. Unless we grasp this, we are blind to what the Scriptures mean.[8]

Third, Luke checks that you have understood that the only way in which this plan will ever come to pass is through ordinary people, like you and me, learning to partner with God's Spirit. This is lost in some English translations of 24:49, where Jesus says literally that *"I am going to send you **the** promise of my Father."* The Old Testament contains 8,000 individual promises (that's one for every three verses) yet Jesus says that one promise so encapsulates them all that it can be seen as *"**the** promise"*. So pay attention.[9] Jesus says that the great promise of the Bible is that God wants to clothe people on earth with his heavenly power. We have read a lot about this promise in Luke's gospel, so don't put this book down without asking God to enable you to partner with his Spirit.

Suddenly the disciples are no longer afraid. They unlock the doors and start making plans to take the Gospel to the world. That's what happens when we truly understand the message of the Bible. It enables us to live as God commands us, without fear.

---

[8] As the only non-Jewish writer of the New Testament, this is one of the big themes of Luke's entire gospel.

[9] Luke actually says it is *"the promise"* of the Old Testament three times. The others are in Acts 1:4 and 2:39.

Starting Pistol (24:48–53)

You are witnesses of these things. I am going to send you what my Father has promised; but stay in the city until you have been clothed with power from on high.

(Luke 24:48–49)

Usain Bolt was a dead cert to win the 100-metre final at the World Athletics Championships in 2011. He didn't just hold the Olympic gold medal for the 100 metres. He also held it for the 200 metres and the 100-metre relay. No one else in sporting history had ever come within a tenth of a second of his record-breaking time of 9.58 seconds for the 100 metres. He appeared to be unbeatable.

Yet Usain Bolt managed to lose the race. He began running before the starting pistol sounded and he was duly disqualified. The medal went to a runner that Usain Bolt could have beaten barefoot. Pounding the wall in frustration, he was asked how he felt by an insensitive reporter. *"I have nothing to say right now,"* he seethed. *"I need some time."*

Remembering Usain Bolt at those World Championships helps me to listen to Jesus when he tells his disciples to wait for God's starting pistol at the end of Luke's gospel. He has invited us many times throughout these twenty-four chapters to follow his example and partner with God by being filled with his Holy Spirit, so even as he reminds the disciples that *"You are witnesses of these things"*, he offers them a word of extreme caution.[1] His ascension back to heaven will mean that, at long

---

[1] They were witnesses of Jesus' resurrection, but we are all witnesses in the sense that we have a story to tell about him. Even if you are still a sceptic, you have something to tell others from having read Luke's gospel.

last, God's Spirit is available to everyone who believes, and they must not attempt to run without him.[2] *"I am going to send you what my Father has promised; but stay in the city until you have been clothed with power from on high."*[3]

Imagine what would have happened had the apostles tried to run before God fired the starting pistol. Embarking on their mission without the Holy Spirit's power would have spelled disaster.[4] The Jewish leaders, let alone the Devil, would have made mincemeat of them. Besides, they would have been far too distracted by their own plans to receive the Holy Spirit when he finally fell on the Day of Pentecost. Thankfully the apostles understood this. Luke ends his gospel by telling us that they watched Jesus ascend to heaven and then they simply waited.[5] They worshipped in the Temple courtyards with great joy and attempted nothing for God until they heard him fire the starting pistol to indicate that it was now time for them to run.[6]

We are not always like the apostles. We are impatient. We are the generation that complains when downloading videos on our smartphones takes a few seconds longer than usual. We are so busy with our own initiatives, our own church programmes and our own plans for God that we all too often miss what he is doing all around us. Because we are too busy to wait for God, we never see the breakthrough that he alone can bring. We have forgotten the words of Jesus in John 15:5: *"I am the vine; you are*

---

[2] Jesus is talking to his disciples in 24:48–49, but Acts 2 makes it clear that this promise belongs to us all. Peter declares on the Day of Pentecost that there will be no more elitism. The Holy Spirit is for everyone.

[3] *Clothed* with the Spirit is a Hebrew metaphor used in Judges 6:34, 1 Chronicles 12:18 and 2 Chronicles 24:20.

[4] To emphasize that even Jesus depended on the Holy Spirit's power for ministry, Luke always uses passive verbs to describe his ascension back to heaven (see 24:51; Acts 1:2, 9, 11, 22).

[5] Jesus ascended from the Mount of Olives (Acts 1:12), which was on the road to Bethany (Luke 24:50).

[6] Although Luke 24:53 says that *"they stayed continually at the temple"*, they slept at lodgings nearby. Acts 2 tells us that they were actually filled with the Spirit while they were together in their lodgings.

the branches. If you remain in me and I in you, you will bear much fruit; apart from me you can do nothing."

Because the apostles worshipped and waited in the Temple courtyards, they were not disqualified from the prize. In the first two chapters of Acts, Luke says that as they waited and prayed, *"Suddenly a sound like the blowing of a violent wind came from heaven and filled the whole house where they were sitting... All of them were filled with the Holy Spirit."* Peter had been so frightened seven weeks earlier that he denied Jesus three times on the night he was arrested, but at the sound of this starting pistol he leaps up and preaches boldly to the crowds. Three thousand are converted by a single sermon. God declares to the believers that it's time to run. The Church begins its long race to victory.

I wonder how good you are at waiting. If you are anything like me, you find it hard. But on the occasions when I stop and wait for God's starting pistol I am amazed at the difference it makes. A little while ago I grew frustrated that I was not leading enough unbelievers to the Lord, so before I left the house one morning I prayed that Jesus would extend to me the same promise that he made to Simon Peter in Luke 5:10. I asked him to help me fish for people and I promised that I would wait for him. I would empty my diary and open my eyes to see what he was doing all around me. I would fit in with his plans, instead of expecting him to fit in with mine.

As I left my house, I saw an alcoholic drinking a can of beer for breakfast on the bench across the road. On any other day I might have missed him, but not today. Taking some food across the road, I affirmed his dignity by asking him questions instead of rushing past him in a busy blur. His name was Nathan and he was in a mess. Suddenly my heart went out to him. The disciples had to wait for the coming of the Holy Spirit, but I did not. The Holy Spirit is at work all around us. Our waiting is simply about taking the time to sense what he is doing.[7] I offered to pray for Nathan and he accepted eagerly. Both of us were soon in tears as I confronted "the demon drink" and commanded it to leave. Later, I asked him if he believed in Jesus. He replied, *"I don't know – but I know I believe in you."*

Some months later, I prayed the same prayer again. I told the Lord that I wanted to partner with his Spirit and that the day was completely his, and not my own. I took my children to the park for a game of football and to my surprise came face to face with Nathan. His eyes lit up like mine, and I had another chance to pray for him. The following Sunday he came to church to find out what I meant when I talked about Jesus. As we knelt on the carpet together and I heard him ask God to forgive him, I felt the same joy that Luke describes in the final verses of his gospel.

This is the Christian life. Not making our own plans and praying that God will bless them, but waiting for God to reveal his plans to us so that we can partner with his Spirit. If the essence of sin is self-centredness, instead of God-centredness, then the essence of discipleship is a return to God-centredness. It is allowing him to hold the starting pistol.

So as we end Luke's gospel, tell Jesus that you want to die to your own ideas of how to help him so that you can fit in with his plan to clothe you with his resurrection power.

The apostle Paul reminds us that *"Anyone who competes as an athlete does not receive the victor's crown except by competing according to the rules."* He echoes Luke's command for us to listen for the sound of God's starting pistol. *"Run in such a way as to get the prize."*[8]

---

[7] They had to wait because the Spirit would not be poured out until Jesus returned to heaven (John 7:39; Acts 2:33). Our wait is about aligning ourselves to what he is now doing in the world (Acts 9:17; 22:16).

[8] 2 Timothy 2:5; 1 Corinthians 9:24.

Conclusion: All of This Happened for You

Tell how much God has done for you.

(Luke 8:39)

Luke is the longest book in the New Testament. Matthew's gospel has more chapters, but the first chapter of Luke contains four times as many verses as the final chapter of Matthew. Knowing that he can only fit 20,000 words onto a scroll, Luke ends his first volume with very little space to spare. It is 19,482 Greek words long.

But Luke had a second scroll. He begins the book of Acts by presenting it as the practical outworking of everything he has taught us in his gospel. *"In my former book, Theophilus, I wrote about **all that Jesus began to do and to teach** until the day he was taken up to heaven, after giving instructions through the Holy Spirit to the apostles he had chosen."* All that Jesus began to do and teach. The implication is clear. When we say yes to partnering with God's Spirit, Jesus continues to work and preach through our hands and mouths. Even as Luke changes scrolls, he makes it very clear to us that his gospel is far from over.

The book of Acts describes the theory of Luke's gospel put into practice. Anyone can see that the apostles are *"unschooled, ordinary men"*, yet they transform the Roman Empire when they listen for God's starting pistol and devote themselves to partnering with his Spirit in the world.[1] Crowds of people are

---

[1] Acts 4:13. The Devil wants you to put the apostles on a pedestal, treating them as special cases you can't follow, but Luke insists that they were ordinary people empowered by your extraordinary God.

healed of illnesses and delivered from demons. Others are raised from the dead. Tens of thousands of Jews respond to the Gospel and are baptized as followers of Jesus, signifying that they identify with him in his death and burial, and that they want to walk after him along the death-and-resurrection pathway.

When the Jewish leaders drive the Christians out of Jerusalem, salvation breaks out among the Gentiles. The rabbi leading the persecution against them has a dramatic encounter with Jesus while attempting to stop the spread of the Gospel to Damascus. An ordinary Christian named Ananias, who spends time listening for God's starting pistol, is told the surprising news by the Lord as he prays: the murderous rabbi has been chosen to spearhead the advance of the Gospel throughout the nations of the world. Ananias shelves his own plans and risks his life to baptize and disciple the rabbi. In just nine years, the converted rabbi Paul plants churches right across Cyprus, Asia Minor, Macedonia and Greece. The book of Acts ends with his arrest and arrival in Rome to stand before one of Caesar's judges. Luke uses the final chapters of Acts to convince Theophilus that Paul is innocent, and he succeeds. We know that Paul was released from prison in 62 AD, partly as a result of Luke's two scrolls.

Luke ends the book of Acts in mid-air because he wants us to grasp that there is still a third scroll to be written. He hands the pen to us and says that it is now time for us to start writing. So as we finish Luke's gospel, we need to understand that its story is only just beginning. Anything can happen through us if we say yes to partnering with God's Spirit. Luke insists that all these things happened for you.

This is why the Early Church advanced so rapidly in its first few centuries. People said yes to partnering with God's Spirit. Irenaeus of Lyons records that *"Without doubt some truly drive out demons, so that those who have thus been cleansed from evil spirits frequently join themselves to the Church. Others foresee things to come: they see visions, and utter prophetic expressions.*

Still others heal the sick by laying their hands on them, and they are made whole.[2] Origen insists that such close partnership with the Holy Spirit was the norm for every Christian and not just for an elite few. *"For the most part, it is uneducated people who perform this work... It does not require the power and wisdom of those who are good at arguing or who are most educated in matters of faith."*[3]

The Church has always declined whenever it has forgotten this, and it has always advanced whenever it has rediscovered that Christianity is an invitation to allow Jesus to continue his work through us as we partner with his Holy Spirit. We may not believe every story about the great medieval church leaders, but we cannot deny all the miracles that are attributed to pioneers such as Saint Patrick, Bernard of Clairvaux, Francis of Assisi and Vincent Ferrer. Those monks withdrew from the clamour of the world in order to hear God's starting pistol, and they re-emerged to spearhead major spiritual advances, having spotted how God was calling them to partner with his Spirit.

The same was true in the eighteenth and nineteenth centuries. John Wesley's journal gives a vivid account of his active partnership with the Holy Spirit. He attributes his revival to the fact that *"The power of God came mightily upon us, insomuch that many cried out for exceeding joy, and many fell to the ground."* When a cynical doctor accompanied a female patient to one of his meetings, Wesley rejoiced that *"when both her soul and body were healed in a moment, he acknowledged the finger of God."*[4] Charles Spurgeon gives the same explanation for the revival that he led in London: *"Is there not such a thing as the power of the Spirit? Yes!... There is nothing like the power of the Spirit; only let that come, and indeed, everything can be accomplished!... Go*

---

[2] Irenaeus wrote this in c. 180 AD in *Against Heresies* (2.32.4).

[3] Origen wrote this in c. 248 AD in *Against Celsus* (7.4). This is simply basic Christianity.

[4] These quotes come from entries in Wesley's *Journal* dated 1st January and 30th April 1739.

out and labour with this conviction – the power of the Holy Spirit is able to do anything!" [5]

The great evangelist D. L. Moody also tells us that this is how so many people were saved through his ministry:

> *I was crying all the time that God would fill me with His Spirit. Well, one day, in the city of New York – oh, what a day!... I can only say God revealed Himself to me, and I had such an experience of His love that I had to ask Him to stay His hand. I went preaching again. The sermons were not different; I did not present any new truths; and yet hundreds were converted. I would not now be placed back where I was before that blessed experience if you should give me all the world.* [6]

I think you get the point, so that's enough of other people's stories. All of this happened for you. As you end Luke's gospel, it is therefore time for you to make your own choice. Will you languish in the shallows of the lukewarm Christianity that masquerades as the real thing in so many churches, or will you ask God to help you partner with his Spirit?

Luke has finished his scroll about the life of Jesus. Now he invites you to write a fresh scroll of your own. Jesus wants to continue the story by filling you with his Holy Spirit. Luke hands you his pen and assures you that all he has recorded happened for you.

---

[5] Spurgeon said this in a sermon on "The Power of the Holy Spirit" on 17th June 1855.

[6] Taken from *The Life of Dwight L. Moody*, published by his son W. R. Moody in 1900.